THE MALE MALADY

MARGARET WALLER

The Male Malady

Fictions of Impotence in the French Romantic Novel

RUTGERS UNIVERSITY PRESS

New Brunswick, New Jersey

Library of Congress Cataloging-in-Publication Data

Waller, Margaret.
    The male malady : fictions of impotence in the French romantic
novel / Margaret Waller.
        p.   cm.
    Includes bibliographical references and index.
    ISBN 0-8135-1908-X
    1. French fiction—19th century—History and criticism.
2. Feminism and literature—France—History—19th century.
3. Women and literature—France—History—19th century.
4. Masculinity (Psychology) in literature.   5. Impotence in
literature.   6. Sex role in literature.   7. Romanticism—France.
8. Men in literature.   I. Title.
    PQ653.W35   1993
    843'.709353—dc20   92-13863
                                                                        CIP

British Cataloging-in-Publication information available

For Ken, who is not in this book

Contents

Acknowledgments

I want to thank Columbia University, the American Association of University Women, the Woodrow Wilson Foundation, the Georges Lurcy Foundation, and the Northeast Modern Language Association for the grants and fellowships that supported my early research and writing. I am also very grateful to Pomona College for numerous research and travel grants as well as a generous sabbatical leave, which gave me the most valuable gift of all, time.

Nancy K. Miller has been graciously supporting me and this project from its beginnings. Without her pathbreaking work on gender and her unfailingly astute readings of my work in all its many guises, this book would not exist. Naomi Schor's long-distance mentoring and illuminating work on nineteenth-century French literature have been equally valuable. While my intellectual debt to Nancy and Naomi can be easily read in the lines of this book, my enormous personal gratitude can best be read between them. I am also indebted to Michael Riffaterre for sponsoring this study early on, to Ross Chambers for his generous reading and encouragement, to Frank Bowman for his nineteenth-century expertise, and to Leslie Mitchner, my editor at Rutgers, who believed that the manuscript could become a book and helped make it one.

The members of my nineteenth-century reading group, Arden Reed, Hilary Schor, and Peter Starr, gave me timely moral support and critical feedback. Special thanks go to Paul Kafka, whose way with words gave polish to my own, and to Peter Allen, Cris Miller, and Helena Wall, ideal colleagues and generous friends. From the beginning, Kate Jensen has sustained me. She makes it possible for me to write and a pleasure to be read. To Kate, as always, I send thanks that go beyond words.

An earlier, condensed version of my argument in Chapters 1 and 2 appeared in "Cherchez la femme: Male Malady and Narrative Politics in the French Romantic Novel," *PMLA* 104 (Mar. 1989): 141–151.

All translations from the French are my own unless otherwise indicated. Emphasis, unless otherwise noted, is in the original text.

Claremont, California
January 1992

Prologue

If we are to believe the popular press and popular culture, the women's movement is over: women have won their struggle for equal rights and men have changed for the better. Nevertheless, as Susan Faludi's *Backlash: The Undeclared War against American Women* argues, recent studies on violence against women, wage differentials, men and women's share of the housework, women's education, and the feminization of poverty show that women are far from enjoying full political, social, economic, or legal equality.[1] Moreover, recent events reveal that the resistance to attempts to "reform" masculinity is becoming increasingly virulent. On the one hand, as Faludi explains, more and more men, in a backlash against affirmative action as well as feminism, are complaining that because the new order does not put men first, *they* are the "new downtrodden" (303). On the other hand, Robert Bly's "men's movement," for example, seeks a return to an atavistic masculinity that would once again exclude the "second" sex and eradicate what is feminine in men.[2] Meanwhile, however, popular culture, from *Tootsie* to *Mr. Mom*, has been heralding the advent of a kinder, gentler, "feminized" version of masculinity to replace old stereotypes of manliness, and is touting this new man as the answer to every woman's dream.[3]

Susan Jeffords argues that this growing myth of a "reformed and performative masculinity" in contemporary American culture represents a disturbing and insidious backlash against the limited gains in equality that women have made.[4] She reveals that the current emphasis on the "feminized" "new man" in television programs, movies, and articles in the popular press serves to essentialize this man's difference from other men and in so doing masks the attitudes or privileges that he shares with them. It also forgives all past abuses of the power he enjoys as a man and, on the basis of his current reform, denies the threat of any such behavior in the future. Furthermore, Jeffords notes, the focus on individual, exceptional men, whether real or imaginary, gives the illusion that individual actions can solve political problems that are in fact endemic to patriarchal structures. Finally and perhaps most tellingly, this attention to a man's supposed reformation effectively erases the woman, silencing her voice and effacing her point of view.

While this feminization of men may seem new, in fact the phenomenon first took on a recognizably modern form almost two hundred years ago in the French Romantic novels that are the subject of this study. Indeed, Jeffords's analysis of the sexual politics at work in representations of the "new man" in 1990 bears an uncanny resemblance to my own conclusions here about the fictions of gender and power in the male-centered novels that were published in the aftermath of the French Revolution and revolutionary women's unheeded calls for women's rights.

With the crisis of paternal authority symbolized by the decapitation of the king—the ultimate father figure—the post-revolutionary era represents a key moment in the development of modern patriarchal power. Although the period from the rise and fall of Napoleon through the restoration of the Bourbon monarchy saw crucial political changes, the political, social, and literary order remained throughout dominated by men. The literature produced during this time of masculinist backlash and counterrevolutionary retrenchment, however, did not express an explicit interest in putting women in their place or even in restoring traditional class privilege so much as an anxiety that newly disenfranchised men were to have no place in the reconstituted patriarchal order.

One of these marginalized men, François-René de Chateaubriand, an aristocratic émigré who became a political essayist and novelist, offered in his semiautobiographical fiction, *René*, a new version of masculinity that would become the model for an entire generation of men. In that novel and in the literature that followed, the tender, sensitive, "feminized" heroes are

overcome with ennui and doomed to frustration. Anathema to
the new orthodoxy of virile and militarist masculinity set in
place by Napoleon and, later, to the social, political, and religious conformism of men (and women) under the Restoration,
these men are portrayed as social outcasts. Indeed, the new Romantic version of man claims that he is barred from partici-
pating in the new paternal order and is thus unable to take
advantage of its privileges. Nevertheless, this new avatar of
masculinity would discover that in modern times a man wields
far more power over a woman when he bemoans his weakness
than when he displays his strength.

Contemporary America and postrevolutionary France thus
offer two variations on a similar masculinist response to times
of great social change and periods of gender crisis. In today's
counterreaction against the women's movement, the burning
question is: What is to become of men now that women are
becoming like them? In the androcentric fictions of French Romanticism, however, the question is instead: What is to become
of some men now that they have become like women? Because
I want to analyze rather than reproduce the masculinist bias so
common to many of these Romantic works, I also ask: When
some men seem to be becoming more and more like women,
what becomes of women? In other words, when are men's claim
to feminization and their complaints of impotence a ruse that
helps maintain patriarchal power?

My feminist analyses of the paradoxes of power reveal what
is positive and assertive in these fictions of impotence. Exam-
ining not only the power relationships represented *in* the novels but also those that operate *through* them, I study the authors'
paratexts, the implied reader created by the works, and the re-
actions of nineteenth-century critics and readers. My readings
suggest that during this period, male writers in particular and
their male protagonists as well are learning to take advantage
of the "powers of the weak" (silence, withdrawal, and refusal),
which are traditionally associated with women, as underhanded
means of reempowerment.[5]

Although the title of this book and its primary subject is
what I am calling the male malady, I do not intend to contribute
to that insidious modern phenomenon Tania Modleski calls

"feminism without women," which brings men back to center stage as a way of marginalizing women and undermining feminism.[6] Instead, in order to analyze the representations of gender and the paradoxes of power in postrevolutionary France, I have chosen a double focus and a double corpus: the depiction of men *and* women in works by women as well as by men. While this double vision complicates my task, I believe it also offers theoretical and methodological advantages. First, since gender is a system of meaning that is fundamentally relational, the two sexes derive their meaning not from any intrinsic properties but from the ways that they are mutually defined. Second, as these novels make clear, in the protagonist's fiction of social, psychological, or sexual impotence, the other sex has a crucial compensatory role to play. Third, at the time these men and women authors were writing, they did so with reference to each others' works and with a keen awareness of their own relative status to each other in the economic and political struggles between social classes as well as in the literary competition between the sexes for the "rights" to the novel and its growing readership.

I have therefore chosen to study the heroine along with the hero not only in three of the most famous male-authored and androcentric works of this period—Chateaubriand's *René*, Benjamin Constant's *Adolphe*, and Stendhal's *Armance*—but also in two important revisionist variations on this pattern by women authors. As I will show, when Germaine de Staël in *Corinne* and George Sand in *Lélia* imagined their own melancholic men, they did so in part as a way to show that this reformed masculinity did not fundamentally change men's power over women or women's secondary status. In addition, unlike their male contemporaries, both Staël and Sand create extraordinary heroines who resist the traditional definitions of gender in unorthodox texts that defy the conventions of genre.

Because I read all five works closely and within their specific historical contexts, however, I take note of the differences *among* men and *among* women, both as characters within the fictions and as authors of it. Indeed, these works evidence some of the blurring of gender boundaries and the reversal of gender identities typical of later nineteenth-century realist texts, which show gender itself as a fiction.[7] Nevertheless, these early Romantic works, like the societal expectations and conventions they adumbrate, operate according to gendered notions of character and gender-specific principles of causes and consequences. Thus, while the Romantic hero's antisocial malady (*le mal*) is usually said to characterize the entire age (*le siècle*), these works show the mal du siècle as a specifically male malady. Even when this fiction explicitly comes under attack, as in Sand's *Lélia*, which makes the mal du siècle a woman's malady, the heroine still finds herself ultimately bound by society's constraints on her sex.

In the first chapter, "Rereading the Mal du Siècle," I show the way that mal du siècle fiction, revising the eighteenth-century image of the sentimental man, only appears to negate the sexual politics of the libertine novels of male prowess. By underscoring the gender-determined role that women play within these male-centered fictions, I expose the insistence on the hero's disablement as a *fiction* of impotence. The mal du siècle works by women present, by contrast, a feminist protest against these conventions which makes clear what men have to gain and what women have to lose in the new literary, social, and political order. I also set the works in their literary and historical contexts to reveal that the male malady achieved considerable popularity at a time when men were not only gaining increased legal, political, economic, and social power over women, they were also beginning to claim as their own the sentimental novel, which had been associated with femininity, female writers, and women readers.

Chapter 2, "Fictions of the Feminine," explores Chateaubriand's *René* as the production of a new kind of melancholic male subject whose apparent impotence proves his genius. While Chateaubriand claims that this minimalist, confessional narrative rejects plot, I show that both the hero and the text make the telling of René's unadventurous life a compelling story by capitalizing on the prurient interest afforded by the unveiling of a woman's desire for him.

Chapter 3 reads Staël's *Corinne* as a novel that discloses what's wrong with the hero whom the heroine considers Mr. Right. Although the unconventional Corinne, a woman of genius, resists the traditional heroine's plot, in the end she succumbs, the victim of the conventional hero's inability to love a woman of whom his father and the paternal order do not approve. The novel reveals the source of his mal du siècle as the English-style patriarchy then coming into vogue in France.

My analysis of Constant's *Adolphe* in Chapter 4 demonstrates how the novel short-circuits the seduction and abandonment premise of libertine fiction. In its attempt to establish sympathy for another's pain as a new basis for liberal ethics, the text creates for its mal du siècle hero a double bind. I show, however, that the politics of point of view in the novel and the hero's ready acknowledgment of guilt merely modernize male dominance in duplicitous attempts at self-exoneration.

Chapter 5, "Taking the Woman's Part," reveals male impotence as a fantasy of male desirability in Stendhal's *Armance*. I study the preface to the novel, however, in order to explore Stendhal's own anxieties about treating such a subject—albeit anonymously—and in a genre associated with women writers and women readers. In the novel, Stendhal uses a third-person narrative voice to ironize the text's presentation of its hero and in so doing problematizes the reader's relationship to the mal du siècle text.

In the final chapter, "Toward a Feminist Mal du Siècle," I address the question of reading more directly, for Sand makes *Lélia* an ideological *Bildung* for the reader as well as for the hero. Sand's portrait of a melancholy and impotent woman of genius provides a kind of negative counterpoint to Staël's representation of empowered female genius in *Corinne*. Nevertheless, Sand's heroine resists even more effectively than Corinne had both the codes of gender and the necessities of genre. Whereas in *Corinne* the woman genius is destroyed by love, in *Lélia* she defies this expectation. Furthermore, in the novel, Sand does what no writer before her had done: she explicitly makes the mal du siècle, which had traditionally indicated a nostalgia for older forms of male domination, a sign of feminist discontent with a world made by and for men.

In the Epilogue, I briefly explore the fate of the male malady under the July Monarchy in works by Sainte-Beuve, Balzac, and Musset and compare these testimonies to male narcissism with the far more famous works of male masochism and gender role reversal of the 1830s. Finally, I suggest that the figure of the alienated artist in fin-de-siècle decadence and early modernism reveals, as its early Romantic predecessors had, an anxiety about the devaluation of men's literary work and a crisis of male identity not unlike the current one.

I

Rereading the Mal du Siècle

I N 1815, AT THE END of Napoleon's Empire and on the eve of the restoration of the Bourbon monarchy, a best-selling novel in France was Sophie Gay's *Anatole*. In this fiction, a woman falls in love with the enigmatic man who had saved her life. Though handsome and charming, possessed of all possible virtues and talents, Anatole remains mysteriously silent and withdrawn. The hero's secret, the heroine finally discovers, is that he is deaf and dumb. She learns sign language so that her love can conquer his insecurities, and they live happily ever after. According to Mario Praz in an essay on women writers during the Empire, one of Sophie Gay's fans was no less than Napoleon himself, who found solace on his last night as emperor by reading *Anatole*.[1]

This vignette from Napoleonic lore has all the appeal of an apocryphal fiction: he who used to make the world in his own image has lost on the battlefield and been barred from the corridors of power. He must therefore settle for the vicarious gratification offered by an imaginary world in which romantic fantasies offered perhaps the sole remaining arena untouched by failure. This scene of reading, in which man's power over woman provides a kind of consolation prize for otherwise disabled men, nicely encapsulates the subject of this study: fictions of impotence and compensatory empowerment in early nineteenth-century France. Although the figure of Napoleon as reader offers a particularly arresting example of this paradox, the emperor's interest in fictions of male disablement was far from unique.

During this same period, Chateaubriand and the hero of his novel *René* (first published in 1802) became the avatars of melancholy, masculine genius for the Romantic generation. In his memoirs, Chateaubriand offered a derogatory portrait of the progeny his fiction had spawned: "An entire family of René poets and René prose writers proliferated: lamentable and disjointed language was all one ever heard; all they ever discussed were winds and storms, mysterious sorrows delivered up to the clouds and the dark of night. There wasn't a single callow youth just out of school who didn't dream he was the most unfortunate of men; not one lad of sixteen who hadn't exhausted his life, who didn't believe himself tormented by his genius."[2] Young readers' identification with this new kind of writer and his alienated but sublime protagonist served as a rite of passage not only to Romanticism but also to adulthood and to writing itself. Young men patterned themselves after René; young writers imitated Chateaubriand's protoromantic subject and style.[3] This notion of literary genius as solitary, melancholic, and male has become synonymous with the Romantic writer and hero in most traditional literary histories and in the popular imagination.[4] Indeed, the image of a self-absorbed young man lost in moody contemplation sums up the malady (*le mal*) that is said to characterize the entire modern, secular era (*le siècle*).

To read this psychosocial and literary metaphor in its own terms, which is to say medically and morally, one might say that in the first three decades of the nineteenth century the example of René contaminated later representations of men. Some heroes, such as Gay's deaf and dumb Anatole, suffered physical disabilities. Others were visibly disfigured, such as the sensitive and talented man scarred by smallpox in Caroline Pichler's *Olivier* (translated from the German in 1823) or the exiled poet in Saintine's novel *Le Mutilé* (1834), whose hands and tongue have been cut off. In the mid-1820s, Claire de Duras dared make her hero's malady a question of virility: the tender and passionate Olivier's unspeakable secret is his sexual impotence.[5] Soon after, Henri de Latouche and Stendhal followed her lead with their own novels of impotence, *Olivier* (1825–1826) and *Armance* (1827), respectively.

The malady of the most famous and canonical heroes of this period, however, is more figurative than literal, yet no less debilitating. Chateaubriand's moody, troubled René longs to make his mark on the world, but he despairs of any attempt and condemns himself to proud but unhappy isolation. Benjamin Constant's Adolphe, subject to inveterate doubts, is unable to love the woman he has seduced or to leave her, and his irresolution makes him a social outcast and costs him his career. Although these early Romantic protagonists are financially and socially privileged, highly intelligent, and remarkably sensitive, they are unable or unwilling to enter the world on its terms and so they retreat from society.[6]

The authors of these works claim far-reaching historical significance for this antisocial malaise. In his introductory remarks to *René*, Chateaubriand argues that his hero's "vague des passions," a passionate but undirected longing, characterizes the current state of men under the influence of women during the modern, Christian era. In the preface to *Adolphe* (written around 1806 and first published in 1816), Constant makes his eponymous hero representative of an entire generation of sensitive sons incapable of carrying out the libertine principles of their fathers. By the time of Stendhal's *Armance* in the mid-1820s, incapacitated and disaffected young men had become a literary and cultural commonplace. According to the doctors who examine Octave, his only disease was "that kind of dissatisfied and censorious sadness characteristic of the young men of his time and rank."[7] In 1836, Musset makes his hero's malaise the story of his generation in the much discussed second chapter of *La Confession d'un enfant du siècle*. Critics in the nineteenth century also declared this malady endemic to the age and dubbed it "le mal du siècle."[8] In the twentieth century, literary scholars made this representation of dissatisfaction with the modern world an obligatory opening set piece in anthologies of nineteenth-century French literature, and many praised the works as stirring portraits of eternal adolescent angst or stunning evocations of "Man's" timeless spiritual malaise.[9] Despite these sweeping claims by the authors and by literary critics, the novels remind us that "universal Man" does not include women.[10] The mal du siècle afflicts only certain men, certain *mâles du siècle*.

To read these works as stories of men rather than as embodiments of Man is to begin to see that the mal du siècle represents, precisely, the hero's failure to be a "man." In each case, the protagonist's difficulty has to do with his inability to take up the traditional male role in a man's world. If the later nineteenth-century French novel is, as Joan DeJean for example has argued, the novel of the father, a fixed, linear form based on a chronological time of generations,[11] its predecessors, the mal du siècle fictions, seem to have broken that patriarchal continuity and called it into question in their portrait of impotent sons unable to follow in their father's footsteps.

Mal du siècle novels recount the hero's tragic tale of male disempowerment as both the cause and the effect of his alienation from the patriarchal status quo.[12] Because Chateaubriand's René has no place in his father's house, he has no home in society; Etienne Pivert de Senancour's Obermann rejects the social order but fails to make a world of his own; Constant's Adolphe, sidetracked by a woman, will never assume his father's position; Stendhal's impotent Octave can neither play a socially useful role nor carry on his aristocratic family name. The mal du siècle tradition did not just offer a new kind of protagonist, it promoted a new image of man. These heroes are, to varying degrees, outcasts who give voice to a profound social alienation. Unable to fulfill their ambitious dreams, they find themselves outside the paternal order. Their propensity for introspection leads them to ask hard questions about their roles and their worlds and prevents them from assuming either the deep faith or the smug self-confidence of the men around them. Their failure to conform to standards of male behavior and achievement, whether social, sexual, military, or entrepreneurial, calls into question received ideas about masculinity and the options society makes available to men.

Although the nineteenth-century canon of Romantic fiction favors the depiction of men by men, women writers of the time also featured disabled heroes in their novels. Germaine de Staël chose a melancholic Scotsman as the ill-fated love interest for

her extraordinary heroine, Corinne. Claire de Duras wrote not
only about the impotent Olivier, but also about the bourgeois
Edouard, who allows class differences to come between him
and the noblewoman who loves him despite his lower social
status. George Sand peoples her *Lélia* with three *mâles du siècle*:
a lovelorn poet, an older but wiser ex-convict, and a madman.
Despite critical differences, the heroes of these women's novels
have much in common with the inveterately melancholic and
emotionally crippled protagonists of male-authored novels.
Like them, the women writers' heroes doubt their attractive-
ness, desire but fear relations with a woman, shrink from the
social order, and withdraw from the world. Nothing, it would
seem at first glance, could be further removed from this preoccupation with male impotence than the earlier, libertine celebration of male power and prowess. I will argue, however, that
the obvious and important distinctions between these two avatars of masculinity also mask the interest they share in fictions
of gender difference and in strategies of male empowerment.

Plus ça change . . .

One of the male protagonists of Claude-Prosper de Crébillon's
Lettres athéniennes (1771) seems to speak for countless other
eighteenth-century libertine heroes who were equally explicit
about the pleasures men hoped to gain from their social and
erotic interaction with the opposite sex: "To please, indeed, to
be passionately loved; to see myself as the object of the wishes
and desires of every woman; to enjoy by turns their ecstacy and
their despair; to sacrifice them constantly to one another; and
to find them in the end, despite their pride and even their
plans, subject to all the emotions I want to have them feel."[13]
No matter how devious or cruel, no matter how many women
suffer, the hero acts with impunity. In their libertine representations of the rites (and rights) of men, the libertine writers
make no apologies for his privileges. Instead, this literature is a
tribute to man's mastery over the world, which he demonstrates
by manipulating a series of women.

The early Romantic hero, by contrast, is far more submissive than controlling, chooses to avoid society rather than swagger through it, and attempts a relationship with only one woman. He thus resembles not the libertine rake but the man of feeling of the eighteenth-century French, English, and German sentimental traditions. Like Saint-Preux, Yorick, or Werther, the mal du siècle protagonist demonstrates the passivity, sensitivity, and vulnerability associated with the era's idealized image of woman.

By all appearances, this feminized version of male subjectivity of the eighteenth and early nineteenth centuries would seem to represent some progress toward equality between the sexes and increased reciprocity in their relations. Recent feminist work on the eighteenth-century feminized male in English as well as French sentimental literature has shown, however, that the promotion of "feminine" sensibility can be oppressive as well as liberating. In the fictions that have become canonical, almost all of which are by men, the praise of "feminine" ideals and the ostensible reign of women merely reinforce men's domination of them. In the most famous example, *Julie, ou la Nouvelle Héloïse,* Rousseau elevates woman as exemplar only to make her the spokeswoman for the patriarchal order that subjects her. In such fictions, writes Nancy K. Miller, "woman permits man to celebrate himself; feminocentrism underwrites androcentrism."[14] On the other hand, some women authors of the eighteenth century, who are only now being reread and rediscovered, used sensibility as a form of protest against the rights of men and the constraints on women,[15] or as an empowering language that allowed them to resist the plot of seduction and imagine for their heroines a polymorphous pleasure that goes beyond love.[16] In other words, the sexual politics of sensibility depends in large part on the uses to which this apparent valorization of the feminine and breakdown of gender difference is put.

While mal du siècle fiction's debt to the novel of sentiment and sensibility is considerable, the later authors make different use of sentiment.[17] Eighteenth-century sentimentalism involves a high dose of pity and concern for others; the mal du siècle protagonists direct that attention to themselves. Whereas the sentimental novel arouses pathos in the name of virtue, the mal du siècle authors elicit pity for the hero on the basis of his undeserved victimization and unrealized greatness. Even more significantly, while sentimental literature tends to place the heroine on a pedestal, the early Romantic novel gives her positive qualities to the exceptional man. Although on the one hand, the mal du siècle hero's feminine sensitivity makes him superior to his fellowmen, his feminine indecisiveness is also a frustrating source of his difficulties. Thus, Laurence Sterne's Yorick is proud of his feminine weakness, but René resigns himself to it, Adolphe struggles with and against it, and Octave overcompensates for it with violent displays of strength. In other words, in the early Romantic novel, the feminization of the hero is no simple paean to femininity, either in women or in men.

Whether feminine by nature or feminized by circumstances, the mal du siècle hero is introspective and sensitive to the point of paralysis. This aspect of his femininity is played out as a character flaw, a weakness that traps him in situations of emotional bondage more common to women characters than to men. René, for example, who is his sister's soul mate, is sensitive, indecisive, and continually subjected to the will of others. Obermann, who rejects manly concerns, dreams of submission to a master and returns obsessively to thoughts of the married woman who may have loved him. Staël's Oswald remains in the shadow and under the spell of Corinne in Italy, though his duty to father and country calls him back to England. Because Adolphe feels sympathy for the woman he has seduced, he cannot abandon her, and his inveterate irresolution fatally binds them. Stendhal's Octave, homebound, remains devoted to his mother. Unable to accept Lélia's love on her terms, Sand's Sténio turns to debauchery and, in a gesture of final despair, to suicide. Each of the male protagonists finds himself tied, inextricably, to the heroine,[18] and the main subject of these novels is almost always the psychological effects of these ties on him, not on her, even though she usually has more to lose.

In its fascination with the hero's debilitating social and emotional constraints, both external and self-imposed, the mal du siècle novel makes a sharp contrast with the literature that precedes and follows it, where attention is much more likely to focus on the literal and figurative ties binding the heroine. Miller's study of the eighteenth-century sentimental and libertine "heroine's text" in England and France spells out the inexorable logic of sexual consequence that confines the female protagonist to marriage or condemns her to death.[19] Writing about French novels of the mid-nineteenth century, Naomi Schor argues that "realism, far from excluding woman from the field of representation draws its momentum from the representation of bound women" and "depends to an unsuspected degree on the binding of female energy."[20] What remains to be seen is to what extent the early Romantic depiction of bound men confirms or undermines earlier and later narrative conventions that establish men's power by depicting women's subjugation. In other words, is the hero's feminization incapacitating or empowering or both? And when man becomes feminine, what becomes of woman?

The mal du siècle protagonist must suffer the consequences of choosing the wrong partner. In this sense, he resembles the sentimental heroes of *Manon Lescaut* or *La Nouvelle Héloïse* rather than the impervious libertine male. But in both the sentimental and mal du siècle traditions, it is the heroine who almost invariably faces the ultimate punishment, which is death. In Prévost's and Rousseau's eighteenth-century fictions as in Staël's *Corinne*, the heroine is sacrificed so that the prodigal son may ultimately return to the paternal fold. In most mal du siècle fiction, however, despite the heroine's traditional victimization, this final reconciliation of son and father does not come about. The hero himself decides that he cannot go home again. Chateaubriand's René, for example, offered a second chance in the New World with two paternal substitutes instead chooses internal exile; and for Senancour's Obermann, self-imposed banishment is a foregone conclusion. Unfit for life and ready for death, the hero of Constant's *Adolphe* wanders aimlessly over Europe after Ellenore dies instead of returning to his all-forgiving father. As penance for a relationship gone awry, the mal du siècle hero makes himself a stranger to the fatherland. Despite these protagonists' many similarities to the hero of Goethe's *Sorrows of Young Werther*, only Duras's Olivier, Stendhal's Octave, and Sand's Sténio follow Werther's lead by committing suicide.

Although the novels insist on making the hero bear the consequences of his own inadequacies, the fascination with the hero's self-punishment in traditional mal du siècle fiction is strongly mitigated, as the analyses in this study will show, by an even greater interest in his self-preservation and aggrandizement. The novels of this tradition only seem to test the limits of man's desirability. "Can such a hero inspire love?" asks the epigraph to Pichler's *Olivier*. Whether he shamefully conceals or belligerently parades his failure to conform to norms of masculinity, this question drives the mal du siècle hero to distraction. And although his antisocial behavior opens him up to mockery, remonstrance, or attack by other characters, the novels themselves belie that vulnerability by giving the male protagonist pathos, dignity, and a highly alluring air of mystery that elevate him above his fellows.

Even more important for the mal du siècle plot, the very qualities that make the hero's masculinity suspect—sensitivity, tenderness, and vulnerability—are those that the heroine values. Whereas he adopts the culture's narrow ideas about masculinity to his own detriment, she is generally more than willing to love a man who is, in society's eyes, less than a "man." Indeed, following the eighteenth-century sentimental tradition, a "feminized" man is a woman's ideal. In the traditional mal du siècle novel, however, she has one main function: to convince him of her love, whatever its consequences for her happiness. In the euphoric version of these plots, typical especially of the works now judged minor, the heroine succeeds in persuading the hero that he is desirable. In the dysphoric version characteristic of androcentric mal du siècle literature, however, despite the heroine's love and devotion, the hero himself decides he cannot accept her love because he is not a "real man."[21] The latter novels thus do double ideological duty. Through the heroine, they show an androgynized version of masculinity as desirable; through the hero, they reveal it as unbearable.

Although the hero may doubt the heroine's love, the novels make it clear to the reader that there is little room to question her devotion. In this sense, the early Romantic fascination with

male disablement surreptitiously engineers for the reader what
its apparent ideological opposite, the libertine novel, flaunts ostentatiously: a text establishes man's dominion by showing his
power over a woman. The valorization of the feminine in the
male disguises a modern, liberalized but no less entrenched
rule of men.

Despite this fundamental similarity between the heroine's
role in the sentimental and libertine traditions, mal du siècle
fictions give the heroine a very different function than their
eighteenth-century predecessors do. Whereas sentimental fiction by men generally focuses on the hero's quest for the elusive
woman who can satisfy his romantic fantasies, and libertine fiction uses her so that he may further his ambitious erotic wish
and revel in his conquest of her, the early nineteenth-century
novels of male introspection by men pay more attention to the
hero himself as an enigmatic subject of frustrated desire. In the
postrevolutionary society adumbrated between eighteenth-century worldliness and realism's "world," a youth must still possess
a woman to become a man. This conquest is not enough, however, and can even be harmful, for attachment to a woman
keeps the mal du siècle hero locked within a domestic plot at a
time when power is shifting to the public sphere, which is, increasingly, the province of men.

Nevertheless, because these antisocial texts offer few public
outlets for the hero's ambitious wish, the heroine plays a crucial
compensatory role. She provides him with one of the few remaining arenas at his disposal for exercising and displaying the
powers and prerogatives he still possesses as a man. In the novels, no matter how unable the hero may be to secure a place
for himself in the world of men, no matter what his liabilities
(whether social, moral, financial, or physical), no matter how
badly he may mistreat the heroine, and no matter how strongly
she may resist her own desire, the heroine dramatically reveals
the hero's power over her, thus confirming, despite his disablement and self-doubts, his desirability and dominion. In shifting
the focus from woman to man and from object to subject, the
mal du siècle novel marks an important transition in the
representation of ideologies about gender. Whereas the libertine and sentimental works hid their androcentrism under

an apparent feminocentrism, the early Romantic novel openly advertises its fixation on the male.

Despite the masculinist bias that is endemic to the mal du siècle, a few works successfully resist this standard sexual politics. In very different and even conflicting ways, Staël's and Sand's novels offer a radical challenge to these stories of troubled men by opening up this resolutely androcentric model to representations of female subjectivity. Both *Corinne* and *Lélia* call into question the power of vulnerable, melancholic men by setting them up against the will, desires, and intelligence of defiant women. In Staël's *Corinne*, Oswald's paternal plot—the hero's melancholy mourning of his father and desire to follow his father's will—must compete with another narrative of equal if not greater interest and importance centered on Corinne, an extraordinary woman renowned for her talents and crowned for her achievements. In Sand's similarly feminocentric *Lélia*, the stories of the three *mâles du siècle* revolve around the enigmatic heroine who resists their desire and their plots for her. More remarkably still, Sand subverts and revises the meaning of the male malady by making it female. The suffering of her proud, independent heroine is not the mal du siècle of a man unable to be a "man" but that of a woman who sees the role which society prescribes for women exactly for what it is: a dead end. By reversing gender roles in the novel, Sand reveals the degree to which the famous impotence of canonical early Romantic heroes is a disguised form of power. Far more than interesting variations on the mal du siècle theme, *Corinne* and *Lélia* are remarkable examples of feminist revisionist fiction, which evidence the four major strategies of this literature outlined by Miller in *Subject to Change*. The two works display "a self-consciousness about woman's identity," demonstrate the difference between woman and Woman by making "a claim for the heroine's singularity," contest the available plots for literary heroines, and figure "other subjective economies, other styles of identity."[22]

Though far less radical than either *Corinne* or *Lélia* in its feminist revision of literary form and content, Duras's *Ourika* (1824), the story of a woman who feels herself condemned to live as an exception to her sex and at the margins of the upper class because of her race, has a special status in the history of the early Romantic novel: Ourika is the only heroine other than Lélia to suffer from the "male" malady. Although her symptoms resemble those of René, Ourika's psychological torment is particular to women as they have been socially constructed in that it translates into self-loathing rather than self-aggrandizement and is far more physically debilitating. Furthermore, in despair at finding herself without a future, this freed slave reexamines the tenets of the liberal French aristocracy that had adopted her as she notes the hypocrisy of the Enlightenment and the limited application of the "universal" ideals of the French Revolution.

Duras's fiction thus brings the mal du siècle down to earth by using it to address timely and pressing questions about racial prejudice and human rights. The more conventional novels, by contrast, evoke instead a vague psychological or metaphysical mal du siècle and establish only in very general terms its relationship to contemporary political and social questions. Nevertheless, as I have shown, the prefaces of these works claim that the heroes are far from alone and that the mal du siècle is symptomatic of larger social forces. In the pages that follow I shall briefly sketch out the general social and political context of the mal du siècle novels, first, to give a sense of the historical—and political—significance of these fictions of impotence and, second, to suggest possible correlations between the power relationships represented in these works and the relative power of their male and female authors in the world.[23]

Literary Men and Literary Women in a Man's World

In his important and illuminating work on the mal du siècle, Pierre Barbéris shows the extent to which this fiction represented real social and political malaise and argues that the identity of those alienated changed significantly over time.[24] In the beginning, during the Consulate and Empire, aristocrats such as Chateaubriand, who had been disenfranchised by the French Revolution and marginalized under Napoleon's reign, thematized the malaise to represent their nostalgia for the Old

Regime and their alienation from the postrevolutionary world. For the bourgeois and liberal Staël, who was exiled by Napoleon, her hero's mal du siècle by contrast represented both an admirable Romantic sensibility and a horrific vision of the future in which an English notion of separate spheres forever hobbled women's ambitions. After 1815, those who wrote fictions of disempowerment tended to be bourgeois liberals, such as Stendhal, who were being shunted aside not only by the restoration of the monarchy but by the rise of industrial capitalism. Thus, from the 1800s to the 1830s, writers of each marginalized group in turn told the story of an alienated hero in the interests of very different, even opposing, political agendas.

Given the class interests that distinguished and divided writers as diverse as the monarchist, aristocratic Chateaubriand on the one hand and Staël, Constant, and Stendhal on the other, what is striking about the mal du siècle novels is how many fundamental similarities they share. As I have shown, whether the setting is aristocratic or bourgeois, the figure of alienation is almost invariably a man. Although the hero is incapable of social production, the plot revolves around his inability to carry on society's reproduction, a figurative incapacity made literal in the novels of male impotence such as Duras's and Latouche's *Olivier* and Stendhal's *Armance*. The widespread social upheavals that critics such as Barbéris see at the root of the nineteenth-century malaise are relegated to the subtext of the mal du siècle novel. Instead, the hero's disempowerment appears as a problem of gender identity and is dramatized in his relationship to a woman. To use gender in this way to figure power or the lack of it is hardly new. What makes this particular refiguration of gender and power interesting, however, is its paradoxical timing.

Whatever their struggles with other men and whatever the barriers to their own success, during the French Revolution and in the decades that followed, men of all classes enjoyed ever greater dominion over women.[25] Influential men of all political persuasions condemned both the "reign of women" in the eighteenth-century salons and the radicalism of women who had fought for the Revolution or had fought the revolutionaries for women's rights. The Napoleonic Code, set in place in 1804, institutionalized long-held cultural prejudices against women as full-fledged citizens and subjects by legalizing a sexual double standard and multiplying the legal constraints on women's control over their lives and livelihood. Bonaparte himself, who embodied a virile militarist ideal, promoted a masculinist ethos as well as a misogynist politics. During the Bourbon Restoration, moral rectitude, religious devotion, docile domesticity, and other such ideals precluded noblewomen from engaging in nonconformist activities. Throughout the postrevolutionary period, the public domain was increasingly defined as male, while women were relegated to the private, domestic sphere, a tendency that would be further intensified by the rise to power of the bourgeoisie in the July Monarchy of the 1830s. Given this sobering picture of women's social roles, legal rights, and economic status, what seems curious is that the mal du siècle novels by men do not openly celebrate men's new power over women and that the works by women do not even more strenuously protest it. The lives of these authors and their own personal and political circumstances, however, suggest that there may be biographical reasons for this apparent anomaly.

All of the writers whose works I discuss in the following chapters found themselves outside the inner circle of power in postrevolutionary France. The first three authors were barred from full participation in the public, male domain by their social class, by their politics, and, in the case of Staël, by her sex. For them, writing was a form of political dissidence, but it was only a second-best substitute for more direct political activism.[26] When he first drafted *René*, Chateaubriand was an aristocratic émigré living in England. By the time the novel was published in 1802, he had returned illegally to France but was only beginning to curry favor with Napoleon. In the same year, Napoleon, fearful of the power of his formidable liberal adversaries, exiled Staël from France and dismissed Constant from the Tribunate.

Despite a shared identity as political outsiders, the decision to become a writer had a different meaning for Staël than it did for Chateaubriand and Constant. Although during this period women in general were actively discouraged from writing professionally (and sometimes even from reading),[27] Staël was ridiculed, harassed, and finally exiled for doing so. For her, writing was a defiance of the narrow definition of women's roles, an audacious attempt to join the male political fray by wielding her pen against Napoleon's sword. For the men of the period, on the other hand, intellectual and artistic pursuits—unless they were accomplished at the emperor's request and to his specifications—had lost their status to political, military, and technological careers, which were considered more properly virile. For such men as Chateaubriand and Constant, therefore, writing signified an exclusion from the male, public sphere, and thus a disempowering feminization.

Faced with a similar problem of marginalization, contemporary male authors in England worked to recode writing in general, and poetry in particular, as a heroic, manly calling. As Marlon B. Ross explains, because of the efforts of the English Romantics, "poetry becomes a form of masculine empowerment rather than becoming, as it threatens to, a sign of 'feminine' or boyish vulnerability, and it becomes a paradigmatic form of manly action in the world rather than an ineffectual and puerile preoccupation." These English writers give the poet a far more elevated position than anyone before or since and envision him "as man of action, as masculine quester, as ruler of visionary empires."[28]

In the mal du siècle fictions, by contrast, the male protagonist's action is severely limited; his quest, if he undertakes one at all, is pointless or doomed. Though early French Romantic novels share with their English counterparts a similar fantasy of empowerment and arrogate a comparable form of discursive power (as, for example, René on Mt. Etna contemplating the meaning of human existence), they insist much more strongly on the futility of the hero's efforts and his failed manhood. It would not be until the 1820s with the full-blown Romanticism of Victor Hugo's poetry, for example, that the poet in French literature would openly declare himself a seer, magus, and spokesman for humanity.

The far different prestige the French mal du siècle writers lent their heroes may have been due in part to the literary genres they chose. Confined to the margins of the public sphere, they adopted for their own purposes not the elevated poetic genre, but a far less prestigious form: the novel, more specifically, the sentimental or personal novel, which, because it was associated with feminine values and ideals—tender love, passionate feelings, and an active inner life—was linked to women writers and women readers.

The early mal du siècle authors, like other essayists of the time, acknowledged this link between the feminine and modern times but strongly disagreed on what the connection meant. For conservatives, such as Chateaubriand, the "feminization" of man represented modern decadence and a fall from classical models of literary, social, and political virility. For liberals, such as Staël and Constant, the attention to sentiment in men meant the dawning of a new, progressive age. By the 1830s, the novel was no longer a woman's genre. The advent of realism, for example, made the novel a serious form with pretentions to social commentary, and the serialization of novels in newspapers made writing novels a commercial enterprise and a workaday job for men.[29] Like earlier mal du siècle authors, however, particular men who were new to the sentimental genre, most notably Stendhal and Sainte-Beuve, had reason to be jealous of the literary success of some of their female contemporaries, such as Duras and Sand.

Despite the dangers of emasculation, male writers' adoption of a traditionally feminine literary genre was not an entirely self-defeating exercise. In fact, the personal novel with its predilection for vulnerable characters subject to fits of emotion and predisposed to self-reflection, served them well, for it gave these marginalized men a ready-made form for the literary expression of their own experiences and assured them they had a story to tell and a reason to write. On the other hand, their insistence on the semiautobiographical hero's "feminine" weakness in a genre associated with women seems to have come at some cost to the authors' sense of their own masculine identity. As the chapters that follow show, the prefaces of all three male writers demonstrate an uneasiness about women's influence on men in general and themselves in particular. Despite the growing ascendancy of men over women in postrevolutionary France, these male authors figure the second sex as a source of power—whether malefic or beneficial. While Chateaubriand

and Constant claimed that women's own weakness had made men weak, Constant also invoked, as Stendhal would too, the success of their female literary rivals as an underhanded way of ensuring their own.

The women authors experienced their own very different anxiety of authorship. Both Staël and Sand had to overcome considerable obstacles—not the least of which were cultural prejudices against women writers—in order to authorize themselves to write at all. Their anxiety would seem to surface, for example, when the plot culminates in the punishment of the heroine who, like her author, is an exception to society's rules for her sex. Inasmuch as the novel in general was already associated with women, and its themes—disempowerment, introspection, and emotion—were standard for female protagonists, the genre itself did not represent a step out of bounds for them. On the other hand, Romantic works both updated and reinforced the assumption that subjectivity is male, and thus made it difficult to imagine women characters as full-fledged subjects.

Staël and Sand, however, refused to remain within these social and literary conventions. In *Corinne*, Staël's heroine not only refutes the idea of woman as object, her achievements put the ambitious wishes of the mal du siècle heroes to shame. In *Lélia*, too, the heroine refuses to be an object of man's desire and, in so doing, drives a priest mad and a poet to suicide. It is the audacity of these reversals of gender stereotypes and the empowerment they openly claim for the female protagonists that offers the most significant difference between these women writers' work and the men's. Male mal du siècle fiction tends to offer a melancholic exercise in debilitating sensitivity and guilt that hides a furtive empowerment, the two novels by women by contrast present an anticonformist display of ambition and moral courage that is nevertheless doomed to failure.

The difference between these two kinds of mal du siècle works is just as striking formally as it is thematically. Whereas Chateaubriand (like his male successors) favors the intimate, pastoral, and elegiac mode characteristic of early Romanticism, Staël, far ahead of her time, explodes the genre with the Promethean ambition, grandiose designs, and awe-inspiring enthusiasm that would be taken up by the later Romantics, such as Hugo, Balzac, and Sand.[30] In general, the male writers pare down the novel as genre to its barest essentials and concentrate almost exclusively on a single male subject.[31] In these first-person narratives, a man often tells his story as a confession to another man or to other men. Although the hero may be involved with other people, and is always in a relationship with a woman, it is the male self in isolation who takes center stage. As a kind of corollary to the hero's feminization, the male novelists privilege feeling over adventures and explicitly reject plot as the driving force behind their texts.

Chateaubriand says himself that, "*René* is, as it were, only a single thought; it is the painting of the *vague des passions* without the addition of any adventures."[32] Constant presents his work as an attempt to write an interesting novel about two characters whose situation never changes. Within the mal du siècle texts, narrators such as Obermann echo René in contending that they cannot relate their adventures—since they have not had any—but can only reveal the secret feelings of their souls. Sainte-Beuve's Amaury, for one, admits that his narrative describes "a monotonous . . . life, blank pages, empty days, . . . little action, endless feelings."[33] Envisioning these kinds of constraints on the male protagonist seemed to cramp the male writers' imaginations and temper their literary audacity. Except for Chateaubriand's *René*, with its curious admixture of styles and genres, their works hold relatively few surprises and offer little experiment in literary form.[34]

Staël and Sand's versions of the novel, by contrast, resist easy compartmentalization and represent a veritable explosion of the sentimental genre, which was traditionally associated with women. For both writers, the mal du siècle novel becomes a serious vehicle for the expression of ideas and an iconoclastic challenge to traditional linear and monological literary form. In Staël's work, Corinne's descriptions of Italian art, history, and monuments and her discussions of politics, aesthetics, and cultural differences interrupt and delay the main narrative, which itself does not have one center of interest, which is traditional in mal du siècle fiction, but two: Corinne and Oswald. In Chapter 3, I analyze the difficulties that this doubled novel posed for early nineteenth-century critics who could not decide

whether to label the text a travelogue or a love story, but who
knew in any case that they could promote neither the feminized
hero nor the virilized heroine as role models for their readers.
Sand effects an even more radical confusion of genres as she
shifts in *Lélia* from an epistolary mode to a third-person narrative interrupted by two voluminous first-person confessions.
Not only does Sand multiply her novel's points of view, as Staël
had done in *Corinne,* she also defies the laws of verisimilitude
and of genre by creating a new style novel of idealism.[35] Both
Corinne and *Lélia* call into question the traditional demands of
plot by forestalling, reversing, and highlighting narrative expectations, innovations that disclose the connections between
genre and gender, and what links them both to the representation and exercise of power.

For purposes of introduction, I have set up the masculinist
and feminist traditions as opposites. In the readings that follow,
I shall explore the complexities in this apparently simple opposition and reveal the ways in which these fictions of impotence are different from each other and, often, in contradiction
with themselves as well. Thus, while iconoclastic writers such
as Staël and Sand do in fact offer a challenge to masculinist
ideology, unconventionality alone is no guarantee of revisionist politics. I will show, for example, that the radical critique
implicit in the women writers' representation of remarkably
strong heroines in fact contains fundamentally conservative assumptions about the limits of women's power. On the other
hand, it seems to me that for too long we have been taking the
mal du siècle works at their word. Although these novels are
clearly exercises in "loss, absence, sterility, solitude,"[36] reading
the men's works along with the women's shows that they are all
in fact seeking new forms of empowerment usually at the expense of the other sex.

To examine the literary texts of men *and* women is to work
against the trends in both mal du siècle criticism and feminist
criticism. On the other hand, traditional criticism on the mal du
siècle novel tends to look only at the canonical works which are
by and about men and regard these fictions about men as if
they were about Everyman and every woman. Thus, to examine
the canonical texts of early Romanticism in terms of gender is,

as I suggested earlier, not only to call into question the universality of the heroes' claims but also, and ultimately, the canon itself. My choice of women authors to exemplify a countertradition is, however, also somewhat canonical: Staël and Sand are the two women writers who have received the most attention from feminist critics working on nineteenth-century French literature. Feminist work generally and feminist criticism on the literature of eighteenth- and nineteenth-century France in particular, however, have tended until recently to focus almost exclusively on fiction either by or about women. This emphasis on women has meant that feminist critics have focused on Staël and Sand's strong heroines to the exclusion of their problematic heroes.[37] By giving more attention to Oswald in *Corinne* and by seeing *Lélia* in the context of a male tradition, I hope to complete an otherwise one-sided view of the women writers' feminist protest. Indeed, the full implications of Staël's and Sand's gender reversal cannot be appreciated without a knowledge of the conventions of the male malady from which these authors draw their critique.

If it is illuminating to see women's work in the context of a male tradition, it is equally enlightening to see men's writing in the context of women's literary production. In the case of the works discussed here, personal relations, political antagonisms, and professional rivalries place the writers in three different historical configurations of connection and influence. Thus, as I will show, Germaine de Staël takes on the mal du siècle paradigm established by her contemporary and political adversary, Chateaubriand, to expand its import and expose its politics. *Adolphe* may be viewed in turn as Constant's answer to Staël's fiction of impossible love. The two writers' previous intimacies and their similar political views multiply the possible interconnections between the works while underscoring the striking differences. In a later mal du siècle phase, we find two bourgeois men hoping to outdo an aristocratic female rival. Latouche's *Olivier* sought to capitalize on Duras's work of the same name by taking her premise as his own and pretending his work was hers. Stendhal too wrote *Armance* with and against Duras's unpublished *Olivier*. His preface reveals his desire to replace Duras as the successor to a female novelistic tradition dating all the way back to Marie-Madeleine de Lafayette's seventeenth-century *The Princess of Clèves*. Another convergence of interest in the mal du siècle occurs in the 1830s. While in *Lélia*, Sand both sums up and undoes the work of her predecessors by multiplying her melancholic heroes and making her main mal du siècle hero a woman, none of her immediate successors, Sainte-Beuve in *Volupté*, Balzac in *Le Lys dans la vallée*, or Musset in *La Confession d'un enfant du siècle*, take on Sand's iconoclastic, feminist challenge. Instead, these novelists attempt to outdo each other with their semiautobiographical fictions of male disablement which recall the male tradition set in place by the original mal du siècle text, Chateaubriand's *René*.[38]

2

Fictions of the Feminine
in Chateaubriand's *René*

IN THE BEGINNING was *René*. Chateaubriand's 1802 tale of a
young man overcome with ambitions and desires but incapable of acting upon them was the first, the most famous, and
the most influential French novel to feature a hero afflicted
with the mal du siècle. This pathbreaking work and the imi-
tations it inspired marked a key turning point in the ideologies of gender and conventions of genre in French literature.
Whereas eighteenth-century novels tended to solicit the reader's interest by featuring female characters as object or subject,
René relegates women to the margins; it is the hero who names
the work and dominates the text. Plot played a significant role
in the eighteenth-century novel, while in *René* the frustrated
and aimless hero has no adventures and the minimal narrative
concentrates instead on the lyrical exposition of his malaise and
frustration. This tale of a vulnerable, sensitive, and disempowered hero rewrote the traditional fictions of idealized masculinity. Did it thereby dismantle patriarchal assumptions about
male dominance or merely adapt them to changing times? Inasmuch as Chateaubriand and his works played an important
role in the counterrevolutionary backlash that characterized
early nineteenth-century France, the beginnings of an answer
can be found in contemporary politics.

B<small>Y</small> 1800 <small>REVOLUTIONARY REPUBLICANISM</small> and anticleri-
calism were beginning to wane. Napoleon was prepar-
ing to sign the Concordat, reestablishing Roman Catholicism as
France's state religion and thus solidifying the reaction against
the revolution. François-René de Chateaubriand, who had emi-
grated to England, seized the moment to return illegally to
France. Hoping to become the spokesperson for this ideological
shift to the right but barred from most of the traditional elite
avenues of advancement, this aristocratic émigré sought to
make his fame through his writing. Chateaubriand, to generate
interest in his forthcoming apology for Christianity, excerpted
from this work his story of a virtuous Indian maiden who com-
mits suicide rather than break a vow of chastity. Published in
1801, *Atala* was an instant bestseller. *Genius of Christianity, or the
Beauties of the Christian Religion*—which appeared a year later in
1802 and included both *Atala* and, for the first time, *René*—
also enjoyed phenomenal success. In his work Chateaubriand
sought, as he put it, to move unbelievers to faith by showing the
effects of Christianity on "the arts, morals, mind, character, and
even the *passions* of the peoples of modern times."[1] An essential
part of his campaign involved revealing "the effects of Gothic
ruins, compared to other kinds of ruins, monasteries set in solitude, the poetic side of popular religion which used to place
crosses at forest crossroads" (35).

The exotic and erotic *Atala* and the ponderous yet poetic
Genius of Christianity thus made religion appealing to a new age
by repackaging Christian myths, rites, and culture to suit this
new sensibility, which, in turn, gained legitimacy by being tied
to age-old Catholicism. Although wildly successful, Chateaubri-
and's use of secular arguments and earthly pleasures to serve a
religious revival did not come without contradictions. We will
see some of the many ways in which the two discourses, value
systems, and ideologies clash.

For the most part, however, these very different ideological
forces proved mutually reinforcing and nowhere more so than
on the question of gender, where they simultaneously served
the interests of a burgeoning bourgeois culture and a reactionary backlash against women's participation in the public

sphere.[2] During the Revolution and its aftermath, countless writers of widely varying political stripe, from republican revolutionaries to ultramonarchists, attributed the decadence of the eighteenth century to the corrupting influence of aristocratic women and feared a recurrence of the direct and sometimes violent political activism that women of all classes had engaged in during the French Revolution.[3] Their remedy to this "unnatural" situation was to reestablish a patriarchal order in which men would have a place in the public sphere while women would know that their place was the private sphere. In his comments on *René* in the preface to the novel, Chateaubriand extols just such a world and openly states that the fantasy guiding his fiction is a reign of men. Nevertheless, according to Chateaubriand, this virile ideal, which had been realized in the ancient world, remains for modern men a distant memory and an elusive goal. Times have changed, and so have men.

Civilization and Men's Discontents

The introduction to *René*, which first appeared in *Genius of Christianity* and was reprinted with some revisions as the preface to the novel in later editions, presents the story as a fictional example of the "vague des passions," an objectless longing that characterizes the contemporary, Christian era.[4] Chateaubriand shows this psychological malady as a modern phenomenon by putting it in historical perspective: "The more advanced the civilization, the more this vague stage of longing increases. . . . The ancients knew little of this secret anxiety, this bitter ferment of stifled passions; extensive political involvement, games in the gymnasium and on the military esplanade, the business of the marketplace and the public square filled all their moments and left no room for sorrow of the heart" (63). Inasmuch as the activities Chateaubriand cites—politics, sports, commerce, and war—were the sole prerogatives of the ruling class and the dominant sex, the ancient world Chateaubriand eulogizes is an elite world of men. Indeed, for Chateaubriand, the difference

between the decadent nineteenth century and the utopian classical age rests precisely on the exclusion of women from the public sphere. Segregation of the sexes in ancient Greece and
Rome, he argues, safeguarded what is masculine in the male by
preserving men from the perils of intimacy with women: "They
were not inclined to exaggerations, hopes, and groundless fears,
to ever-changing ideas and feelings, and to a perpetual fickleness that is nothing but a continual source of disgust: tendencies that *we* acquire in the intimate company of women" (63;
emphasis added). Inasmuch as keeping women's company results in the insidious feminization of men, undermining their
moral rectitude and resolve, the female as Other presents a
clear and present danger for "us," the male author and his male
addressees.

The destabilizing and feminizing effects of women's contagious influence are so pervasive in modern times that they
threaten to spread beyond the affairs of the heart—woman's
traditional realm of power over men—to contaminate every
sphere of man's domain: "In the modern age, women, indepen-
dently of the passion they inspire, have an influence on all
other feelings. They have a certain self-abandon in their existence that they introduce into ours; they attenuate our manly
character; and our passions, weakened by being blended with
theirs, become both uncertain and tender" (63). In contrast to
the sympathetic portrayal of the sociohistorical determinants
of men's "vague des passions," the text links women in an
essential relation to emotional excess, indecisiveness, exaggera-
tion, and inconstancy. But if Chateaubriand's denunciation of
modern women's influence on men in particular and the public
sphere in general struck a common, misogynist theme, his
stand was also full of ambiguities and contradictions.

Although the feminization of modern men is an object of fear
in Chateaubriand's argument, it is also a subject of fascination.
What makes their passions "uncertain" also makes them "tender" (*tendre*), an adjective whose positive connotations—sensitive, good, sweet, generous, compassionate, loving, or drawn to
love or friendship—mitigate the explicit criticism of emasculated virility.[5] Even more significantly, Chateaubriand presents

men's "vague des passions" as a direct consequence of the "genius of Christianity," whose salutary effects Chateaubriand's larger text is intended to prove. In a qualification of his earlier statement, Chateaubriand notes that the advantages of the ancient, patriarchal world pale before the higher, Christian consciousness of the modern: "The Greeks and Romans, scarcely gazing beyond life and never suspecting more perfect pleasures than those of this world, were not led, as we are, to reveries and desires by the nature of their religion" (63). Thus the same argument that censures feminization as a form of emasculation also praises certain feminine traits in men as a sign of modern, Christian superiority and recodes them as manly.[6] In his preface, Chateaubriand thus shows a dream of absolute gender difference to be illusory. Even so, he does not see the sexes as equal. In this brave new world, men may adopt feminine characteristics, but it is never a question of women taking over traits traditionally associated with men. Whatever their failings, men are still on top. Thus, the breakdown of gender difference is a one-sided affair, which maintains rather than undermines the hierarchy of the sexes.

Fiction as Moral Antidote

According to Chateaubriand, making the historical argument about the genius of Christianity is not enough. His apology for Christianity requires "proof," which must come in the form of a fictional example, which is *René*. In his moral combat against the unbelievers, Chateaubriand admits that he borrows his tactics—literature—from his enemies, but claims that he has expunged their impieties: "The author had to combat impious poems and novels with pious ones; he took up the same arms his enemy bore" (65). Nevertheless, *Atala* and *René* make their case not through edifying examples but through far more seductive counterexamples to their moral message. *Atala* praises female virginity by offering a sensual tableau of sexual temptation. In *René*, the hero, dazed by the beautiful mysteries of

Christian culture, remains deaf to the Church's moral teachings. Given the moral ambiguities of his methods, Chateaubriand works to convince his readers that his religious ends justify his secular means.[7]

The author describes his strategy in *Genius of Christianity* as a reversal of the approaches of contemporary apologists of Christianity which have failed, he argues, because they do not take into account the skepticism of their post-Enlightenment and postrevolutionary readers. "It was necessary to go in the opposite direction," he states, "move from effect to cause. Rather than prove that Christianity is excellent because it comes from God, assert instead that it comes from God because it is excellent."[8] *René* targets an even more specific audience: young men. Chateaubriand in his preface presents his text as an antidote for the "poisonous germ" introduced by the "impious" texts of Rousseau and Goethe, which have led readers to "disastrous and guilt-ridden reveries" and even to suicide. As a cautionary tale of cause and effect, *René* is designed to save the reader who identifies with the hero from a similar fate by displaying "the fatal *consequences* of an excessive love of solitude" (66; emphasis added). Chateaubriand argues that without *Atala* and *René,* an "innocent trap for the nonbelievers" (65), the "real" work from which they are taken, *Genius of Christianity,* would not even have been read.[9] He thus portrays the seductive appeal of fiction as a necessary evil employed in the interests of loftier designs. If *Atala* and *René* are the traps set to lure the unsuspecting reader, what exactly is the bait?

On the one hand, Chateaubriand's preface claims that literature is not necessarily immoral; on the other, it asserts that *Atala* and *René* are unlike any other fictions—"I do not know whether the public will appreciate this story, which does not follow any of the usual paths and which presents a kind of nature and mores that are completely foreign to Europe" (41). Indeed, *Atala* is described not as a novel but as "a kind of poem, half descriptive, half dramatic" (41) that defies the reader's expectations and precludes fiction's traditional pleasures. He cites, in particular, the novel's minimal plot, its few characters, and the extensive space it gives to description. Repeating terms used to describe the originality of *Atala*, Chateaubriand warns that "*René* is, as it were, only a thought; it is the painting of the *vague des passions*, unadulterated by any adventures" (64). As in *Atala*, plot takes second place, but here is it upstaged not by description but by affect, for *René* is, according to Chateaubriand, a case study of "a prodigious melancholy . . . which is of a somewhat confused nature . . . [and which] is created among passions, when these passions, without object, consume themselves in a solitary heart" (64). Adventure has been superseded by self-destructive solipsism.

Although Chateaubriand insists that his fictions eschew events, he declares that the conventions of genre and the constraints of ethical intention oblige him to interpose an exemplary twist of plot: "One would need only to add some misfortunes to this indeterminate state of passions for it to serve as the setting of an admirable drama." This exception to the refusal of adventure is "a great misfortune sent to punish René and to frighten young men who, given over to useless reveries, criminally shirk their responsibilities to society" (64). The efficacy of the precept and its example depends on meting out disastrous consequences for failure to conform to the social script. Crime must have its punishment for fiction to work its intended effect.

Chateaubriand's preface justifies *René* morally by noting that the novel assigns the hero full responsibility for his deeds and makes him bear the full weight of their consequences. The story thus achieves an exemplary circularity—"Indeed, René's mad reveries begin the evil, and his extravagances bring it to an end: through his reveries, he leads astray the imagination of a *weak woman*; through his extravagances, in wanting to take his own life, he *obliges* this unfortunate woman to join him; *thus unhappiness arises from the subject, and punishment derives from the offense*" (67; emphasis added). What determines the self-reflexive turn of the screw is not fate or even God but this young man's own failings. The psychologic that dictates René's character—his "mad reveries" and "extravagances"—also determines the punishing twist of the plot. That the hero's sister must also bear the weight of his crime is, for the author, only an ancillary consideration. Although Amélie provides the edifying example of Christian sublimation in *René* and is crucial to the "great misfortune" to which the preface alludes, she is elided in the novel.

In shifting the traditional focus of the novel from woman to man and by reducing the novel as genre to its barest essentials, *René* paradoxically reveals all the more clearly the role of the feminine and the heroine in this narrative of masculinity in crisis. It is through his feminine qualities and position that the hero, like the novel itself, solicits interest in his story. And it is the heroine's suffering and her secret that give the tale the heightened drama the author claims is necessary to its moral message. The frame narrative, which is staged in the luxuriant wilderness of colonial Louisiana, establishes the ground rule for male feminization: the exclusion of women.

In the Company of Men

From the very first sentence, the narrator identifies the telltale symptom of the hero's social alienation as his anomalous sexual status. "On arriving among the Natchez Indians, René had been obliged to take a wife in order to conform to Indian customs, but he did not live with her" (147).[10] Conjugal union, for this hero, is not a freely exercised male prerogative. Instead, it is an act imposed from without which forces him into a position of social and sexual submission that, in earlier fiction, was more typical of women than of men. Bridling at finding himself bound to a woman against his will, René thus deploys the strategy of the weak, which combines outward compliance with passive resistance. But if René is, in this sense, *like* a woman, the unnamed woman who would be his spouse is nowhere to be seen, and marriage, which was in the eighteenth century the be-all and end-all of feminocentric fiction, is reduced to a single declarative sentence. Though René's retreat from connubiality poses the central enigma of his character, neither his marriage nor his wife is the focus of this story.

René's compromise between his personal desires and social obligations allows him a place within Indian society; he lives nevertheless on its margins, "a melancholic tendency constantly drew him deep into the woods; he spent entire days there in solitude and seemed like a savage among savages" (147). Despite this hyperbolic characterization of his self-imposed exile, the forlorn young man is less a "savage" than an *enfant sauvage*, a painfully withdrawn child and prodigal son who yearns to return to the arms of the Father. The stranger who has no commerce with woman is also said to have "renounced commerce with men," with the exception of the Indian Chactas, "his adopted father" (147), and Father Souël, a missionary and spiritual father. René's adoption by not one but two father substitutes hints at the extent to which the orphan's "savagery" is always already tamed, if not actually contained, by his submission to paternal authority.

The hero and the two father figures create a homosocial family in which men play all the roles. The maternal, consoling Chactas with his "kindly indulgence" provides the necessary counterpoint to the rigid, paternal Father Souël and his "extreme severity" (147). Abnegating heterosexuality (but denying homosexuality as well), the three men triangulate women's exclusion: René refuses sexual union; Chactas, the aged, blinded warrior, is beyond it; and Father Souël's vow of chastity precludes it. The defining social contract of the hero's narration is thus not man's relationship to woman but rather the male bonding to which that relationship gives rise. Nevertheless, in an attempt to seal the ties that bind them, René's commerce with men will involve discursive traffic in women.

Despite his subordinate position in the all-male family, the protagonist wields power over his "fathers." In a paradox characteristic of the mal du siècle narrative, the hero's obvious incapacitation—here, the disjunction between his high birth and current exile—makes him an object of fascinated speculation. The two patriarchs' curiosity acts to state the narrative's central enigma and figure the reader's desire for its solution: "Chactas and the missionary had a keen desire to know what misfortune had brought a well-born European to the strange resolution to bury himself in the wilds of Louisiana" (147). René's reference to "the event that determined him to come to America" confirms the existence of a secret and hints broadly at a scandal, which the hero claims he must "bury in eternal oblivion" (147). This reference to something buried, however, is tantamount within the terms of the genre to advertizing its imminent excavation. And *René* quickly conforms to this timeworn convention.

The hero's secretiveness serves to inflate the value of his discourse and compound its interest. It also assures his hold over his interlocutors. "Secrecy—the claim to be in possession of a secret, together with an implied willingness to divulge it—forms the paradigm of . . . tactics of narrative authority," writes Ross Chambers in his work on narrative seduction.[11] Nevertheless, the protagonist's narrative "authority" is only a discursive illusion. In fact, "the character's freedom [to recount or to refrain from recounting] is dominated," writes Roland Barthes, "by the *discourse*'s instinct for preservation."[12] In other words, René is not free to refuse to tell his story because the story is not "his." The hero is, instead, subject *to* the story. If the mimesis of "psychology" in the text's presentation of the character is in fact overdetermined by a higher logic, which Barthes calls the "story's interest,"[13] whose interests does the story's interest serve?

Despite the hero's vow of eternal silence, the novel is clearly interested in telling the story, not in postponing it. In the space of a few sentences, readers are transported several years into the future. The arrival of a letter from Europe intensifies René's grief and compounds the curiosity of his paternal audience whose solicitousness and influence produce the foreordained result: "they used so much discretion, gentleness, and *authority* that [René] was finally *obliged* to satisfy them" (148; emphasis added). Once again, the text portrays René as a subject who is himself subjected, thus attenuating his own responsibility for his actions.

Before introducing René's confession, the framing discourse sets the exotic scene: "on the twenty-first day of the month that the Savages call *the moon of flowers*," "under a sassafras tree, on the banks of the Meschacebe" (148). The site, which commands an imposing view of nature, sets the select few above and apart, but within sight of, the excluded community as René shares his secrets. The careful delineation of outside as inside designates René's two addressees and, by extension, the reader, as a privileged audience and envelopes them as it forges a homosocial bond.[14]

The hero's narrative is more than the telling of a tale, it is

also the revelation of a (guilty) secret. In *René*, as in later mal
du siècle novels, the narrative pact which offers a story in exchange for absolution is also a confessional contract, more often than not between men.[15] As Michel Foucault notes in *The
History of Sexuality*, confession requires "the presence . . . of a
partner who is not simply the interlocutor but the authority
who requires the confession, prescribes and appreciates it, and
intervenes in order to judge, punish, forgive, console, and reconcile."[16] In Chateaubriand's novel, the power that literally and
figuratively frames the hero's disclosure is paternal authority.

Although, on the one hand, the text insists on René's subjec-
tion to the authority of his "fathers," on the other, the hero as
narrator has and claims a certain degree of power. René yields
to the father figures' will to knowledge, but he controls the
terms of his narration. Indeed, with his first words, the hero
states his embarrassment but then predicts his audience's reaction as a way of determining it: "How you will pity me! How
wretched my perpetual anxieties will seem to you!" And then,
in a sudden switch to the third person, "Alas, do not condemn
him; he has been punished too much already!" (148–149).

Despite the abhorrence for mixed genres that Chateaubriand states in his preface, his hero's first-person narrative,
which makes up the bulk of the novel, does not adhere to the
conventions of a single narrative genre. Instead, it offers in
quick succession three distinct kinds of novels: autobiographical, philosophical, and Gothic. Each represents the perils and
pleasures of male feminization according to its own literary
conventions and together the three-novels-in-one show how
women are at once necessary and incidental to a young man's
tale of his malaise.

Male Femininity

Echoing Chateaubriand's own defense of the audacious re-
newal of genre in the novel, René adds an exclusionary clause
and disclaimer to his narrative contract: "He therefore set a day
to tell them, not the adventures of his life, for he had not had

any, but the innermost feelings of his soul" (147). Although the
hero had claimed that his story held "little *interest* and was limited to the story of his thoughts and feelings" (147; emphasis
added), the exclusion of the dramatic is no sooner said than
undone. Responding to his listeners' interest, intent on protecting his own interests and following the higher logic of "the story's interest," René's narrative does not, in fact, restrict itself to
the purely subjective depiction of secret thoughts and feelings.
Instead, this first part of his story, which recounts his childhood
and adolescence, begins and ends with the death of his parents,
dramatic events that establish him in the most pathetic terms as
innocent victim. As in the reference to René's Indian wife, here
too a woman—in this case the hero's mother—is mentioned
only to be elided. The son's desire for fatherly love and his loss
of paternal inheritance takes precedence.

THE STARK BEGINNING of René's life story establishes in
schematic terms the exchange of life for death and male for
female that characterizes his entire narrative. With his very first
sentence, René announces that the price of his life was his
mother's death.[17] The mother's loss is thus the male child's (unhappy) gain. Bereft of his mother, the second-born son is also
excluded from the paternal. "Soon abandoned to outsiders, I
was brought up far from my father's house" (149); by contrast,
his older brother, first in paternal succession, enjoys the father's
favor. From the beginning, then, René establishes himself as
emotional orphan.
   This first part of René's tale ends abruptly a few pages later
when his father passes away in his arms, making René a real
orphan. Whereas the mother's death was the hero's original
sin, the father's demise provides the rejected son with an occasion for transcendence: "I learned to know death from the
lips of he who had given me life. . . . It was the first time that
I saw clearly the soul's immortality. . . . And in my holy sorrow that bordered on joy, I hoped one day to join my father's
spirit" (150). Although the patriarch exhibited only cruel indifference to him, the orphan's fondest wish is not reunion with
his mother, but rejoining the father.

Despite a pronounced interest in being his father's son, in his self-portrait, René insists on his deviation from traditional masculine attributes and his exclusion from the paternal line. As a child, the emotionally orphaned protagonist acts out his drama of alienation and dream of reconciliation as an unhappy oscillation: "I had an impetuous temper and an erratic nature. By turns boisterous and joyful then silent and sad, I gathered my young friends around me; then, abandoning them all of a sudden, I would go off to sit by myself" (149). In the preface to the novel, Chateaubriand attributes this moodiness in modern man to a process of feminization caused by the contaminating influence of the fickle, weaker sex. In the novel, however, René's moodiness seems to come from within as well as from without. Though he does not explicitly ascribe his character to the company he keeps with his sister Amélie, the feminine qualities they share do draw them close: "Timid and inhibited in my father's presence, I found pleasure and contentment only with my sister, Amélie. A sweet affinity of temperament and tastes bound me closely to her" (149). The family is thus divided into two opposing camps: the privileged father and older brother on the one hand, the marginalized René and his sister on the other. Socially emasculated, psychologically feminine, and female-identified, Chateaubriand's hero portrays himself as triply feminized and thus triply disadvantaged.

This femininity has its compensations, however. *René* recodes the hero's disempowering feminine weaknesses as a means of empowerment, thus setting the paradigm for future mal du siècle fiction. First and perhaps most important, René's feminization makes him a sympathetic figure who merits center stage. It earns him the right to be the subject, precisely, of a story in which he is both hero and victim. But in René's case, male femininity has more specific benefits as well. René turns his antisocial feminization to advantage by recoding his marginalization and melancholia as emotional sensitivity, aesthetic sensibility, and poetic reverie, as in the following idyllic tableau of the times he shared with his sister when they were young: "Sometimes we would stroll in silence, listening to the muffled rumbling of autumn or to the crackling of the dried leaves that we would trail sadly under our feet; sometimes, in our innocent games, we would follow a swallow into the meadows or the rainbow on rainy hillsides; sometimes we would murmur verses that the sight of nature inspired in us. When I was young, I cultivated the Muses" (149). Despite René's earlier assertions of blissful sibling similarity, the sudden shift from "we" to "I" spells out the gender difference: only the male self courts the poetic muse. René's feminine qualities are a sign of the superiority that sets him above the woman whom he claims is his soul mate. Indeed, in later years, at the height of the Romantic movement, René would become the very model of young artistic genius for his readers, an example more commonly and easily taken up by young men than by young women in a culture that assigned subjectivity, even alienated subjectivity, exclusively to men.

René is not alone in coding his heightened sensitivity as a sign of superiority. At several points in the hero's storytelling, the third-person narrator intervenes to record René's emotions and Chactas's sympathetic reaction:

> René had fixed his gaze on a group of Indians who were gaily passing through the plain. Suddenly his face *softened*, and *tears* fell from his eyes. "Happy savages!" he exclaimed, "oh, why can I not enjoy the peace that always goes with you!" . . . Chactas, stretching out his arm in the dark, and taking the arm of his son, exclaimed, *deeply moved*, "My son! my dear son!" At this, Amélie's brother came out of his reverie, and *blushing* at his *distress*, begged his father to forgive him." [155; emphasis added]

Although the hero's flush of embarrassment registers the inappropriateness of his feminine sensibility, his outward display of emotion seems to guarantee his sincerity and evokes a responsive chord in Chactas, who affirms its pathos. Through the feminine, the orphaned male protagonist is once again a new father's son. Chactas goes so far as to make René's emotional vulnerability a sign of the hero's spiritual nobility: "If you suffer more than others at the experiences of life, you shouldn't be surprised: a great soul necessarily holds more sorrow than a small one" (155). If René and the other mal du siècle heroes possess the related "female virtues" of tenderness and chastity, it is less by design than by default. Despite Chateaubriand's elaborate justification of *René*, his novel is more concerned with the titillating representation of vice than with the exemplary depiction of virtue, just as René in his self-presentation is more interested in demonstrating his unrealized greatness than in paving the way to future goodness. It is this shift in interest from man's ethical goodness to his artistic greatness that may be said to mark the difference between eighteenth-century sentimentality and nineteenth-century Romanticism.

In his study of Samuel Richardson's *Sir Charles Grandison*, a classic eighteenth-century English novel of male femininity, Terry Eagleton notes that the hero blends the feminine virtues of tenderness, feeling, goodness, and chastity with male socioeconomic power to create an ideal of the womanly man.[18] René, by contrast, is neither good nor charitable though he is definitely tender. Unlike Grandison, he is economically and socially marginalized, first as the "younger son," but even more significantly by his own refusal to take a place in society. Yet, as Elaine Showalter has remarked, it is precisely the power Grandison asserts as an aristocrat and a man which makes his "goodness [seem] priggish, chastity pointless, and tenderness merely effeminate."[19] Does René's dependency and powerlessness, more typical of women than of men, more characteristic of the poor than the rich, make his feminine sensibility appealing?

Eagleton shows Richardson's meek and mild hero as an attempt to co-opt the tide of feminization for patriarchy by explicitly centering it on a man: "The 'feminization of discourse' witnessed by the eighteenth century was not a sexual revolution. . . . Male hegemony was to be sweetened but not undermined; women were to be exalted but not emancipated" (95). Chateaubriand's *René* effects a similar recuperation, over fifty years later and in France. But, Eagleton concludes, "what is at stake in *Grandison* is nothing less than the production of a new kind of male subject. If this is a recuperative gesture, raiding the resources of the feminine to 'modernize' male dominance, it is also in its own way an admirable one" (95–96). Is this gesture admirable in *René*? Is the figurative cross-dressing in Chateaubriand's novel a subversive redefinition of gender? One way of answering these questions is to ask whether the blurring of the boundaries of sexual difference in *René* works in the interests of the heroine as well. Before René turns to Amélie to regenerate interest in his tale, however, he first becomes mired in philosophical speculation.

Lost in Time, Lost in Space

With the death of their father, the motherless René and Amélie are truly orphaned. Soon after, the older brother, who now occupies the father's place, exercises his legal dominance, submitting René and Amélie to a patriarchal order that appears all-powerful but cruel and unjust: "I had to leave my father's house which my brother had inherited" (151). Amélie joins a convent, but René acts out his banishment as a picaresque hero whose irresoluteness and excess of passion leads him through a series of aimless geographical displacements, a choice his mal du siècle successors, Obermann and Adolphe, will also make. Once the hero leaves the father's estate, his highly plotted tale of paradise lost loses its thread. It is as if the loss of paternal order precluded the standard conventions of plot.

Losing the minimal elements standard to the novel genre, René's narrative becomes a series of poetic and metaphysical variations on the theme of death in life. In the schematic recounting of his travels from the ancient world to the modern, from the monuments of nature to the ruins of civilization, from solitude within the crowd to a life in exile, René makes little pretense of "realistic" exposition or connection. Each stage of his journey serves instead as an occasion for lyrical apostrophes and ponderous speculations on mortality—"Nothing certain among the ancients, nothing beautiful among the moderns. The past and the present are two incomplete statues: one, quite disfigured, has been drawn from the debris of the ages, the other does not yet have its future perfection" (154).

While the first section of René's tale is clearly a portrait of the artist as a young poet manqué, hero and writer merge even more clearly in this middle section. In passages such as the following, it is difficult to distinguish the portentous lyricism that was characteristic of Chateaubriand's protoromantic style from

René's remarks, impossible to separate the hero as narrator from the author as essayist. "O power of nature, weakness of man," René intones, "a blade of grass may pierce through the hardest marble of tombstones, which the dead, once so mighty, will never be able to move!" (152). Similarly, the hero, like his creator, asserts the "genius of Christianity," as in this passage on monasteries: "These shelters in my country, open to the unfortunate and weak, are often hidden in little valleys, which give the heart a vague feeling of misfortune and the hope of a refuge; sometimes, too, you can find them on high places where the religious soul, like a mountain plant, seems to rise toward heaven, offering up its perfumes" (151).

Whatever René's failings, they are counterbalanced in such passages by the power of expression, depth of emotion, and profundity of insight with which he offers his universalizing pronouncements. In her work on gender and Romantic poetry, Susan Kirkpatrick notes that although Romanticism was "an extension of the 'feminizing' trend in bourgeois culture . . . the Romantic self was also built on aspects of the liberal subject that the redefinition of gender difference had subtly denied to women: both the implicit imperiousness of the liberal subject, arbiter of right, wrong, truth, and falsehood, and its liberatory interests were carried to passionate extremes in the Romantic 'I.' " [20] In other words, what authorizes the grandiose statements of the otherwise ineffectual hero is his (male) ego.

Each stage in this dysphoric prose poem merely repeats the pattern of failed integration and philosophical defeatism established by its predecessors. René himself expresses dissatisfaction with the continual dislocation that moves him from one geographical place to another with no end in sight and from one philosophical topos to another with no occasion for transcendence: "I wearied of the repetition of the same scenes and the same ideas" (158). Only in the final third of the novel, where his continually frustrated ambitious wish becomes channeled within the erotic plot, does René's life gain meaning and his story conventional fictional interest. It is as if, to have a story, a man needs a woman—the wrong woman.

In the meantime, René will, like Obermann, Adolphe, and Amaury, fantasize about the path not taken and dream of an ideal mate, a mirror of the self. In retreat from the world, René nevertheless feels that he has a "power to create worlds" and conjures up for himself a female double: "Ah! if only I had been able to share the delights I was feeling with someone else! O God! if you had given me a woman after my heart's desire; if only you had drawn from my side an Eve, as you did once for our first father, and led her to me" (160). In despair at ever achieving this adolescent fantasy, René, contemplating suicide, writes to his sister, who hastens from the convent to save the hero from death and his narrative from inconclusive circularity. The heroine's arrival brings about an abrupt shift in genre, from soliloquy to melodrama, and in gender, from an exclusive concern with the hero to his specular fascination with the heroine. Here, at the precise midpoint of the story, what René had first announced would be a tale only of its teller, without incident or plot, becomes more traditionally novelistic, resorting to such conventions as multiple characters, intrigue, dialogue, and dramatic confrontation—all organized around a woman who has a secret.

Female Trouble

In his description, the woman in René's life is all good—part woman, part angel. "Amélie had received some divine attribute from nature. . . . She had a woman's timidity and love, an angel's purity and melody" (162). Nevertheless, with the arrival of Amélie, the portrait of a man caught between the strictures of the finite and a longing for the infinite comes abruptly down to earth. As in later mal du siècle novels, the presence of a woman makes the metaphysical decidedly physical. Although René depicts his sister as a paragon of virtue, his love for her is coded in the hyperbolic language of amorous rapture: "To comprehend the bitterness of my later sorrow and my utter transport at seeing Amélie again, you have to understand that she was the only person in the world I had loved. . . . I therefore received Amélie in a kind of emotional ecstasy" (161–162). In

their paradisiacal reunion, the hero portrays the heroine herself as somewhat less than kin and more than kind: "Amélie
looked at me with compassion and tenderness, and covered my
brow with her kisses; she was almost a mother, she was something more tender. . . . I surrendered to Amélie's domination"
(162). Sexuality, heretofore absent from the novel except as an
enigma of abstinence or a fleeting erotic fantasy, returns to the
text with a vengeance to become its ubiquitous mainspring. Although in retrospectively describing this brotherly-sisterly love
René intimates its debt to desire, he sensationalizes the later
revelation of incest by recounting his tale as if he did not now
know its secret, the better to save its scandalous disclosure for
his own dramatic ends.

Borrowing from melodrama in this, the third and longest
section of his tale, René makes woman the site of a struggle
between truth and its expression. After a brief period of euphoria, René discovers that the cost of Amélie's ameliorating
presence is her own dysphoria. In this zero-sum game, his happiness precludes hers. In his retelling, the heroine becomes a
literary commonplace, a walking symptomatology of desire and
its repression: "Amélie was losing the peace of mind and health
that she was beginning to restore in me. She was growing thin;
her eyes became sunken; her manner was listless, and her voice
unsteady" (163). René records in great detail his alter ego's increasing incapacitation: "she would take up her work and set it
down, open a book without being able to read it, start a sentence that she would not finish, suddenly burst into tears and
withdraw to pray" (163). Although this description evokes literary commonplaces of the pangs of unrequited love and/or
repressed sexual desire, René as narrator offers no such diagnosis; he merely confirms the persistence of an enigma and delays its revelation until the final, shocking end. Thus the story
that had started out as the divulging of René's secret shifts to
focus interest on unveiling hers: "In vain I attempted to discover her secret" (163).[21]

Amélie leaves without warning, but leaves a letter that en-
codes, by indirection, clues to her secret. To decipher them
correctly, the hero—and the reader—must subject her text to

a literal rather than a figurative interpretation. "Forgive me, then, for stealing away from you *as though I were guilty*" (164; emphasis added), she writes. Somewhat later, she details at great length the delight a wife would find in René and he in her and she ends by saying, "In your presence she would become all love and innocence; *you would feel that you had found a sister again*" (165; emphasis added). The letter's double entendre unites René in a blissful union with a woman who, in one reading, would be like a sister to him, but in another, would *be* his sister. In retelling his interpretation of the letter, the hero touches on the truth, while apparently remaining blind to it. "Who was forcing her so suddenly to take up religious life?" he asks. "Perhaps Amélie had fallen in love with some man and didn't dare admit it" (166). Despite hints of this kind, René continues to equivocate, thus emphasizing his ignorance and "proving" his innocence.

The climactic moment of female self-disclosure comes in the convent, where Amélie has made her final retreat from René and the world. As a secluded haven for the sublimation, repression, and transcendence of illicit female desire, the convent also provides an occasion for intensifying sexual desire through religious fervor. "For the most violent passion," Amélie explains in a later letter, religion "substitutes a kind of burning chastity in which lover and virgin are one" (173). The erotic and the religious merge in the convent as a source of oxymoronic and sacrilegious titillation. Indeed, for Chateaubriand, the drama of a "burning chastity" is precisely what gives Christianity its appeal: "Only Christianity," he writes, "has set up these terrible struggles between the flesh and the spirit, which are so conducive to dramatic effects."[22] But who suffers the consequences of these dramatic effects and who serves to gain from them?

René records the heroine's final religious vows as a highly charged series of dramatic scenes and tableaux. In despair at the loss of his sister and, it would seem, desperate to become the center of attention, René feels the strong pull of melodrama, which he calls the work of the devil: "Hell goaded me into thinking that I should stab myself in the church and thus

join my last breath to the vows tearing my sister away from me"
(168). Although the hero ultimately resists this temptation, he
succumbs as narrator to "the melodramatic imagination."[23] The
scene of Amélie's taking of the veil weaves the semes of religion
with those of Eros and Thanatos in a characteristically Gothic
mix. The accumulation of graphic details of setting and scene,
action and reaction, builds narrative suspense while putting the
hero—and with him the reader—in a specular relationship to
the female protagonist's unveiling. The reader is made voyeur
of Amélie's confession of illicit desire.

At the height of the ceremony, "a confused murmur
emerged from under the shroud" as Amélie whispers her
shameful confession to God, inadvertently revealing her secret
incestuous desire to René: "may Thy blessings be lavished on
my brother, who has never shared my forbidden passion!" At
these words, the hero, not to be outdone, throws himself on
Amélie's ceremonial shroud, pressing himself into her arms as
he cries out his final adieux: "Chaste bride of Jesus Christ, receive my last embraces through the chill of death and the
depths of eternity, which already have parted *you* from *your
brother*" (169–170; emphasis added). At this moment of truth,
and in his final words to his sister, the hero reveals his fundamental egotism. Barbara Johnson writes of a similar revelation
in Balzac's "Sarrasine": "What is at stake is not the union between two people but the narcissistic awakening of one."[24]
Amélie's avowal of desire makes René aware of his own desirability. Both at the time and in its recounting, René thus makes
the revelation of Amélie's secret a scene, one that sensationalizes virtue and, not incidentally, establishes him as the object of
a love so great it defies the prohibition against incest and led a
virtuous woman to immure herself forever in a convent as a
way of guarding against temptation.

If this shocking climax represents the "victory over repression" (4), which Brooks says is characteristic of melodrama, the
triumph is mixed. While the heroine's brief confession seals her
death to the world, it gives the hero a reason to live, opening a
floodgate of words and emotions and a plenitude of narrative
discourse and pleasure where there had been nothing but emp-

tiness: "O my friends, I realized then what it was to shed tears
for a misfortune that was not imaginary! My passions, indeterminate for so long, avidly seized on this, their first prey.
I even found a kind of unexpected satisfaction in the fullness
of my anguish, and I realized, with a secret sense of joy, that
sorrow is not a feeling that consumes itself like pleasure"
(171). Through a woman's desire, the male self escapes solipsism the better to revel in narcissism. His life now has meaning
because he has a scandalous place in her story. She provides
him with an Other, without which he was condemned to
"le vague des passions," a self-consuming ardor, aimless and
objectless.

As in the eighteenth-century feminocentric tradition, the
heroine is sacrificed and the hero survives.[25] In the eighteenth-
century epistolary novel, however, the hero often lives to mourn
the heroine and reunite with the father figure, but he does not
necessarily tell the tale. Instead, an impartial observer compiles,
edits, and introduces the letters of the hero, heroine, and their
correspondents. *René*, however, follows the pattern of first-person male retrospective novels such as *Manon Lescaut,* in which
the heroine dies *so that* the hero may tell her story.[26] In *René*, it
is not until the heroine's death, announced in the mysterious
letter that has arrived from Europe, that the male protagonist
agrees to tell his story, which is to say her sinful desire. Just as
the hero's presentation of self was founded on a female corpse—
that of the mother—his narrative, too, is predicated on female
death. René is the sole survivor and to the survivor go the spoils
of narrative. The form his narrative takes reveals not only the
hero's vested interests and the "story's interest" but the larger,
ideological interests it serves.

René's confessional narrative has, as I have shown, three
main sections. The first, a family romance and childhood idyll,
sets up an autobiographical situation that follows strict chronological lines from birth through adolescence. With the death of
the father, this story of self becomes a travel narrative cum
metaphysical prose poem. In it, the insight provided by hindsight thematically organizes the discourse as a fruitless quest,
pulled toward the universal. Its sweeping generalities feature

scenes over actors, geographical sites over interpersonal situations. Thus, the first two sections both capitalize on and refashion certain cultural prejudices about what is "interesting" or worthy of a story. They redefine the boundaries of gender and genre by focusing on the introspective musings of a powerless and sensitive male self to the exclusion of standard notions of plot and character.

In the final section, however, René's tale becomes a fragmented, semiepistolary novel of suspense featuring the melodrama of incestuous sexual desire and its revelation. Here, the dynamic of plot clearly delineates a beginning, a middle, and an end, and leads the reader along René's path from ignorance to melodramatic disclosure and final knowledge. In its shift from a concern with "feelings and thoughts" to a chronicling of "adventures," René's narrative moves from internal musings to dramatic external events, from subject to object, and from exposition to plot. The spiritual malady of a male self becomes a *story* by capitalizing on the traditional exigencies of plot and the traditional lure of sex.

In *René*, interest in the hero and his discourse is raised by the *price* a woman paid for loving him and the loss she incurred.[27] For Amélie, that price was a figurative death to the world in the convent, a literal death to the world through yet another altruistic self-sacrifice, which in turn authorizes René to tell her secret.[28] The fiction of female desire and death lends *René* its drama, its point, and its appeal. Woman provides the seemingly minimalist narrative with a more traditional enigma—female desire—to be exploited for its dramatic interest and tragic consequences. Woman is the bait used to arouse the reader's desire for a story always already read.

The hero's narrative may constitute a confession, but the sin he confesses is the *heroine's* illicit longing. The male protagonist refuses to make his tale the occasion for introspection. Though he announces he will reveal "the secret feelings in his soul," he does little soul-searching of his own. René never puts his desire in question and displays no anxiety about his implication in Amélie's. The hero's own desires, hidden perhaps even from himself, are instead disclosed by his interlocutors. In the confession of sex, this "truth" can only be told through the voice of authority, in this case, René's paternal addressees.[29]

The Voice(s) of Truth

René ends his tale with the last sight of his fatherland viewed from the ship that will take him to the New World. The disclosure of Amélie's secret and this conclusion do not coincide with the end of the novel, however, because René's story is also a confession, for which he has yet to receive analysis, absolution, or acquittal. "Throwing himself into Chactas's arms and stifling his sobs," René breaks off his narration with an embrace of the maternal father figure. "Chactas clasped René in his arms; the old man was weeping" (174). Given the success with which René's narrative has turned every weakness to his advantage, and given the warm embrace he again receives from Chactas, the abrupt, censorious ending of the novel which immediately follows comes as a surprise. Father Souël, who up until this point has not uttered a word, cuts short René and Chactas's display of sensibility with "la parole du père."

René's spiritual father finds René contemptible and his misfortunes trifling compared to the virtue and saintliness of Amélie. For Father Souël, René's story is one of exacerbated individualism and condemnable narcissism, which discloses the truth of René's desire. "Your sister has atoned for her sin," he declares, "but if I must speak frankly, I fear that through some terrible justice, that confession from the grave has in turn stirred up your own soul" (175). The voice from beyond the grave, which would be Chateaubriand's own trope of truth in his autobiography, *Mémoires d'outre-tombe*, here names the truth of René's desire, the secret pleasure in pain which allows him to inflame rather than extinguish his passions and relish his recital of their effect on his life.

The priest ends his sermon with an admonition and a warning. He exhorts René to renounce antisocial feminization and self-indulgent melancholia. Nonconformity and isolation, he argues, are the royal road to misery. Chactas hears in Father

Souël's diatribe a condemnation of his own misplaced sympathy and seconds the missionary's judgment with an extended allegory and his own aphoristic pronouncement: "Happiness can be found only in the common paths" (176). Given the author, the text, and the times, such a moral could not help but have a political meaning. Applied to the case of Chateaubriand, it would justify his own return to France and his unholy alliance with his political adversary, Napoleon. The "common paths" were at once a call for other aristocrats to rally to the regime in power as well as a nostalgic evocation of the ideology of pre-revolutionary France, which is the setting for the novel.

The commonest "common path," however, and the one that the fathers oblige René to take involves sexual politics. The hero complies one last time even as he resists adapting to social and sexual norms: "It is said that, encouraged by the two elders, he returned to his wife, but he found no happiness there" (176). A deus ex machina makes short work of the end. Along with Chactas and Father Souël, René "perished soon after in the massacres of the French and Natchez in Louisiana" (176). The characters' premature deaths not only short-circuit the promise of redemption through conformity, they also foreclose a divine retribution that might have been directed specifically at the hero for the reader's edification. The reader may well wonder whether the common path had ever been a viable—or attractive—option.

The text's closing image confirms rather than denies the link between René and his "useless reveries," thus negating Father Souël's role as the repository of truth and value. Instead, René lives on in local legend: "People still point out a rock," writes the narrator, "where he used to go off and sit at sunset" (176). His "resting place" is not a tomb but a cenotaph, which memorializes the hero in and by his absence, just as the text presents the hero as an exception to the rule he is supposed to exemplify. Though marked as a cautionary tale by Chateaubriand's preface and Father Souël's sermon, the novel gives short shrift to its moral. Resisting its pedagogical and moralistic moorings, the text instead follows the lead of secular fiction, which sacrifices the didactic in the interests of a good story. Furthermore, it follows what will become a characteristic Romantic impulse that involves privileging the individual alone, withdrawn from society. The "story's interest" and its author's undercut the novel's elaborate moral framework.

Nineteenth-century reader response to the novel seems to have elided the moral completely. René's claim to fame, which has been considerable, was (and remains) his resistance to the ostensible lesson of the text. In the second and third decades of the nineteenth century, great numbers of contemporary readers—primarily adolescent, bourgeois, and male—identified with the hero and adopted him not as an admonitory example but as a role model. For many mid-nineteenth-century authors, *René* and the mal du siècle were empowering fictions that served as inspiration for their lives as well as their work.[30] For them, the superiority of artistic alienation to social conformism, was the lesson of Chateaubriand's pathbreaking fiction.

New Novel, Old Story

In defining the malaise that for contemporary readers seemed to characterize the age, *René* redefined "man" and rewrote the terms of the novel. At the same time the text reinforced many of the genre's conventions and their traditional ideologies of gender. In the preface, for example, Chateaubriand, like many of his mal du siècle successors, presents his hero's malady as a social, collective phenomenon. The narrative itself, however, focuses on a single individual. Indeed, this early Romantic text, setting the pattern for the works that would follow, so exacerbates the individualism endemic to the novel that this fundamentally introspective work takes on a solipsistic quality. As René does in his story, Chateaubriand in his preface explicitly rejects plot as the driving force behind his texts, thus narrowing the fictional focus on subjectivity still further.[31] But sentiment alone does not make a story. *René* shows that, to merit telling, a metaphysical meditation needs a strong story line, in this case a narrative told as the confession of a secret that hints at a scandal and caters, at least subliminally, to prurient interest.

Like its successors, Chateaubriand's novel offers a titillating

premise, narrative suspense, and climactic closure by capitalizing on a commonplace: the confession of sexual desire and
the narration of its consequences. The mal du siècle novels—
disclosure narratives all—thus appear to exemplify the imbri-
cation of sexuality and confession that, according to Michel
Foucault, has given rise to a "metamorphosis in literature."
Since the eighteenth century, he writes, Western society has
passed, "from a pleasure to be recounted and heard, centering
on the heroic or marvelous narration of 'trials' of bravery or
sainthood, to a literature ordered according to the infinite task
of extracting from the depths of oneself, in between the words,
a truth," which is sex (59). In Foucault's analysis, confessing one's
sexuality is not a liberation from repression but a submission to
the power relations that make such a confession compulsory.
Chateaubriand's novel presents its scene of confession as the
hero's reluctant compliance with just such a discursive imperative. But these power relations are also a transparent fiction that
follows an injunction of a different order, the "story's interest."
In making sex the novel's secret, the mal du siècle novels do not
so much defy a prohibition as conform to genre conventions
that, in turn, offer the narrator ample compensations.

When the subject who confesses in the canonical mal du
siècle novel is heterosexual and male, which is almost invariably
the case, his confession of sexuality follows an age-old adage of
narrative causality. To understand the riddle of man's behavior
one need only "chercher la femme."[32] The truth of sexual desire that must be extracted, in Foucault's words, "from the
depths of oneself" is instead displaced onto the heroine. It is
she who allows the hero to combine the hermeneutic with the
prurient in the telling of his tale. The strategy in René, as in
later mal du siècle novels, consists in creating interest in character through the feminine in the man while providing melodramatic interest in plot through the often fatal effect of the
man on the woman.[33] By linking commonplaces of literary causality with ideologies of gender difference, the hero ensures his
discursive empowerment. Thus, in the mainstream early Romantic novel, the author uses traditional strategies of narrative
and sexual politics to compensate his alter ego's feminized disempowerment. If, on the one hand, the mal du siècle novel

breaks down gender stereotypes by feminizing the male, in doing so it does not so much dismantle the imbalance of power
between the sexes as maintain it in a modern, more camou-
flaged form. In Chateaubriand, the hero may be feminized, but
the heroine is not virilized. Staël's *Corinne*, by contrast, experi-
ments with sex role reversal for both sexes and uses far different means for very different ends.[34]

3

What's Wrong with Mr. Right

Staël's *Corinne, or Italy*

GERMAINE DE STAËL'S *Corinne, or Italy,* published just five
years after the first appearance of *René,* could not be
more different from Chateaubriand's novel in form, in sub-
stance, or in sexual politics. In contrast to Chateaubriand's
minimalist, elegiac novel of a hero's self-serving confession,
Staël's long, iconoclastic work sets up Oswald, her own version
of the mal du siècle hero, against Corinne, a woman of genius
who is almost Promethean in her powers and achievements.
René shows the advantages that accrue to the hero in telling the
secret of a woman's guilty desire and its terrible consequences.
The challenge to Staël's heroine and text is, precisely, to resist
this premise of female guilt and defer the fatal causal logic of
this traditional plot. Although midway through, this experi-
mental novel succumbs to a traditional notion of narrative
consequences and shows a problematic and self-defeating idealization of female masochism, *Corinne* was a work of defiant
formal and ideological iconoclasm in a profoundly conservative
age. What, then, is a mal du siècle hero doing there?

Oswald, Lord Nelvil, a Scotsman far from home, is, like
René, in mourning for his father and has lost all interest in life.
Reserved, timorous, and incapable of taking a stand, he has
posed a problem for readers ever since the publication of Staël's
text. Why does the heroine see this melancholy man as Mr.
Right? I will argue that the hero's mal du siècle, which makes
him so wrong for the heroine, is precisely what makes him right

for this novel of feminist protest. In *Corinne*, Staël reveals the new feminized man not as a sad exception to patriarchal rule but as the latest incarnation of the law of the fathers.

B Y THE TIME *Corinne* was published in 1807, a modern version of the male-dominated social order of the ancients, which Chateaubriand had eulogized in his preface to *René* in 1802, had been set in place by Napoleon. Bifurcating the world, this new order sought to make the public sphere male while it relegated women to hearth and home. The emperor's campaign of imperial conquests put the nation in a constant state of war, thus reestablishing a military ethos as a masculine ideal and making affairs of state the exclusive province of men. The Napoleonic Code tightened the loopholes in the patchwork of previous laws by codifying the political, economic, and legal subordination of women to men in a thorough, systematic fashion. According to the new domestic ideal, women—even aristocratic women—were to be obedient, submissive, and devoted daughters, wives, and mothers, the very antithesis of Germaine de Staël's claims to fame as a writer and salonnière—a woman to be reckoned with. Writing prolifically and wielding influence in and through her liberal salon, Staël defied the new constraints on women's activities and ambitions. As a price for her high visibility and outspoken engagement in public affairs, she was mocked, condemned, and finally exiled by Napoleon.

Unlike many of her feminist contemporaries who fought for women's rights and political equality, and despite her own status as defiant exception, in her writings Staël embraced the new order that relegated women to the home as a way of ensuring social power for women.[1] In Staël's vision of a post-revolutionary world governed by principles of economic and political liberalism, it was the private not the public sphere that would be preeminent. Given what Staël believed was their capacity for ennobling sentiment and sensibility, women would provide a countervailing ethos to curb the excesses of self-interest necessary to a liberal economy. Agents of social enlightenment, women would preside as they had in the seventeenth-century French salons over the free exchange of ideas and take the lead in the field of literature. Thus, in contrast with Chateaubriand's dark view of a modern, feminized world in his preface to *René*, Staël's essays posit women's influence on men and society as a civilizing, moral force that merits their claim to the private sphere, which is redefined as the social, intellectual, and artistic realm.[2]

Although Staël believed that the essence of ordinary women's role was to keep the home fires burning, thus ensuring the status quo and the new economic order, she also argued that exceptional individuals—male or female—had a far more public and progressive function in society. Extraordinary men and women, she wrote, had the right to develop their genius according to their own lights, even if this meant resistance to the powers that be.[3] To Napoleon's policy of coercive conformism through repression, censure, and exile, Staël thus opposed an ideal of liberal individualism.

Though a central theme in her essays and other writings, the case for the exceptional woman is made most spectacularly in *Corinne*. In the novel, a woman of genius is free to develop her talents to rousing public acclaim not in France, where such an ambitious wish had been foreclosed for women (and was becoming less and less possible for independent-minded men as well), but in Italy before its conquest by Napoleon. Contemporary response to *Corinne* and to Corinne registers the range of views on the Napoleonic ideology of conformism and on Staël's clear defiance of this new social order.[4]

Gender and Genre: Neither and Both

Staël's iconoclastic novel and its extraordinary heroine enjoyed immediate and prolonged success. Reviewing the forty extant private letters written to Staël about the novel, Simone Balayé notes that these readers were enchanted, electrified, and moved by the text and its heroine. As two readers' letters to Staël put it: "All Paris shares [Oswald, Lord] Nelvil's love for Corinne. If only you could be here to see the sensation she is making," and for the novel, "all society is enchanted . . . I hear only cries of admiration."[5] To the extent that the novel's consid-

erable popularity was due to an appreciation of the female protagonist's exceptional talents and the woman writer's audacious
ambitions, contemporary reader response marks a form of resistance to official ideology that confined women and the novel
within strict limits.[6]

The contemporary press, which was dominated by Napoleon
and his supporters, was, predictably, far less favorable to Staël's
work. Objections to the accomplished, independent, and strong-
willed heroine were couched in the language of the new gender
orthodoxy. In his review of *Corinne*, for example, the abbé de
Féletz, the most influential voice among Staël's reactionary op-
ponents, writes that her heroine could not be considered admirable because "woman's greatest charm, indeed her greatest
glory" is in the "practice of all the soft, pleasant and modest
virtues." Woman's best and only destiny is "first to be a timid
and respectful daughter, then a lovable and virtuous wife, a
sensitive and tender mother."[7]

The anonymous reviewer at the *Gazette de France* makes the
gender distinction even clearer as he shows that what is wrong
about Corinne is that she is more like a man than a woman:

> If you are looking for someone who, since earliest childhood, dreams
> only of glory, who longs to escape the peace of the domestic hearth,
> and flees from it to run from one public stage to another; someone
> who dreads men's opinion much less because of his morals than be-
> cause of his talents; someone who with no shade of timidity or reserve
> seeks love as he seeks fame, and shows himself always ready to sacrifice
> himself for one or the other; someone who is said to feel a profound
> *melancholy*, but who always wants a crowd to witness his tears and his
> successes, *you will find that man in Corinne*.[8]

The reviewer concludes that a woman who is like a man is not
a woman at all: "A woman who has the talents and qualities of
a man should not be counted as a woman any more than a rose
bush that bears laurel leaves would be counted as one of its
kind" (591). Corinne, who is literally crowned with a (masculine) laurel wreath in the novel is at best a bizarre hybrid, at
worst a monstrous hermaphrodite. Indeed, the latter accusa-
tion was the one leveled at Staël herself for arrogating what
were considered male prerogatives by writing, speaking, and

acting in the public world.[9] Echoing the moral that Chactas directed at René in Chateaubriand's novel, the majority of reviewers drew from the text the conformist credo intoned by the abbé de Féletz: "Every woman must remain on the road that nature and the social order indicated for her" (3).

Though the conservative critics of 1807 found much to criticize in Staël's audacious heroine, they were particularly puzzled and irritated by the indecisive and phlegmatic Oswald, Lord Nelvil. The *Gazette de France* reviewer sees the question as the flip side of Corinne's gender reversal:

> Are you looking instead for someone who is reserved and shy, full of respect for her parents, someone who would die rather than marry without their approval, who dares not resolve to be the first to speak of the love she feels, who loves being mysterious and delights in making a secret of her life; someone who never defies the authority of opinion and customs, and whose idea of her duties makes her continually worried and timorous about her least little action; *you will find that woman in the melancholic Lord Nelvill* [sic].   [592; emphasis added]

Like Staël's heroine, who enjoys the powers and privileges associated with masculinity, the hero, who takes on the weaknesses connected with femininity, clearly transgresses gender boundaries. But in both cases, the new ideology of increasingly separate spheres recuperates the reversal as proof and reinforcement of an "essential" sexual difference.

Corinne, or Italy defies the ideology of separate literary spheres on the formal level as well. It does so not by reversing the terms of the binary opposition but by refusing the logic of either/or. Staël's work is two texts in one: a love story *and* a travel narrative. For contemporary reviewers, even those sympathetic to her project, this coupling broke a fundamental law of genre, that is, uniformity. "Good taste rarely approves works *of an ambiguous genre* where truth is mixed with fiction and two different goals are proposed."[10] In a strategy that recalls the medical reaction to biological hermaphrodites and their sexual ambiguity through the ages,[11] the reviews all agreed that the text consisted of two genres and even which two genres these were, but they insisted that one must predominate. The critics were evenly divided between those who considered the love story merely a vehicle for the didactic description of Italy and those who saw Corinne's oral tour of Italy as an irritating distraction from the main love plot. For the critic at the *Mercure de France*, for example, "Corinne interests readers only at the expense of Italy."[12] For the *Gazette de France* reviewer, however, the description of Italian sites, art works, and customs disserved the work, which he believed was essentially a novel, by making its fictional components all the more obviously a lie.[13]

Setting the two genres alongside and against each other in a radical innovation of literary form is, nevertheless, precisely what allowed Staël to make the novel, which was generally considered a frivolous and insignificant genre concerned only with love, both a serious forum for ideas and a powerful form of social critique. *Corinne, or Italy* explicitly demonstrated that the representation of individual lives and private emotions, which was the sine qua non of the novel as genre—one reduced to its minimalist essence in Chateaubriand's *René*—, has everything to do with larger questions of cultural ideology and sexual politics. Specifically, the descriptive passages in which Corinne holds sway and which characterize the first half of the novel, offer cultural, political, and narrative alternatives to conventional wisdom and traditional plot. The love story, which ultimately reasserts its dominion in the second half, demonstrates the devastating personal costs of the demands for conformity to that "wisdom" and those laws of genre. To discuss the premise let alone the plot of Staël's feminocentric novel, however, we must begin not with its heroine but with its hero.

Mr. Right?

Nancy K. Miller argues in *Subject to Change* that the challenge for an exceptional heroine is finding a man who would be her match, a problem that troubled contemporary readers of *Corinne* as well.[14] How could Oswald, wrote one contemptuous reviewer, "who is finally the weakest, the most insignificant of men," capture the heart of a woman who was so clearly his superior?[15] Even Staël's friends, who were enthralled by the heroine and the new ideas and sensibility the novel offered, had trouble being sympathetic to Oswald. A year after the publication of *Corinne*, in "Un héros allemand," an essay intended for her treatise on Germany, Staël acknowledged the problem: "I chose an Englishman as the hero of *Corinne* and people thought, perhaps with good reason, that I had not depicted a man who was equal to the woman who loved him."[16] She revealed, however, that this inequality was essential to the novel's basic premise: "I wanted to highlight the misfortunes that result from certain qualities in a woman, and what misfortune could there be for a woman if she were perfectly loved by a man worthy of her?" (94) Inasmuch as Staël's experience with Napoleon had shown her precisely what some of the other misfortunes befalling an exceptional woman might be, her failure of imagination on this point testifies to the constraints that literary conventions and the myths of romantic love exercised on her imagination and thus on the politics of her text. Despite the work's attempts to expand the purview of the novel beyond the narrowly interpersonal and to resist the traditional love plot, in *Corinne*, the question is nevertheless not *whether* the extraordinary heroine will come to a bitter (which is to say unloved) end, but *how* and *with whom*. In order to tell this story, Staël had an interest in sketching out a portrait of the Wrong Man, a hero who will neither equal the heroine nor love her enough.[17] For there to be any dramatic interest created by this state of affairs, however, the hero must nevertheless *seem* to be Mr. Right and the heroine, following a familiar pattern, must remain blind to his faults or their ineradicable nature until it is too late.

Part 1: The Fine Art of Deferral

From the very first sentence, the narrator of *Corinne* leaves the reader no doubt that the novel's male protagonist has all the standard social advantages of the most conventional literary hero—looks, brains, noble blood, and wealth—and the traditional emotional advantages of the sentimental hero: "His was a restless nature, sensitive and passionate."[18] Like other mal du siècle protagonists, however, Oswald, Lord Nelvil, is besieged by melancholy. At twenty-five, Oswald "had wearied of life; his mind prejudged everything, and his wounded sensibility no longer had any taste for the illusions of the heart" (3). As in *René*, the loss of the father makes the hero first and foremost his father's son, but Oswald's grief is compounded by guilt. As the inconsolable young man sails away from home and toward Italy, the narrator sketches out a geography of affection in which filial love is inextricably tied to the centripetal pull of the fatherland. Oswald's mal du siècle is, in more ways than one, a *mal du pays*.

There are obvious resemblances between Oswald and the exiled and orphaned René, but Staël's narrator establishes early on that on two major counts Oswald resembles none of the mal du siècle protagonists before or since. Whereas melancholy leads René to blind self-centeredness and pointless wanderings, Oswald's own depressive state makes him self-abnegating to a fault and capable of great physical heroism. Within the first few chapters of the novel, Oswald proves himself the swashbuckling hero of a *roman d'aventures*. Strong, fearless, and calm, Staël's protagonist, caught in a storm at sea, takes the helm of the ship in a storm, commands the crew, and comforts the other passengers. Upon arriving in Italy, he single-handedly saves the town of Ancona from a fire and rescues those whom the townspeople would have let die: the Jews in their ghetto and the inmates in their asylum. Though Oswald shows the brave heroism so central to the new Napoleonic ideal of military manliness, his valor gives it an important ethical twist—he does not conquer enemies but instead rescues victims—which shows his enlightened lack of prejudice against those whom society had cast out. None of the other mal du siècle heroes come anywhere near displaying Oswald's selflessness or derring-do.[19] Indeed, unlike all of them, Oswald *does* something, and even *excels* at what he does. Thus the single exception to the marked feminization of the male protagonist in mal du siècle writing is in a novel by a woman. The unique combination of melancholy and virility that Staël gives Oswald is linked to the two other factors in the novel that make it so unusual, not only in this tradition but in any novel before hers: Staël's cosmopolitan vision and her extraordinary heroine.

Staël sets the action of her story and draws her characters from not one but three European countries. In the schematized Europe of 1794–1803 represented in *Corinne*, the French men are courtiers, dispossessed and displaced by the Revolution, while Italian men are busy patronizing the arts and pleasing their lovers. Only in democratic and parliamentary England are men, such as Oswald, called to traditional masculine pursuits: military service and civic duty. In his 1807 defense of the novel, Benjamin Constant argues that "Corinne's lover had to be an Englishman, which is to say the inhabitant of a country where men's careers have been predetermined, their duties are concrete, where public opinion is harsh, mixed with prejudice and strengthened by force of habit."[20] The reason is that in the new, nineteenth-century version of the novel, with its emphasis on the inner self, there must be impediments to love and these must come from within. In other words, what Staël's novel about female genius requires is a man who has internalized a cultural value system so thoroughly that it is of a piece with the man himself—and at odds with the happiness of the exceptional woman. More significantly, however, Staël's choice locates the crux of the problem as an ideal of masculinity which takes as its corollary the subordination of women in the private sphere, a point to which I return below.

To make the extraordinary heroine's love for this man plausible, Staël must raise her hero to her heroine's elevated level. She does so by giving him the highest possible qualities in this masculine domain: selfless devotion and superior courage. However, she rewrites these terms of gender difference to her gifted heroine's advantage. By confining Oswald's superiority to the domains of military daring and physical courage, she is able in a bold, revisionist move to claim the artistic and intellectual sphere for her female protagonist—a division of labor that is anathema to the England of Staël's novel and to the Napoleonic France from which Staël herself had been exiled for precisely this defiant wish.

Triumphant Heroism

Having proved his mettle under fire in Ancona and fleeing the public approbation of his heroism, the gloomy and taciturn hero arrives in Rome. There "he was told that this very morning the most celebrated woman in Italy was to be crowned at the Capitol: Corinne—poet, writer, *improvisatrice*, and one of the most beautiful women in Rome. . . . Nothing could have been more opposed to an Englishman's customs and opinions than focusing the public eye on a woman's fortunes" (19). While Oswald's stay in Italy will cause him to call into question what he takes for granted, the narrator implies early on that his suspension of his English values will last only "for a time" (19). Oswald's grand European tour is nothing but a long detour on his way back home.

What Oswald witnesses is the spectacular public triumph of a woman genius. Her gala coronation on the steps of the Capitol takes place to the universal cries of "Long live Corinne! Long live genius! Long live beauty!" (21) This crowning of a woman and of artistic genius implies a notion of power completely foreign to the British officer and to Napoleonic France. Unlike the "statesmen borne in triumph by the people" in Oswald's native land, Corinne's "triumphal chariot had cost not a single tear to anyone; and neither remorse nor fear checked admiration for those most beautiful gifts of nature: imagination, feeling, and thought" (22). In this idealized version of the artist, her power is stripped not only of its competitiveness—there are no male or female rivals for her throne—but also of its potential for abuse. Unlike Napoleon's conquest of Italy in 1805, Corinne's victory comes at no cost and much happiness.[21]

Given the hyperbolic representation of the heroine's superior talents and her formidable success, it would be tempting to call the Corinne–Oswald couple an example of gender role reversal, as some of the contemporary reviewers did. The narrator who had established the "feminized" Oswald's "manly" virtues and courage with the dramatic account of his two rescue missions is also quick to undercut the "virilization" of the heroine by underscoring her traditional feminine qualities. As if to reassure the reader, the narrator insists that the woman of genius is still a woman. Shy at seeing herself celebrated, and self-effacing, Corinne is vulnerable to the opinion of others and apologetic for her success.[22] More than modesty, however, Corinne's Achilles' heel is her eyes. Having caught sight of Oswald in the crowd, Corinne turns back again to see him as she descends the throne. In her eagerness to catch another glimpse of the perfect stranger, her crown falls.

All in the Family

In her illuminating essay on *Corinne* in *Subject to Change*, Miller argues that the heroine's faux pas is emblematic of the power relations inherent in the "work of the gaze" that is central to the novel. The gaze exchanged between hero and heroine is a "gendered and (gendering) asymmetrical operation of looks [which] from the beginning structures [their] relations of power and desire."[23] Miller shows that inasmuch as Oswald sees *as a man* and constructs Corinne as a woman who needs a man, Corinne's desire to see and be seen *as a woman* means that her private relations with him will be traditionally gendered and fundamentally disabling (187). From the very beginning, however, the gaze is shown to be an uncanny *recognition*. For both hero and heroine, love at first sight is in fact a scene of repetition that operates with the force of what has been not only foreseen but preordained.

Corinne singles out Oswald from the crowd, *recognizes* him as an Englishman and feels thereby impelled to match her words to his obvious state of grief. What might, in an eighteenth-century sentimental drama have been a recognition scene courtesy of a shared bloodline becomes the acknowledgment of *cultural* affinities in *Corinne*. The heroine, unbeknown to anyone but herself, is the orphaned daughter not only of an Italian mother but also of an English father, who was Oswald's father's closest friend. Stifled by England's conformist social

order and its repressive treatment of women, she had fled to
Italy as a young woman where she took on a new name, Corinne, and made a reputation for herself through her inspired
public verse improvisations and other literary and artistic ac-
complishments. What Corinne sees in Oswald is thus a return
of the repressed—her paternal heritage. In this sense Oswald
is, in Gutwirth's words, "the heroine's *Doppelgaenger*. He embodies the internalized self-destruction inherent in Corinne's
daring stance: he is her alter-ego, the other through whom she
is destroyed, but with whom she herself cannot help identifying."[24] Thus, although Staël's novel breaks out of the narrow
confines of the sentimental novel to include the entire European continent, the world she invents ends up replicating the
repressive constraints of the family circle.

Though hardly uncommon in literature, in *Corinne, or Italy*
this genealogical repetition compulsion gains a decidedly feminist resonance. The father explicitly represents both the heroine's past and the entire patriarchal order—English style—
and, in particular, its construction of woman as the sex that is
rarely seen and seldom heard. By contrast, in Italy, her mother's native land, father figures and even families are conspicu-
ously absent. Corinne leads a free and independent existence
as a woman artist under a name of her own choosing and without a patronym. Falling in love with Oswald will mean having
to confront not only the father's name, which she had rejected,
but also the interdiction she had defied, which had sought to
deny her not only the full development of her talents but also
her happiness in love. Years before the heroine's coronation on
the steps of the Capitol and the protagonists' love at first sight,
Lord Nelvil, Oswald's father, had rejected the gifted adolescent
girl as an inappropriate match for an Englishman's son. In resisting a script that has already doomed them as a couple, Corinne's only hope is that her love and Oswald himself will prove
stronger than the fathers' ability to create sons and daughters
in their own likeness who can do no more than toe the patriarchal line. Sustaining this hope for both protagonists as well as
for the reader is the knowledge that Corinne has made a life
for herself on her own terms in Italy and that Oswald is on
foreign soil, his ties to the fatherland temporarily broken.

Throughout the first half of the novel, both Oswald and Corinne see in each other the fantasy of a second chance and strive,
he out of ignorance and she despite her knowledge, to disprove
the father's prediction. From the beginning, however, their desires are of a different temporal order. For Oswald, unaware of
his father's explicit disapproval of Corinne and tormented with
remorse for his previous dalliance with a French woman, Corinne inspires a dream of continuity: "what if he could recover
memories of his native land and at the same time gain a new
life through the imagination; what if he could be reborn to the
future *and yet not break with the past?*" (33; emphasis added). To
be perfect, Oswald's future would have to be blessed by the father and continue what has already been. The heroine, on the
other hand, knows the past and suspects that such a future is
both imperfect and impossible. Therefore she sees in their time
together a chance to construct a world for two, *in the present*. In
her fantasy of having it all, "all" is a present time of stolen moments in which she might be both celebrated and loved, despite
the father's interdiction. The tension between these two desires
dominates the novel. While one drive, represented by the hero,
moves imperiously toward a familiar goal—settling the heroine
down to marriage or abandoning her for a more conventional
mate—the other, represented by the heroine, attempts to fore-
stall this terrible teleology by opening up another space and
another time not subject to the constraints of the proper and
plausible love plot.[25]

Timeless Pleasures

The hero, captivated by the exotic Other who is also so reassur-
ingly the Same, defers to the heroine and prolongs his stay in
her city. Seizing the opportunity offered by this interlude, Corinne proposes herself as Oswald's guide to Rome and later to
Italy. As they listen in reverie to the fountains at Saint Peter's,
the narrator notes that "in this place above all *time is powerless*"
(58; emphasis added)—a remark that would serve equally well
as a comment on the novelist's ability to make Rome a space

that arrests the insistent forward drive of plot and its attendant conventions of gender and genre. For over three hundred pages, *Corinne, or Italy* becomes an intellectual travelogue instead. In this most unusual fiction, the lovers' courtship is staged within and as a sightseeing tour, complete with Corinne's lectures on Roman history and monuments, discourses on Italian art and literature, and lengthy discussions between the characters comparing European aesthetics and mores.

During this interlude, writes Marie-Claire Vallois in her study of the novel, "narrator, protagonists, and reader share the euphoria of amorous ecstasy in a timeless present, the present of tourist descriptions."[26] Here Staël allows the heroine to delay obeying the father's imperative that she choose between love and glory. Instead, she is able to enjoy, for a time, both a traditionally masculine and a traditionally feminine triumph, in the public as well as the private sphere. Staël offers in *Corinne, or Italy* what few novels have: a sustained representation of a companionable and passionate love that is compatible with the *heroine*'s ambitious wish. In stark contrast with other mal du siècle novels, the idyll in Staël's work is a substantive interlude for adults in the present, not a nostalgic glimpse back at childhood as in *René* or a momentary adolescent euphoria turned psychological nightmare as in Constant's *Adolphe*. Furthermore, in *Corinne*, the heroine's glory is not a fantasy of future success but a realized goal, confirmed again and again by both the lovestruck hero and public adulation of artistic genius in Italy.

In Chateaubriand and Constant's novels, every new site, no matter how unique, merely reflects the melancholic protagonist and confirms his unchanged condition. In Staël's novel, by contrast, a change of venue offers viable alternatives to other cultures' truisms and reveals them as contingent upon cultural differences and subject to change over time. In Italy, free from the tyranny of public opinion, Corinne is able to engage Oswald, otherwise blindly subject to the values of English society, in an ongoing conversation in which society itself is subject to analysis—sometimes in pointedly feminist and surprisingly modern terms. Corinne explains to Oswald, for example, that in Rome, he will see educated women who are "professors at the academies, . . . giving public lectures; and were you tempted to laugh, people might ask you: *Is there any harm in knowing Greek? Is there any harm in work to earn a living? So why do you laugh at something so simple?*" (102).

Although in the novel one nation provides a point of comparison from which to criticize another, *within* two of those countries—France and England—the logic of social interaction is not only restrictive but inescapable. This social and geographical determinism is most evident in the sexual arena. France is portrayed as torn by the Revolution but still mired in libertine deception and victimization. England is shown as a land locked in a narrow-minded insistence on domestic virtue bound by marriage. In Italy, on the other hand, Oswald and Corinne are free to choose a path in which seduction, virtue, and marriage are not the reigning issues. Placing the bulk of the action of her novel in that country, Staël subverts—at least temporarily—long-standing fictional conventions that make love the exclusive subject of novels.

Most previous literary heroines are defined primarily by their desire to love and be loved. Staël shows that her desire for the heroine includes this wish but goes beyond it as well. Though Corinne is tempted and will finally be doomed by her love for Oswald, she expresses profound doubts that love is worth the price of leaving Italy and the independence, pleasure, and fulfillment it represents. "For this heroine," writes Gutwirth, "no less than for Eugène de Rastignac or for Julien Sorel, the power to act on the world, to be free, rivals love in importance and vies with it as supreme value."[27] Corinne's love of liberty transforms her notion of love into an ideal of equality and even fraternity. Unlike Oswald, the heroine desires "not so much a match in marriage," writes Miller, "as the perfect *destinataire*: . . . a privileged interlocutor and reader in the form of a friend and lover."[28] Inasmuch as Staël has created a heroine who has something substantive to say and a hero who will listen (although he will not always hear), she revises the love plot as a courtship that is also a conversation. The lovers' conversation is an exchange of information, moreover, and a debate from widely divergent views about ideas as well as feelings.[29]

Although Oswald holds his own in these debates, Corinne

dominates. In her own territory, she is the expert, the primary subject of discourse and of knowledge, while Oswald is her ignorant and inexperienced pupil. As they tour the monuments of Rome, it is she who teaches him to see and to feel: "'Stand here, next to the altar,' Corinne told Lord Nelvil. 'You will see the church of the dead through the iron grating under our feet, and when you raise your eyes, your gaze will barely reach the top of the vault. Even seen from below, the dome inspires a feeling of terror'" (60). Like René, she draws the general rule from the specific example: "What we know is as inexplicable as the unknown; but you might say we are practiced in our routine vagueness, whereas new mysteries are terrifying and upset our mental faculties" (60). Many of Corinne's descriptions and universalizing pronouncements are almost indistinguishable in form and content from those of the omniscient narrator.[30] As in *René*, this confusion of character and narrator (or even author) gives the protagonist's views considerable weight. Both René and Corinne serve in their respective novels as the principal spokespersons for the new Romantic aesthetic of dizzying contrasts and as prime examples of a sensibility that privileges feeling and, in Corinne's case, enthusiasm.

In the mal du siècle novel, however, there are other, more dominant traits in these impassioned protagonists: a profound melancholy and decided anomie. Chateaubriand combines both sides of the Romantic equation within his hero René. Staël splits the mal du siècle protagonist in two and gives each character focused attention and the chance to discourse at length. To her sensitive hero, she assigns the melancholic side of the "unfulfilled potential" equation. To her heroine she gives the expansive energy and enthusiasm as well as the unparalleled ambition and talent that make Corinne the prototype of Romantic genius in its most empowered and triumphant form.

The contrast with the heroine's role in Chateaubriand's novel could not be more striking. In *René*, Amélie is primarily the enigmatic object of the hero's inattention. Corinne, on the other hand, is unquestionably a full subject in her own terms. In fact, Staël's heroine articulates a politics and embodies an ethics that call into question precisely the kind of role Chateaubriand's heroine plays as sympathetic witness, unwitting cause, and tragic victim of the male protagonist's plot. This challenge is possible in part because woman in *Corinne* is not, as she is in Chateaubriand, a metonym for sex.

Practicing Safe Sex

In sharp contrast to the sentimental as well as the libertine tradition, Staël's novel short-circuits the sexual component of her protagonists' love relations. Passive, indecisive, and proper to a fault, Oswald is far from a vile seducer. It is the heroine who captivates the hero, but she does not seduce Oswald with her sexual charms, nor does she enchant him as the means to a specifically erotic goal. Strikingly attractive, thoroughly charming, and keenly attuned to beauty in all the senses, Corinne's sexuality is nevertheless only suggested, never displayed. Although neither character comes to the other a virgin, the novel does not make the specifically sexual content of their experience a focus, nor does it portray the passion between them as primarily a matter of sexual longing.

The absence of sexuality in the novel sends a mixed message. On the one hand, it emphasizes the heroine's "feminine" virtue and would thus seem to be of a piece with Corinne's equally "feminine" modesty, which was duly noted by the narrator in the heroine's first dramatic appearance in the novel. Claudine Herrmann links this doubly coded femininity in *Corinne* to the difficulty inherent in portraying a woman of genius: "It is not—[Staël] seems to be saying—because a woman is free and famous that she becomes either indecent or pretentious."[31] Thus, the heroine's modesty reflects the limitations set by the culture's sexual double standard.

On the other hand, Corinne's virtue and the hero's high sense of honor allow Staël to write against the implicit ideology of her predecessors and the lowest common denominator of most love stories. Her heroine is not a sexual prey as in libertine fiction, nor is Oswald's love for her merely the decorous manifestation of his—and the reader's—desire for a sexual fix, as in certain sentimental works. By sidestepping sexuality, Staël obviates the commonplaces of seduction as well as the moral of her most influential predecessor. Rousseau's *La Nouvelle Héloïse* exemplifies the ideology of the eighteenth-century sentimental novel in which the "drama of the aggressive male checked by the virtuous woman is paradoxically a reaffirmation of the patriarchal authority of the family."[32] Although the patriarchal family is central to *Corinne*, Staël makes its purview more emotional and moral than explicitly sexual, and she criticizes rather than praises the effect it has on those in its power, a point to which I return below.[33]

In *Pudeur et romantisme*, Janine Rossard argues that Staël's valorization of sexual modesty was part of a general movement of protest against the hypocrisy of conventional morality in the late eighteenth and early nineteenth centuries, which included both men and women writers.[34] Nevertheless, among these authors, "modesty" takes very different forms for very different purposes. In an illuminating comparison of Chateaubriand and Staël, for example, Godelieve Mercken-Spaas notes that Chateaubriand gives Eros a secondary position in his fiction, while in Staël, love is a central preoccupation.[35] She goes on to argue what I have shown as well: in Chateaubriand, sex gets maximum play when the woman is a figment of the hero's wish-fulfilling fantasy or when the heroine is literally dead or figuratively dying. In *Corinne*, however, Staël desexualizes desire and makes her heroine a full subject in her own right. Corinne is neither a full-time spokesperson for a patriarchal order that oppresses her, as in Rousseau, nor is she primarily and most spectacularly the (dying) object of a man's scopophilic gaze, as in Chateaubriand.

And yet, by the end of the novel, Corinne will succumb to a similar literary imperative. Though she avoided trial by sexual seduction, Corinne will be made to face the hero's abandonment and its inevitable outcome, her death. Despite the novel's explicitly feminist critiques of the sex-gender system, despite its subversion of gender stereotypes, and despite its radical suspension of plot, *Corinne, or Italy* finally capitulates to many of the traditional ideological and narratological conventions about men, women, and power. As I have shown, these assumptions are not imposed from without but instead are embedded within the novel from its beginning as a matter of recognition. They define its central tension as the struggle between the idea of a proper plot and ending (as exemplified by Oswald) and a desire to sustain some other plane of existence (as Corinne attempts to do in their Roman interlude).

Midway through the novel, the dynamic definitively changes in favor of Oswald and the father. The novel describes this shift in terms both archaeological and geological. Like the men he admires who study Roman history through its ruins, Oswald works not only to uncover but to resurrect the buried relics of Corinne's past: "I know no other study that might appeal to me more . . . *it is as if you bring back to life what you discover,* as if the past reappears beneath the dust that has buried it" (72–73; emphasis added). The hero will reveal his own past to Corinne midway up Mount Vesuvius, "on the border between life and death" (207), a fitting image for the potentially destructive force of what the novel has, up until then, managed to bury below the surface of the text.

Part 2: The High Cost of Conforming

When the repressed returns, as it does with a vengeance in the second half of the novel, it appears as a long-delayed revelation of secrets and the figurative exhumation of the father figures. In a rare show of initiative, Oswald offers to make his confession first. With this first assertive move, the balance of power between the two protagonists definitively shifts and the third-person omniscient novel suddenly becomes a first-person narrative not unlike that of Chateaubriand's *René*. Oswald begins, in what will be a familiar mal du siècle refrain, with a declaration of love for the father—"I have never loved anything more deeply than my father" (208)—and then outlines, as Adolphe would later do in Constant's rewriting of Oswald's story, how he had done his father wrong on account of a woman. Oswald presents himself as an innocent young Englishman abroad and, borrowing from *Les Liaisons dangereuses,* the unwitting victim of a French libertine plot and a French woman's plotting. To fulfill his "duty" to his lover, the beautiful but despotic Mme d'Arbigny, the hero continually defers returning to England and his patriotic and filial obligations. He discovers, too late, that she has been deceiving him and returns home to make amends only to learn that his father has just died. Although Oswald presents himself as the victim of unscrupulous manipulation, like most of the mal du siècle heroes who will follow him, he insists on bearing the full burden of his failure as a son.

In the mal du siècle novel, revelation entails punishment—but not for all characters equally. For the hero, confession has its customary positive effects. Staël's hero revels in the guilt that torments him, even while admitting that his culpability is more self-inflicted than real. Since Corinne regards Oswald's sense of guilt as a proof of his innocence and further confirmation that he is worthy of her love, he wins both ways. The cost of confession for the heroine, by contrast, is far higher. Her comment to Oswald as she asks for one final postponement before telling her own secret reveals its stakes: "Forgive me a *last* act of authority. Soon *you* will decide for us both" (236; emphasis added). Like the Sibyl to whom she is often compared in the novel, Corinne can foresee that telling Oswald her story will be the beginning of the unavoidable end.

The medium of the hero and heroine's messages reveals how much the tables have turned. Whereas the silent, reserved Oswald *tells* Corinne his secret, the heroine, renowned for her public improvisations, cannot recount her story in the hero's presence, but must write it instead. Unlike her spontaneous performances, which depend on the magic of the moment, the story that she *writes* is beholden to the past and follows narrative conventions. Corinne's text, however, thematizes the link between conventional narrative imperatives and a repressive paternal line.

Land of the Living Dead

Unlike Oswald and in contrast with *René*, Corinne's narrative does not reveal a sexual secret with its implicit message of guilt.

Instead, hers is a secret of heritage, the revelation of her father's English identity and, therefore, her fatherland. Half-English herself, Corinne not only knows Oswald's beloved England, she had already, with good reason, given up on it. Whereas Oswald's French love story was a throwback to the eighteenth-century libertine novel, Corinne's reveals English domestic life as a modern Gothic horror story.

Corinne recounts her adolescent years in cold, gray Northumberland, England, to make a pointed indictment of complacent and narrow-minded provincialism with its mind-numbing insistence on routine. The prototypically English ritual of afternoon tea becomes, in Corinne's description, an apt image for all that is stultifying about that society, particularly for women:

> Every quarter of an hour, a voice would be heard asking the dullest question, only to get the most unresponsive answer; boredom would lift briefly, only to fall back down on these women all the more heavily. . . . When it came time to leave, they all went off with their husbands, ready to begin right over the next day lives differing from the day before solely by the date on the calendar, and by the traces stamped on their faces by the passing years just as if they had really lived during that time. [256–257]

A mechanical doll, Corinne reasons, could have easily replaced her in this charade of social interaction, the empty shell of a life.

Although Staël personally admired England as a modern example of political liberty and noble public ideals, in her novel she makes the dark side of English liberalism—its repression of difference and its oppression of women—abundantly clear. The notion of separate spheres, which Staël presents as synonymous with England, may condemn men to a dull home life, but it dooms women to a living death, since they have no access to life in the public sphere. Gérard Gengembre and Jean Goldzink describe *Corinne*'s indictment of English women's predicament: "The English woman could be a part of the nation's grandeur only by sacrificing her talents and desires. Her heroism would thus consist in that silent submissiveness, stubbornly maintained even when enraged, through which a collective destiny gloriously dedicated to liberty comes about by making all individuals the same and excluding all deviances."[36] Public liberty comes at the price of a terrible homogenization that suppresses women as a class and any individuals who dare to be different or better than the norm.

Corinne, who is marginalized on both these counts, describes the effect of this reign of mediocrity; she also analyzes its methods. Outright oppression is not necessary since the more subtle techniques of repression—insinuations, glances, and disapproving silence—are just as effective forms of a behavior modification that amounts to a kind of mind control. Despite all her efforts of resistance, Corinne finds herself internalizing the small-mindedness of those around her.

The novel's social and geographical determinism makes change from within a culture impossible. Within England, Corinne is forced to adopt her father's adage of conformism, "You must not fight the customs of the place where you live: if you do you will inevitably suffer" (253). Given the text's cosmopolitanism, however, the heroine has a viable alternative, Italy. The analysis of the power of place in Corinne's narrative thoroughly justifies her decision to move to her mother's homeland after her father's death; moreover, it explains and foreshadows everything that follows in the novel. Once Oswald leaves Italy, he will be unable to resist the pressures to adopt once again the mores of his native land, despite his best intentions. Under the spell of the English countryside, weather, and customs, Oswald will fall head over heels for Corinne's stepsister, Lucile, the quintessentially English angel of submissive domesticity. When the heroine follows the hero to England, hoping to find that he has not in fact abandoned her, she becomes the spectator of a domestic love story from which she is excluded. The improbable coincidences to which she is subject there are overdetermined by a fact Corinne has already established: England is no place for her. Although these peripeteia add drama to what has been foreordained, they do not affect its final outcome. Being in the wrong place provides the scene and the reason for Corinne's downfall by revealing what is so irrevocably wrong about Oswald. To understand what happens to mal du siècle heroes such as Chateaubriand's René and Staël's Oswald, one must "chercher la femme." To understand what happens to Corinne, by contrast, the reader is asked to "chercher l'homme conformiste." The heroine, who is attracted to the hero despite his conformism, is also tied to him because of it.

The Melancholy Face of Patriarchy

Unlike many of her eighteenth-century predecessors, Corinne would never fall for a rake or a brute. In the new literary order taking shape under the influence of *Werther* and *René*, what makes a man especially worthy of a reader's interest and a woman's love are instead his tender, "feminine" qualities, an emotional vulnerability that makes him both sensitive and kind. Even when Oswald is smugly self-righteous, he shows that, despite the authority vested in him as a man and as a leader of men, he is ill at ease with his own power. The narrator notes that "however distinguished, no man would have so captivated Corinne's imagination had his character lacked contradiction and struggle" (151). Oswald's doubts lead Corinne to believe that if he is not yet what she wants, he could become so, for he seems open to her influence.

Like the stereotypical woman of fiction, Oswald is a jumble of contradictions and, like her, he is an enigma: "Inwardly disturbed, Oswald sought to control himself outwardly, and the woman who loved him was endlessly absorbed in trying to read the mystery he presented" (150–151). Unlike Amélie who has no trouble "reading" her brother, René, Corinne finds that Oswald is *not* an open book for her. And it is precisely Oswald's mysterious unpredictability that binds Corinne to him. Indeed, the French passage reads: Corinne "trouvait dans ce mystère un *intérêt* continuel" (1: 214; emphasis added). Oswald's suffering and contradictions represent a challenge that holds Corinne's interest even as they bind her to him against her own better interests; Oswald's sensitivity is also a symptom of the spinelessness that makes him unable for most of the novel to decide whether to love her or leave her.

By making his body a theater of vulnerability, this modern version of masculinity makes it impossible for Corinne to reverse typical gender roles and abandon *him*: "Twenty times Corinne decided to tell Lord Nelvil that she was offended by his indecisiveness, that she was determined to go away. But then she would see him leaning his head on his hand like a man weighed down with painful feelings, or breathing with difficulty, or dreaming on the seashore, or raising his eyes to heaven when harmonious sounds were to be heard. These very simple actions, whose magic she alone perceived, would abruptly upset all her efforts" (278). The repertoire of self-absorbed postures and pathetic gestures, which Chateaubriand's René used so effectively and which would soon become synonymous with the Romantic hero and the male Romantic writer, make Oswald irresistible. This new version of manliness may be said to be the beginning of not only the Romantic ethos that would later come to dominate French literature and society but a certain kind of modern man. The lesson for modern heroines, and—by extension—modern readers, is clear: the new man's power over woman stems, paradoxically, from his *display* of weakness. *Her* vulnerability lies precisely in seeing *his*, for the hero's real suffering disguises that his apparent impotence is the new face of patriarchal power. Although this thoroughly modern heroine had escaped the old-fashioned rule of the fathers in England, what the otherwise lucid and independent Corinne cannot resist is its latest, "feminized" incarnation—old-time patriarchy with a melancholy, Romantic face.

The New Patriarchal Order

For Chateaubriand and male writers of the tradition, tragedy results because the mal du siècle hero cannot or will not follow the path laid out for him by the fathers. In Staël's feminist rewriting of this commonplace, Oswald's inability to do anything *but* follow in his father's footsteps will be the heroine's undoing. This difference is crucial. Staël shows Oswald as a father's son in order to undermine rather than strengthen the paternal line. She does so by disclosing that the apparent weakness of fathers is precisely the source of their power.

Neither the hero's nor the heroine's father is anything like
the epitome of the autocratic patriarch in *La Nouvelle Héloïse*.
Brutal and inflexible, Julie's father rules the house with the
threat of violence. His word is irrevocable, his power absolute.
In the years between the publication of Rousseau's and Staël's
novels, much had changed in European, particularly French,
society, and with it, as Tony Tanner shows in *Adultery in the
Novel*, the representation of the father. During this period and
the years following, he writes, the father's "hold on the negative
voice [the voice that says no], as on the commanding one, tends
to grow considerably weaker."[37]

In Staël's 1807 novel, neither father is a tyrant or a bully.
Instead, they are both shown as relatively permissive, vulnerable, and even weak-willed. Corinne presents her English father, Lord Edgermond, as a man resigned to a life lived within
the narrow constraints of English provincialism with a domi-
neering and meanspirited second wife. Oswald makes an even
more telling analysis of his father's ways: "he found it difficult
to exercise his paternal authority when duty did not command
him to do so. He always feared that authority might spoil the
true and pure affection which depends on what is most free
and involuntary in our nature, and above all, he needed to be
loved" (209) So that he may enjoy affection freely given, Oswald's father abdicates the coercive authority his position affords him. In this modern variant on paternal rule, however,
the father's relative indulgence gives him far greater power
than an autocrat's domination, for it operates as a force that
binds with love as much as by law. His word is law not only
because of his status in the family and in society, but also because his sons—and daughters—see his tenderness, which further consolidates his power over them.[38]

Oswald takes it as his sacred duty to make the laws and logic
of paternal rule his own, stating "I did not want to do anything
without his consent" (213). He goes so far as to attribute absolute power to the father's Word and words: "I had faith in
my father's words as in an oracle, and the ambivalence that is
unfortunately a part of my character always ceased the moment
he spoke" (216). Early critics of the novel found Oswald's hyperbolic loyalty to his father both objectionable and implau-

sible. One reviewer writes that "a wish or an invitation, even when it comes from one's dying father is not really an order."[39] Another critic agreed that "giving the father so much influence makes his power ludicrous and makes that poor Oswald a veritable puppet."[40] By making her hero "plus royaliste que le roi" on the question of patriarchal power, Staël defies verisimilitude, but she also exposes the efficacy of a patriarchy no longer embodied in the father.

From the beginning of the novel, both father figures are dead, but that absence only increases their hold over their descendants, Oswald and Corinne. Their words carry the weight of unchangeable decrees from the grave. As Oswald explains about his father in his letter to Corinne: "Had he lived, I would have thought I had a right to oppose his authority. . . . but those who are no more cannot hear us, and their ineffectual will [leur volonté sans force] bears a touching and holy character" (406). The father figure's impotence thus assures his final authority. His absence means that his power is nowhere and therefore everywhere, impossible to combat. The lesson Corinne learns is that modern patriarchy does not depend on its embodiment and enforcement by individual fathers. Indeed, the fathers are more powerful dead than alive.[41]

In Staël's novel, more than in any other mal du siècle novel before or since, the male malady is linked to this absent but omnipresent father who rules the individual from within. Governing the private world of the family with an absolute power tempered and disguised by paternalistic indulgence, the father also stands for paternal law in a wider, public sphere. In *Corinne*, the law of the father is less the result of any individual father's authority than a consequence of the pervasive and self-replicating power of paternal thinking within individuals and in society at large. Similarly, Staël shows that the father who rules the family romance so characteristic of the novel as a genre is intricately bound up with national mores and state interests. By linking Oswald's relation to his father with the relations of the fathers to the nation, and by connecting the paternal ethos to the workings of traditional plot, Staël reveals that the obstacle to the heroine's happiness is not just a single spineless son, or an inflexible father, but an entire ideology and social system, founded as much on the repression of women as on their oppression.

While the patriarchal order in question is undeniably English, the example of England also holds a lesson for France. As in the novel's representation of English patriarchy, France's father is dead. With the decapitation of the king in 1793, France found itself literally and figuratively without a head, without a legitimating father figure; under Napoleon, headless patriarchy tries on a new, English face. Indeed, the England of 1795 in the novel is not only the France of 1807, when *Corinne* was published, but the France of the future.

While Napoleon fought to legitimize his new version of an absolutist regime and finally lost the right to rule, the social system he established remains more or less in place even to this day. Its strictures made it very clear who would *not* reign. Codifying woman's exclusion from the public sphere and her secondary status, Napoleon gave male rule a new face, which was paternalism in the English style. While France would not adopt bourgeois, capitalist patriarchy wholesale until mid-century, when it did, as Staël's analysis would prove, it was able to foreswear the rule by force in favor of an ever more refined discipline of the bodies and minds of individual subjects. Staël shows the force of conformism most vividly in the case of Oswald, who, despite his inner turmoil and ultimately to his own dissatisfaction, succumbs to the law of the land.

The 1807 reviewers, as already noted, had little patience for this melancholic shell of a "real man." Pointing out the similarity between *Corinne* and Staël's previous novel, *Delphine* (1802), one such critic remarks that the heroines of both works "sacrifice themselves to men who are like well-dressed automatons; deep down they have neither soul nor character; the only thing they know how to do is to follow the dictates of outside appearances; they pretend to think *as men* but we see that they are incapable of acting; bizarre and impotent idols, they are gods only to the women blinded by love for them."[42] According to this argument, Oswald arrogates the male prerogative of thought but shows himself impotent in that he is incapable of "manly" action. Thus, in a curious twist, the fundamentally conformist Empire critics attack Staël's male protagonist for his *failure* to defy public opinion and, in particular, the father's law. Opinion and the "law" in this case, however, are English, and the sentimental power and moral prestige of the father would not reassert itself in French society until a later reign of the bourgeoisie.

Not surprisingly, despite their criticism of Oswald's submission, the French critics fail to praise the heroine's resistance, thus reserving (limited) nonconformity as a prerogative of men. In her *Mélanges*, Staël's mother, Suzanne Necker, put this conventional wisdom about the double standards of conformity in a nutshell: "A man must know how to defy public opinion, a woman how to submit to it." Although Staël uses this aphorism as the epigraph to her first novel, *Delphine*, neither there nor in *Corinne* does the heroine or the hero follow this gender-specific prescription. Instead, in both works, the heroine represents a challenge to crippling orthodoxy, which is embodied by the hero. Whereas Oswald is weak, indecisive, and always dominated by what others might think, Corinne has the moral courage that identifies her with *die schöne Seele*. Staël in *Corinne* formulates a Romantic ethos in which true superiority ultimately requires taking a stand against the status quo. Put another way, in Staël's novel the individual is not just different from the norm, as in *René*, she vigorously opposes social conformism in the name of her difference. Nevertheless and despite her resistance, the heroine yields. As we have seen, Oswald is not the only character to have internalized patriarchal rule; already, at her first sight of him, Corinne *recognizes* in him her own patrimony. As in the traditional script, a woman who defies the father nevertheless finds herself succumbing to the son.

Sacrifice and the Double Standard

When Corinne falls prey to the new Romantic face of masculinity, it is because she is subject to old as well as new romantic notions of love, both of which are based on women's subservience to men. Echoing Staël's own views, Corinne asserts that a woman, even a woman of genius, needs above all else to love and be loved. "All the while I sought glory," Corinne tells Oswald early in the novel, "I have hoped it would make me loved. What use would it be without that hope, for women at least!" (55). The novel sets up Corinne's new, Romantic vision of love as an intense, revitalizing exchange between partners in clear opposition to the socially mandated relations between the sexes, as exemplified by Oswald's marriage to Corinne's stepsister, Lucile. There, the woman functions as a blank screen the better to reflect Oswald's desires and serve his society's interests. But even within the sphere of Corinne's more egalitarian, Romantic version of love, men and women are still not created equal. On the one hand, Staël gives the man greater responsibility and with it greater guilt, for she will show that he is unworthy of the heroine's more perfect love. On the other hand and paradoxically, however, the woman will bear the heavier burden for *his* inadequacy. According to the conventions of the novel and as Staël's own 1796 treatise *De l'influence des passions* makes clear, passion is tantamount to unhappiness, particularly for women, and the cost of its failure is the heroine's death.[43]

Corinne's wholehearted embrace of self-immolating love as a glorious and terrible destiny midway through the novel marks the radical difference between the first and second halves of Staël's work. The heroine who had more or less directed the course of events and jealously guarded her independence becomes the hero's slave. "Do as you will with me, chain me to your fate like a slave" (289), she tells Oswald. Corinne abandons herself to an ideal of love as a form of fusion, a plenitude achieved through the illusion of complete reciprocity. In this dream of a shared and boundless love, sublime disinterestedness guarantees the self's exalted transcendence through union with another. Although the ideal is one of *mutual* devotion, the reality is far different. Once the heroine abandons Rome and agrees to follow her lover's lead, she follows a familiar script in which a woman makes a series of ever greater sacrifices to a man who will, in the end, sacrifice her. The French Count d'Erfeuil warns Corinne that this is precisely what will happen, but Corinne, happy to prove the depth of her devotion, abandons both home and friends for Oswald and declares, "I find a cer-

tain peace in leaving myself no recourse" (188). Not content
with her own total submission, Corinne, following the example
of previous heroines, reserves the right of self-sacrifice for herself alone. By giving Oswald his freedom even as she declares
her own servitude, Corinne insists that their relations are *not*,
nor will they ever be, reciprocal.

Staël criticizes, through the voice of the narrator, Corinne's
self-sacrifice as a form of idolatry wholly inappropriate to any
object, certainly any man, and especially Oswald.[44] Nevertheless, the narrator concludes by conceding that such love, characteristic of ardent souls, is admirable in its power and that
Corinne, who suffers her humiliating pain in silence, is "worthy
of pity" because her "fatal love was destroying no one but herself" (338). Thus is female masochism justified.

Though clearly debilitating, sacrifice and the gender asym-
metry on which Corinne insists give the heroine the pleasure of
claiming a noble disinterestedness, while depriving the hero of
the moral high ground. By submitting to Oswald, Corinne also
rises above him. By making herself a martyr to the cause of
love, she proves herself morally superior. In her self-sacrificing
devotion, Corinne joins the ranks of other French women writers' heroines whose primary talent is loving more nobly and
selflessly than the men of their dreams.[45] Love in this view
serves to elevate women—but only to a limited degree and with
disastrous consequences. For woman's enoblement takes place
within the traditional feminine domain and only through a display of her weakness. Nor does the heroine's moral triumph
save her from her sacrifice's devastating effects. Indeed, because Corinne is not just any woman but a woman of genius,
she has even more to lose than any of her many predecessors—before it takes her life her sacrifice comes at the cost of
her art.

For Corinne, as for Staël, woman's need for the Other is a
given. Yet the love that is necessary to the heroine is also, by
definition, fatal to her genius. Thus, Corinne is doomed from
the beginning. As Herrmann explains, "if she is denied love,
the woman of genius will dissolve in sorrow, but if she is
granted love, that love will efface her."[46] Because both Corinne
and Oswald accept the premise of female self-abnegation, the

woman artist in love will be unable to maintain the independence necessary for her art and her survival. While presenting intersubjectivity as an ideal in love, Staël also reveals its costs. As in love, so too in art.

Caught between Alienation and Affection

After Corinne's devastating discovery of Oswald's love for Lucile, she returns to Italy, a black-veiled shadow of her former self. The heroine will live there in isolated retreat, unable to exercise her talents. The narrator explains her incapacitation: "Good writing requires a base of genuine—but not harrowing—emotion. Happiness is necessary for everything, and most melancholy poetry must be inspired by a kind of verve implying intellectual energy and pleasure" (368). This notion of art— even at its most melancholic—as the result of an affirmative and joyful enthusiasm comes in sharp contrast to a paradigm of art as the empowering consequence of alienation, which was promulgated by male writers of the Romantic tradition.[47] While most Romantic writers have their heroes, such as René, seek transcendence in isolation, Corinne seeks fulfillment in relation. Susan Kirkpatrick notes that Staël and other women writers, notably Mary Shelley, "depict marginalization as a crippling experience, one best represented as illness or as a polar waste." In their work, "alienation [is] a state of declining rather than renewed creative powers."[48]

Nevertheless, I would argue, Corinne too is empowered by her alienation in the final chapters. No longer able to direct the course of the plot or her life at its end, she nevertheless shows herself able to understand and move beyond it. Deprived of audience and addressee, Corinne is devoid of energy, desires, and strength. Unable to write according to recognized conventions, she produces only a set of fragmented thoughts. These disjointed "ravings" of a woman driven mad by sorrow nevertheless offer a coherent defense of moral and intellectual superiority, a moving cry of self-pity, an explicit protest against women's restricted sphere, and a complex expression of her self-doubts and personal contradictions. Even at her worst, Corinne never stops making sense.[49] In fact, the breakdown of conjunctive logic gives the heroine another kind of power, a renewed resistance to conventional ideas and their standard plots and, more specifically, a refusal of Oswald's teleological version of narrative logic and its self-serving demands.

In a replay of René's plea, Oswald's wish in the end is for all to be forgiven so that he may have the pleasure of knowing that he is still loved, despite his guilt. Begging Corinne for a final interview before she dies, he writes, "May the one who goes first feel that he is missed, that he is loved by the friend he will leave in this world! Only the innocent should have this pleasure, but may it also be granted to the guilty!" (407). While acknowledging Oswald's continuing power over her, Corinne refuses his desire to make a spectacle of his contrition and her forgiveness, and in this way reestablishes her power over him and his demands. The mal du siècle hero and Staël's Romantic heroine are both empowered by alienation. What distinguishes them is the nature, means, and ends of this empowerment.

Unsettling the Conventional Ending

Despite Corinne's final acts of resistance, in the last episode of the novel, she succumbs to the ideological and narratological imperative that requires a woman and the story to come to an "edifying" tragic end. The heroine's dramatic submission to the bonds of love and her pious transcendence of them through a gradual decline of her powers until death is, of course, a familiar literary convention, which would continue to dominate nineteenth-century, particularly Romantic, fiction.[50] In Staël's *Corinne*, as in Chateaubriand's *René*, it is the women who love better; and it is they who die for love. As Mercken-Spaas's comparison of the two authors in "Death and the Romantic Heroine" shows, however, the differences between the male and female authors' works are crucial. In Chateaubriand's *René* and *Atala*, the obstacles to love are powerful sexual taboos—incest in the first case, a mother's oath of virginity on the other—and

the heroes indulge in "autoerotic mourning" for the perfect
love the heroine showed them—a desire Staël's hero shares. Oswald loudly proclaims his own culpability, but in terms that reveal the reason he wants to preserve the memory of Corinne:
"he charged himself with being the most barbarous and per-
fidious of men. . . . He repeated endlessly to himself that *no one
would ever love him as she had* . . ." (382; emphasis added). While
René and Oswald gain stature and interest because a woman
loves them no matter what they are or do, Corinne is said to
merit our pity and admiration because she sacrifices her own
life for a man incapable of loving her enough. Thus the heroes
of these novels—through the heroines—are assured a narcissistic satisfaction that is unavailable to the women precisely because of the narcissism of the men.

Corinne focuses instead on the heroine's *disillusion* with the
hero's love. The social conventions that stood in the way *could*
have been overcome, but are not because of Oswald. Although
the hero does not seem to get the message, the reader does
because Oswald's suffering does not become the focus of the
story, nor is he allowed the discursive power that René uses to
his advantage and that most mal du siècle authors would grant
their heroes by letting them become the story's narrators. Thus,
while remaining within the broad lines of early Romantic conventions, Staël significantly revises the masculinist premises of
its standard ending by refusing its traditional frame and by giving equal time to the views and point of view of the melancholic
hero's antithesis, Corinne.

In a final subversive move, Staël establishes the heroine's legacy as a generous gift to Oswald that is also a bittersweet re-
venge. As self-appointed marriage counselor, Corinne teaches
Lucile how to speak her mind in front of her husband. She
trains Oswald's and Lucile's daughter, Juliette, who already
looks like Corinne, to play a lyre-shaped harp as she did. Thus,
the differences that divide the heroine from the Other Woman
dissolve in a willful replication of similarities. In *La Nouvelle Héloïse*, a similar compulsion to repeat takes hold in the final pages
when the deceased Julie seems to reappear as Claire's daughter,
Henriette. In Staël's novel, however, what is being replicated
explicitly flies in the face of the compulsion to repeat that forms

the basis of the English paternal order. Corinne's last acts guarantee that neither Oswald's wife nor his daughter will ever again be daddy's little girl so completely. Thus, Corinne, who suffered from the all-pervasive influence of the fathers from beyond the tomb, will die so that she may come back to haunt the mal du siècle hero in her turn. In the last lines of the novel, the narrator leaves Oswald hanging, raising the question of his guilt by giving it no answer: "The order and purity of Lord Nelvil's domestic life were exemplary. But did he forgive himself for his past behavior? Was he consoled by society's approval? Was he satisfied with an ordinary lot after what he had lost? I do not know, and on this score I wish neither to blame him nor to grant him absolution" (419).

Recuperating the Ending

Whereas I have argued that Staël's *Corinne, or Italy* calls into question men's and women's "natural" spheres, contemporary critics praised what they saw as the novel's conformist moral: if men and women are to be happy, they must each stay within the sphere to which nature has assigned them. Picking up on Staël's own contradictions, they seized on the tragic unhappiness of the heroine in particular to argue that this lesson is particularly applicable to women. According to the reviewer at *Mercure de France*, Staël's "laudable" moral purpose was to show women "that they risk grave dangers when, driven by a vain desire for glory, they seek to raise themselves above the sweet and modest endeavors to which they *naturally* must confine themselves."[51] Another critic concludes that if the two protagonists are unhappy, it only serves them right for being exceptions to their sex.[52] Like his compatriots, he blames the protagonists for their difference from the gender norm rather than indict, as Staël does, the social, political, cultural, and economic system that constructs men and women as separate and unequal. The critics thus read the unhappy end of both characters as proof of their guilt and the novel's moral. The review-

ers' equation of telos and ethos effectively erases the novel's
initial premise as well as its entire first half, which, I have argued, is precisely where Staël offers her narrative and ideological alternatives to the status quo.

Staël did not share her critics' assumption about the meaning
of a novel's ending or the means it should take to achieve its
ends. She argued against the notion of literature as edifying in
any simplistic sense; in a novel, virtue is not necessarily re-
warded nor should the moral be explicit in the conclusion. Novels have instead a different purpose: to create a reader who
sympathizes and identifies with the characters. Constant, echoing the views of the Groupe de Coppet associated with Staël,
explains in his defense of *Corinne* that fiction's moral efficacy
comes from its ability to make us better than we were by making
us capable of nobler feelings and greater disinterestedness.
Through the powers of sympathy and identification, the novel
is designed to create a community of readers which would
extend beyond national boundaries and dissolve "distinctions
among eras and social classes, among authors, readers, and fictional characters" as well.[53]

Though the novel enjoyed immense success, and friends of
Staël wrote to tell her they were swept away in a flood of tears
and feelings by *Corinne*, there were nevertheless limitations on
their identification with her characters, perhaps in part because
Staël's novel was far ahead of its time. One reader, who had
been in love with Staël herself ten years previously, confessed a
preference many readers would share: "after experiencing the
highest admiration for the brilliant Corinne, I was drawn to
letting myself be seduced by the innocent charm of Lucile. Despite the remorse one might feel, one is inclined to excuse Lord
Nelvil, because of a strong attraction for this fresh model of
candor and simplicity."[54] Male and female readers both seem
to have preferred a woman who makes no demands, a virginal
tabula rasa who furthers their *interests*: "I have to admit," writes
one enthusiastic critic, "that Lucile is so *interesting*!"[55] Few readers, writes Balayé, saw the "limits of this character who had
been stunted by a narrow education; no one saw the failed marriage that Staël describes with somber delight."[56] In the years

following the publication of *Corinne*, on the contrary, the Lucile type would enjoy even greater success as a nineteenth-century feminine ideal.

Though the readers of 1807 approved the English model of subservient femininity, they did not, as I have already shown, adopt Oswald. Only later would this masculine Romantic type enjoy favor in France, but by that time, the grandiloquent prose characteristic of Staël's writing would be out of favor. For her contemporaries, the only reasonable, plausible, and likable male character in the novel was the Count d'Erfeuil. Despite the upheaval of the Revolution, this outdated aristocratic type continued to exert a nostalgic appeal. Though Staël portrays the count as kindhearted, she also reveals him as an obsessively self-absorbed, willfully ignorant, and hopelessly frivolous throwback to eighteenth-century French worldliness and its novel of easy seduction. Nevertheless, for these early nineteenth-century readers, the count was a kind of French Everyman whose "good sense" they admired. "It seems to me," writes the critic at the *Gazette de France*, "that all that would be required for a good critique of *Corinne* would be to finish what the Count d'Erfeuil was saying."[57] This reviewer, like the abbé de Féletz, complains that Staël always silences the garrulous count too soon.

To appreciate Staël's feminist challenge to masculinist liberalism, however, I shall turn now to the work of her fellow liberal and erstwhile lover. Benjamin Constant has his hero reject the kinds of universalizing, conventional pronouncements that the Count d'Erfeuil makes but in so doing establishes in their place a far more efficacious and up-to-date rule of self-serving masculinist wisdom.

4

The Double Bind of Liberalism
in Constant's *Adolphe*

I N THE PREFACE to his *Mélanges de littérature et de politique*
(1829), Benjamin Constant summed up his life's work as an
unswerving commitment to the defense of individual liberties.
"For forty years," he writes, "I have defended the same principle: liberty in everything, in religion, in philosophy, in literature, in industry, and in politics; and by liberty I mean the
triumph of individualism."[1] As a member of the Tribunate during the Consulate, as a deputy much later during the Restoration, and in his numerous political, religious, and philosophical
writings, Constant did indeed champion the ideals of liberalism.[2] Nevertheless, the only novel Constant ever published portrays the consequences of one man's exercise of his liberty as a
nightmarish bondage and reveals the dark underside of liberalism by showing the male bias inherent in the nineteenth-
century liberal notion of the individual.

When Constant first drafted *Adolphe* in 1806, the abrupt termination of his early political career and a prolonged period of
emotional paralysis had led him to know firsthand the limits of
freedom. In 1802 Napoleon had expelled him from the Tribunate for criticizing the state's increasing encroachment on individual rights. Soon after, Napoleon exiled Germaine de Staël,
and Constant followed his lover to Switzerland. During those
years of exile, Constant was alternately enthralled by Staël
and convinced their relationship was the source of all his woes.
In any case he was unable to break off his relations with her.

During two months of feverish literary creativity in 1806, a frustrated Constant gave fictional form to his professional and personal dead end. The novel he drafted, like previous mal du siècle works, puts the question of career and politics in the background and concentrates instead on the personal impediments that prevent the hero from enjoying the liberties that are his birthright as a nobleman.[3] In his political writings, Constant conceived the individual as an essentially free (male) subject for whom the major impediment to liberty is state interference. In his novel, however, the hero, a young aristocrat in contemporary Germany, is far from free and the state's role is not his central problem.

Adolphe's sex, class, and personal circumstances provide him with more rights than the heroine, and, moreover, afford him the chance to enjoy with impunity, as she cannot, sexual liberties. *Adolphe*, however, gives a mal du siècle twist to this common eighteenth-century phenomenon: it is precisely by exercising his sexual prerogative that the hero loses his freedom. The novel thus operates according to a premise that is in fact one of the central tenets in much of Constant's writings on liberalism: man is free only to the extent that his actions do not harm others. Thus, whereas the male malady in Chateaubriand's *René* stems from the hero's not being connected to anyone, Adolphe's "freedom" is always already fettered by a deep, internalized feeling of responsibility that comes from the ties that bind him to others and, in particular, Ellenore, an inappropriate woman.

As in *René*, then, to understand the hero, the reader of *Adolphe* is asked to "chercher la femme." In Constant's novel, however, the hero's unhappy entanglement with a woman is the text's subject, not its secret.[4] Unlike René's narrative, which coyly saves the woman question as a suitably scandalous surprise for the end of his tale, Adolphe's retrospective confession follows the model of his libertine precessors by taking his relationship with a woman as the sine qua non of his account. Seducing Ellenore, the first aim in Adolphe's adult life, is the first significant event in the novel and the determining event for all that follows. *Adolphe* sets up the eighteenth-century seduction scenario with its promise of male pleasure, only to reject its cor-

ollary of abandonment. Whereas libertine fiction is about a sequence in which a man's capture of one woman ensures the
conquest of the next, Constant's novel is about consequences.
As the hero remarks after his sexual conquest of the heroine:
"She was no longer an objective, she had become a tie."[5]

The woman, who was to serve as Adolphe's momentary goal,
becomes a permanent, debilitating constraint because, unlike
Chateaubriand's self-absorbed René, Constant's hero is neither
deaf to the heroine nor blind to her needs. Instead, Adolphe
deals seriously and at length with the question of his moral ob-
ligation to Ellenore. Constant's liberal version of the mal du
siècle hero clearly takes to task the unapologetic exploitation in
the male libertine model. Indeed, in his prefaces to the novel,
Constant offers an explicit critique of libertinism and even a
protofeminist analysis of gender.

The Demise of Libertinism?

Echoing Chateaubriand, Constant justifies his work as a chastis-
ing representation of a new social reality, the mal du siècle. "In
Adolphe," he writes in a draft for the preface to the second edition, "I wanted to paint one of the principal moral maladies of
our age: the fatigue, the uncertainty, the lack of strength, and
the perpetual analysis that puts an ulterior motive next to all
feelings, thus corrupting them from the very beginning."[6] Although Constant shares with Chateaubriand a distaste for what
he sees as modern decadence, and although both writers in
their fictions bemoan the loss of faith and certainty that characterizes the modern era, Constant expresses no nostalgia for
the male-dominated societies of ancient Greece and Rome, nor
does he follow Chateaubriand's lead by blaming the corruption
of society on women, whom he sees instead as its primary victims. The focus of his attack is, rather, the legacy of fatuous
self-interest that his generation had inherited from their libertine fathers, and the hypocrisy of his society, "which seems to
have found pleasure in placing women over an abyss, in order
to condemn them, if they fall into it" (27).

Whereas Chateaubriand's diagnosis of the century's malady is grounded on an essentialist notion of sexual difference, Constant describes gender as a social construct that hides what he believes is the essential human nature they share. For Constant, if men and women love differently, for example, it is because (aristocratic) women's lack of occupation in contemporary society leaves them with no other preoccupation. "Men, more vigorous, more distracted from sentiment by imperious occupations, and destined to serve as a centre for what surrounds them, have not, in the same degree as women, the noble and the dangerous faculty of living in another and for another" (27). As in eighteenth-century sensibility, Constant sees vulnerability and sensitivity, qualities associated with femininity, as signs of admirable virtue in both men and women. When men stifle these feelings and consider them a sign of weakness, he writes, they kill what is most generous, faithful, and good in their souls.

Constant not only attacks libertinism as morally bankrupt, but also asserts that it is unworkable. Although a decadent society corrupts and represses men's tenderness and empathy, Constant argues, when a man sees the *consequences* of his dissimulation on the face of the women he has seduced and plans to abandon, his natural sensibility is necessarily called to the surface: "When [women's] tears do flow, *nature* returns in [men's] breasts, in spite of the factitious atmosphere with which they had surrounded themselves" (28; emphasis added). In other words, and as the novel will forcefully demonstrate, the new, postlibertine man cannot escape the trap he sets for woman because it is a *double* bind. Borrowing from the literature of sensibility, Constant's new version of modern man thus offers a progressive view of the relations between the sexes and a sympathetic depiction of women, especially in contrast to eighteenth-century libertinism. Nevertheless, his comments reveal the extent to which his liberal views share with libertinism its fatalistic parti pris, its objectification of women, and its androcentric bias.

The message in Constant's prefaces is decidedly mixed. On the one hand, he protests society's libertine mores, on the other, his work reaffirms the mechanistic determinism characteristic of libertinism and its fiction. Thus, he states his novel's moral: "In order to be happy in life, one must not start such liaisons. Once you start down this road, there is only a choice among evils."[7] Indeed, portraying illicit love as an irrevocably fatal step on the road to degradation and unhappiness precludes the exercise of free will and a belief in progress so central to the notion of the individual in liberal theories.[8] Despite Constant's insights into women's and men's condition as a social construction, he reveals his vested interest in presenting this contingent phenomenon as an unresolvable and unchangeable state of affairs: "[Adolphe's] position and that of Ellenore was *hopeless*," he writes, "*and that is precisely what I wanted*."[9]

Constant's remarks stress women's dependency and vulnerability to such a degree that he ends up reessentializing woman as the weaker sex. Men's mistreatment of them thus appears regrettable but "natural" under the circumstances. Women, he argues, are "weak beings, having no real life but in the heart, no deep interest but in the affections; without activity to occupy them, without career to command them, confiding by nature, credulous by an excusable vanity, feeling that their sole existence is to give themselves up without reserve to a protector, and led incessantly to confound the need of protection with the need of love!" (27).[10] Though such remarks elicit sympathy for women, they represent them exclusively as victims. Constant, like Staël and writers in the sentimental tradition, presents this victimization as ennobling. But whereas Staël uses Corinne's self-sacrifice to demonstrate her moral superiority to the hero, for Constant, women's oppression serves instead another, higher end: the moral regeneration of *men*. While the contradictions in her text are self-defeating (the heroine may be superior but she is dead), his are self-serving. Insisting on a world in which sacrifice is not just woman's lot but man's as well, Constant nevertheless makes this double bind work to men's advantage. Telling this story is a man's right and privilege.

Man is in fact the raison d'être of Constant's argument, which gives the author's understanding of women's oppression a paradoxical corollary: inasmuch as women are accustomed to constraints and conditioned to accept dependence, liberty (and liberalism) is a matter for men. "Without [liberty], *men* have no

peace, no dignity, no happiness," Constant declared in one of
his political writings.[11] According to this logic, men's traditional
independence makes their loss of liberty far more tragic than
women's and of greater interest. In a pattern common to the
mal du siècle turn away from the feminocentrism of previous
novels, Adolphe's bondage, not Ellenore's, becomes the subject
of the text, and it is he who tells the story. Despite its progressive aspects, Constant's *Adolphe* thus has far more in common
with Chateaubriand's reactionary *René* than with *Corinne*, Staël's
iconoclastic, double-focused text. In Constant's novel, as in
Chateaubriand's, discourse is a male prerogative and an object
of exchange between men. Despite the importance of the heroine in Adolphe's thoughts, and despite her paralyzing influence
on his actions, attention focuses on the male subject and his
contradictory nature, not on the woman who had been the object of his desires only to become the obstacle to their
realization.

Adolphe enjoys the discursive privilege associated with men
in both the libertine confessional novel and in the androcentric
mal du siècle novel, as well as the monopoly on point of view
that is his prerogative as a consequence of Ellenore's death. All
of what we know about Ellenore in the novel and most of what
we know about Adolphe is filtered through his far-from-objec-
tive perspective. Though Adolphe uses his right to speak in
order to put himself on trial for his failings, the confession of
guilt that is his text serves as a document in his defense as well
as evidence for the prosecution. While many critics of the novel
note Adolphe's fundamental duplicity, I will be exploring what
his double talk can tell us about its sexual politics. In other
words, in this mal du siècle version of male subjectivity, what
do men have to gain from a literary order that is premised on
male guilt?

Like Father, Like Son

While the reason for Adolphe's confession is his treatment of
Ellenore, in his narrative Adolphe subordinates this concern to

a far deeper remorse: his failure to be his father's son. Like
René and *Corinne*, from its initial pages and in the final analysis,
the novel shows that the heterosexual relationship that is its
obvious focus takes second place to the far more compelling
dyad of father and son. So exclusive is this male bond in *Adolphe*
that the mother does not even rate the standard cameo appearance given her in *René*, where she plays the first sacrificial
victim.

The "I" who is the subject of discourse and begins as the
grammatical subject of the very first sentence becomes by the
next the *object* of his father's intentions. Although the father's
travel plans send the son into the world, their circular trajectory
is designed to bring him back home so that he may "be ap-
pointed to the staff of his [father's] department and trained to
succeed him eventually" (37). The father's ambitious wishes cir-
cumscribe the son's social and political future and serve as the
gauge with which Adolphe—and the reader—will measure his
failure to live up to them.

In this story of desire constituted by lack, the hero mourns
his failure to achieve a bond of tender intimacy with a loving
but undemonstrative father. "Unfortunately his treatment of
me was noble and generous rather than affectionate," writes
Adolphe (37). As in the portrait of masculinity that Constant
gives in his preface, both father and son have tender feelings;
however, raised as men, they stifle and deny these emotions,
which they are incapable of expressing until it is too late. The
hero's retrospective psychologizing dramatizes and sentimen-
talizes their emotional misunderstanding by emphasizing the
gap between past blindness and present insight. "I did not re-
alize that my father was shy even in front of his own son, and
that many a time . . . he left me with tears in his eyes and com-
plained to others that I did not love him" (38).

The father raises his son according to a lenient libertine code
of aristocratic male privilege and power that encourages
Adolphe to enjoy his liberty and assures him that he may do so
with impunity, especially in the pre- or extramarital sexual
realm. According to the father, "So long as marriage was not
contemplated, there was no harm in taking any woman and
then dropping her. . . . *It does them so little harm and gives us so*

much pleasure!" (45). In the beginning, Adolphe obeys his father's precepts, and the plot in *Adolphe* follows the standard
script for seduction, which sharply divides the motives and
stakes of illicit love along gender lines. During the courting
stage, Adolphe persists and Ellenore, an impoverished and orphaned Polish aristocrat who has long been the mistress of another man, resists. While he has a desire for conquest, she has
a need to preserve a reputation of moral, if not strictly sexual,
integrity. The hero's seduction of Ellenore is intended to en-
hance Adolphe's own self-image and social prestige, and then
move him through this woman and on to the next.

In this endlessly replayable libertine scenario, no harm is
supposed to come to the seducer. For the woman, by contrast,
love is a matter of grave consequence. It is precisely the high
physical, emotional, and social stakes Ellenore faces that
heighten the drama of sexual passion in the novel and provide its interest, a principle taken to even more melodramatic
extremes in *René* and *Corinne*. After Ellenore succumbs to
Adolphe's seduction, the hero shows an urgent need to be free
of her. The heroine, by contrast, has no interest in liberty. Hers
is a desire for the security and attachment that was supposed to
result from the bonds of love. Her future depends on him, for
only his loyalty can compensate her for the social ostracism she
suffers as a result of their affair.

Ellenore's sexual submission early in the novel and the extreme sacrifices she makes to be with Adolphe would, in a libertine novel, definitively shift the balance of power to the hero.
But in *Adolphe*, her sacrifice only serves to tighten the chains
that restrain him. Adolphe, who had thought his liberty guar-
anteed by the codes of libertinism, bridles under this constraint,
but does not break the ties that bind. Adopting his father's pleasure principle, the son can seduce; he will not, however, abandon. Far from guaranteeing Ellenore's happiness, Adolphe's
unhappy compromise with libertinism ensures that they both
meet an unhappy fate.

The first part of Adolphe's narrative is thus governed by the
"will he seduce her or won't he?" logic of the male libertine plot,
which is premised on the woman's surrender and resulting
shame.[12] By the third chapter this non-iterative event is already

a fait accompli. The burden, but also the power, of determining the couple's plot then falls on the hero, who vacillates between the poles of a new binary opposition in the first person singular: "Will I leave her or won't I?" Adolphe takes a stand only to reverse his position; he analyzes his position only to offer its counterargument. Like the sentimental hero of the first half of the eighteenth century, however, the self-absorbed Adolphe is not so much overwhelmed by the intensity of his feelings as he is deadlocked by his endless analysis and dissection of them.[13] Even Adolphe's impasse, however, advances his position.

The Master's Voice

If, as Julia Kristeva argues, in the novel as a genre characters are conceived not as manicheistic embodiments of transcendent ideas as they had been in the epic but as a union of opposites, then Constant's hero is the fictional protagonist par excellence.[14] Not only does Adolphe embody this bundle of contradictions and dramatize it as a moral aporia, he also systematizes its functioning and champions its universal validity. The hero's constant vacillation recalls Chateaubriand's preface to *René* and his definition of the feminized male who is contaminated by "ever-changing ideas and feelings . . . and a perpetual fickleness," which Chateaubriand associates with the second sex.[15] Constant's Adolphe, however, dismisses the usual gender connotations of irresolution by identifying it not as a feminine or even a masculine trait but as an unavoidable fact of human nature. "We are such unstable creatures," he writes, "that feelings we pretend to have we really do have in the end" (83). He ties this mobility to an inveterate human ambivalence: "There is never any real consistency in mankind, and hardly anybody is wholly sincere or wholly deceitful" (50). Identifying the irreducible heterogeneity of the self as a universal truth allows the hero to excuse his indecisiveness and to valorize it as a victory of his "genuine and natural feelings" (105) over social hypocrisy. "How comes it that with such feelings I have for so long brought about nothing but my own misfortunes and that of others?" (105). Though quick to note that he is the victim of his own sincerity, Adolphe does not so readily avow his compensatory pleasures.

Unable to control his feelings or take a definitive stand, Adolphe is nevertheless master over Ellenore and master of the plot in his retelling of their story. Indeed, the indecisiveness that proves his weakness is precisely the form that his power takes, both within the story and through it. Since the hero's connection to Ellenore has divorced him from the world, only through her can he exercise his power and watch its effect. Taking on responsibility for his affair with Ellenore allows him to exaggerate his power and deny her agency. Thus, the hero portrays the heroine's shortcomings as his own fault, and describes her behavior as if it were his doing. "But did I not know that *this behavior of hers was of my own making*? Did I not know that in her heart she had never ceased to love me? Could I punish her for indiscretions *I was making her commit*?" (105; emphasis added).

In his role as retrospective first-person narrator, Adolphe is able to reclaim for himself the power that knowledge and hindsight give. He stages a discourse of experience, expertise, and mastery which makes telling his life story the occasion for a dissertation on Life. While following a strict, linear chronology, he offers, as René had, a running commentary on the action that offers the wisdom of hindsight in succinct formulations of eternal truths and universal laws. Adolphe's tendency to punctuate the narration of his personal experience with aphoristic assertions runs counter to what he claims, in a long diatribe in the first chapter, is his "insurmontable aversion from all hackneyed phrases and dogmatic formulae" (41). In an example of precisely the kind of oversimplifying aphorisms he condemns, Adolphe proclaims: "Fools keep their moral code in a compact and indivisible whole so that it may interfere as little as possible with their actions and leave them their freedom in all matters of detail" (41).

Just as the dogmatic statements he attacks leave those who parrot them free to do as they will, Adolphe's pronouncements of universal truth afford him the luxury of pontificating, while paving the way for the absolution he desires, as in the excuse

he gives for his deceitfulness: "This duplicity was quite foreign
to my normal character, but a man deteriorates as soon as he
harbours a single thought that he is constantly obliged to con-
ceal" (108). For Adolphe, who is the analyst as well as the patient in his own discourse, the insights of analysis do not lead
him to change his behavior. Instead, in a pattern already established by his mal du siècle predecessors, René and Oswald,
Adolphe's reflections act within the narrative both as a substitute for action and as a retrospective justification for inaction.[16]

The mal du siècle hero's antilibertine maxims are not, finally,
very different from his father's (and the society's) libertine
pronouncements. Despite variations in content, they are all dictated by self-interest (no matter how disguised) and share a
similar politics of form. Reducing complexity to the aphoristic
expression of a universal law, these generalizations dramatize
emotional paradoxes in a minimalist social environment devoid
of historical or material causes, consequences, and contexts. In
both liberal and libertine discourse, the speaker evidences complete confidence in the validity and general applicability of his
categorical statements, which make the historical and contingent appear natural and inevitable, and endow him with the
voice of Truth. The son's discourse thus rejoins the *parole du
père* he claims to reject, by equating individual (male) experience with universal expertise, and presuming mastery as a way
of (re)asserting power. In this narrative cum confession whose
very premise is the presumption of guilt, such claims act as a
kind of special pleading.

Although the hero is quick to deny that his manuscript is a
document in his own defense, he generally does not blame himself but rather the widest possible extenuating circumstances.
He crowns this exculpating move in a universal maxim that
identifies the root cause of his misfortune as society. Adolphe
describes society as a prison house from which no one escapes:
"[Society] presses down so heavily upon us and its impercep-
tible influence is so strong that it soon moulds us into the
universal pattern" (42). Society is not simply a constraint, it is
man's inexorable fate. He quotes a comment to that effect, which
he had made to Ellenore: "'My dear,' I said, 'we can struggle
on for a time against our destiny, but in the end it has to be

accepted. The laws of society are stronger than the will of men; the most compelling emotions dash themselves to pieces against the fatality of circumstances'" (84). Thus "fate" and its maxims lend finality to a moralist and masculinist psychology that exonerates its exponent. The success of the hero's plea bargaining depends, however, not only on its internal maxims but also on the ideology of gender that "naturalizes" for the reader the politics of its novelistic conventions.

Reader Identification

In the preface to the third edition, Constant presents his novel as an experiment in literary minimalism, which must nevertheless satisfy the one essential criterion of fiction, it must have interest. The text is merely an "anecdote," "which was written with the sole purpose of proving to one or two friends staying in the country that it was possible to infuse a kind of interest into a novel with characters numbering only two and a situation remaining the same throughout" (30). The author's task, then, is to compensate the reader for two of the defining characteristics of the mal du siècle novel, a dearth of characters and the absence of adventure. Although his original idea had been to have Adolphe torn between two women, Constant subsequently decided to have only one female protagonist in the novel. In the 1806 diary entry that records his reasoning, Constant makes a distinction that reveals the essential difference between the representation of the sexes in androcentric mal du siècle fiction: "This reading [to M. de Boufflers] proved to me that I won't be able to make this text work if I add another woman. Ellenore would cease to interest, and if the hero took on obligations to another woman and did not fulfill them, his weakness would become odious." [17] As we saw in *René*, while it is the heroine's task to *interest* the reader as an object, it is the hero's function to elicit the reader's sympathetic identification with him as a subject.

Constant's solution to the first imperative is hardly original. Interest in Ellenore comes at the cost of her victimization through social censure, emotional trauma, and, finally, death. Sympathy for the hero, however, is not so easily won. Constant's diary records, for example, his surprise and disappointment at his listeners' failure to understand Adolphe: "Read my novel to Mme de Coigny. Bizarre effect of this work on her. Revolt against the hero." Months later, he registers a male listener's similar alienation from the protagonist with whom Constant, by contrast, has no problem identifying: "Read my novel to Fauriel. The work had a bizarre effect on him. It is thus impossible to make people understand *my* nature."[18]

In the preface to the third edition of the novel in 1824, however, the author claims that this identificatory process had been all too successful.

> Almost all my readers whom I have met have referred to themselves as having been in my hero's position. It is true that a kind of gratified vanity showed through the regret they displayed at all the pain they had caused; they enjoyed representing themselves as having been pursued, like Adolphe, by the unrelenting affection they had inspired, and as victims of the measureless love somebody had conceived for them. I think that for the most part they were maligning themselves, and that had their vanity left them alone their consciences might have rested in peace. [31].

The pleasure of this text, then, derives from identifying with this otherwise impotent man's power over a woman and, I would add, over narrative.

Peter Brooks argues that narrative binds the energies of plot, thus permitting mastery over the tale told and the dominance of the pleasure principle.[19] It does so for the reader, however, only to the extent that he or she identifies with the "master"'s voice.[20] Inasmuch as the reader relives the story from his—not her—retrospective viewpoint, the novel privileges Adolphe's torment and objectifies that of Ellenore, making it more cerebral, less "real," an object of fascination and pity seen, necessarily, from a safe, voyeuristic distance.[21] In Adolphe's retelling of his life, the reader is privy throughout to the "truth" of his feelings, which was hidden from Ellenore by lies and equivocations, and is thus meant to enjoy not only the pleasure of dominance but the satisfaction of superior knowledge. While the dilatory narrative prolongs Adolphe's and the sympathetic reader's ambiguous pleasure, it draws out the representation of Ellenore's agony, multiplying her sacrifices, and overdetermining her ultimate demise. Moreover, the frequent prolepses in Adolphe's narrative organize events after the fact to make disaster appear not only predictable but inevitable and therefore excusable.[22]

The story of a life becomes fiction in this early nineteenth-century novel through the strategic use of suspense, which requires crisis to ensure catharsis and prepares its release according to predetermined expectations about genre—and gender. These socioliterary codes dictate the dramatic death of the heroine as an ideal form of fictional closure.[23] If, as Brooks argues in "Freud's Masterplot," the dilatory movement of the middle is a way of postponing closure to achieve the proper end,[24] it is more than proper to ask: What guarantees the propriety of the heroine's death? And who is the proprietor?

What Cost Climax?

Through the machinations of the baron de T***, playing a worldly father surrogate to the hero who is far from home, Adolphe's seemingly endless chain of hesitations is broken, and something definitive finally happens in the plot. The baron lends the weight of his age, experience, and social position to the "truths" of dominant ideology to which the hero already half-subscribes by assuring him that Ellenore's pleadings are only emotional blackmail, the oldest trick in women's book. What Adolphe perceives as a drama of life and death, he argues, is mere melodramatic, self-flattering fantasy: "Not one of the passionate women of whom the world is full has not protested that she would die if abandoned, but every single one of them is still alive and has found consolation" (91).

Nevertheless, what the baron promises never happens does come to pass. Ellenore dies, dramatically, of love for Adolphe. The violence of the novel's climax demonstrates the high stakes of this premise and underlines the imbalance of power between the sexes it presupposes. The hero's rational and rationalizing account of emotional distress, and his disembodied representation of sexual passion suddenly become, in the final chapter, a narrative of exaggerated physicality, which makes a spectacle of the heroine's somatized emotional distress while highlighting Adolphe's central role as cause: "Ellenore seemed to have lost the use of her senses. She could not see anything round her. Sometimes she uttered piercing screams and repeated my name; then, horrified, would make a gesture as if asking for something hateful to be kept from her" (113). And later: "Suddenly Ellenore leaped up in bed; I caught her in my arms. Her whole body was shaking convulsively, her eyes were searching for me. . . . It was as if," Adolphe writes, "she were wrestling with *some invisible physical power which, tired of waiting for her last moment, had seized and held her in order to dispatch her on her death-bed*" (119–120; emphasis added).

The last few moments of the story complete the piecemeal annihilation of Ellenore as she quickly loses, one by one, the powers of expression, discourse, will, and then life itself. "She finally yielded to the determined attacks of hostile nature; her body became limp. She seemed to recover some consciousness and pressed my hand. She tried to weep, but the tears would not come; she tried to speak, but her voice had gone. In resignation she dropped her head upon the arm supporting it, and her breathing became slower. A few moments later she was gone" (120). Even though plot is reduced to the minimum in *Adolphe*, attention to the heroine's role in this androcentric tale reveals the plotting at work within this relative stasis.

Ellenore's death is the origin of Adolphe's story. It is the reason behind his need or desire to tell it and the decisive break that gives him a story to tell. In a well-established pattern, man comes to writing over a woman's dead body.[25] To tell this tale as a good story, however, the hero saves for last the shock effect of the heroine's demise as a way to ensure the "proper end," a climax.[26] As in *René*, a man's life thus becomes a fiction with "interest" by melodramatizing and sentimentalizing its determinant origins, the guilt a man feels when he "causes" a woman's death.

In "Text, Ideology, Realism," Terry Eagleton argues that ideology in literature may be compared to the "unconscious" of the text. "Like the subject, the text emerges into existence precisely by the repression of certain (ideological) determinants it *consequently* at certain 'symptomatic' points, begins to betray."[27] Adolphe's first-person narrative operates analogously. It takes shape as a fiction precisely by repressing its *psychological* determinants, which it then dramatically reveals. Similarly, Constant himself explicitly rejects certain *literary* determinants—the libertine plot and its code of female objectification—only to take them up in another, more veiled form. This novel "without a plot," which declares itself sympathetic to woman's plight, is nevertheless plotted against the woman in ways common to the far more obviously misogynist fantasies of female victimization in a libertine writer like Sade.

The ideology of gender in *Adolphe* operates precisely at the point where the psychological and literary "origins" of the text converge. The new notion of male psychology, in which sensibility paves the way through alienation, guilt, and anxiety to narrative power, converges with literary notions about what constitutes a story worthy of interest and the way the hero's narrative may be told about, around, and over a woman's dead body. In this way, Constant's text reveals "the feminine"— which is to say the heroine and the feminized male—as one of *the* symptomatic sites for the collusion of literary conventions and patriarchal premises in the early nineteenth-century French novel. It is through his relation to the heroine that the otherwise emasculated hero exercises his power, and it is through her constitutive absence from his retelling of their story that he exerts narrative control.[28]

In "*Adolphe*'s Appeal to the Reader," Martha Noel Evans argues persuasively that, on all kinds of levels and despite its rhetoric of seduction, *Adolphe* exhibits impotence. "Exhibitionism," she notes, "is not a proud demonstration of power; it does not lead to action. It is the showing, at a safe distance, in a perverse parody of seduction, that what one has is only a pitiful and derisible substitute for the lost, mythic phallus. One shows the place of one's castration."[29] While I would agree that the hero and the text display their self-pitying impotence, indeed they revel in it, I have tried to demonstrate that this game of show and tell, even when it is a demonstration of impotence and a confession of guilt, is itself a privilege and a form of power.

While Constant's mal du siècle hero's discursive mastery makes him the successor to male libertine heroes, he does not assert his power and prerogatives nearly so directly or unabashedly. Instead, as we have seen, Adolphe proclaims his guilt as a way of claiming his innocence and couches his power in declarations of impotence. This duplicity, I would argue, bespeaks a fundamental anxiety of reception. To write is to be read, Adolphe's narrative seems to say, and to write one's confession is to risk being judged contrary to one's intentions. Once proffered, the text is outside its creator's control, reflecting back on him in ways that he had not intended. A similar anxious duplicity characterizes all levels of male discourse in *Adolphe's* paratext.

The Perils and Pleasures of Identification

For the fictional publisher, whose note precedes Adolphe's text, this anxiety shows itself as a fear of guilt by association. He points out immediately that his only encounter with Adolphe and his possession of Adolphe's papers were both accidents of fate and justifies his decision to publish this "anecdote found in the papers of an unidentified man" (the novel's subtitle) on another man's assurance that the manuscript's publication "cannot offend or compromise anybody" (34). He also denies the least role in shaping or editing the text: "I have not changed a single word of the original, and even the suppression of proper names is not my doing; they were indicated in the manuscript, as they still are here, by initials only" (34). Assigning all responsibility to the manuscript's author, the publisher presents himself as a victim of circumstance and an impartial facilitator because, it would appear, he fears the consequences of being *personally* associated with the text's contents.

Publishing and writing have their perils, not only for Adolphe and the "publisher," but for the author himself. In his prefaces, Constant's uneasy negociation between innocence and guilt, between identification with the text and repudiation of it, results in a duplicitous discourse that makes assertions so as to deny responsibility and denies as a way of claiming a connection. Constant's double talk, which evidences an anxiety about losing control, is perhaps symptomatic of the precarious financial and professional position he found himself in.

Though he had first written the novel in 1806, Constant did not publish *Adolphe* until 1816, when he found himself strapped for money and, once again, barred from French politics and living in exile, this time in England. Over the years, Constant had frequently read his manuscript aloud to friends, but in those instances, his acquaintance with his listeners and his highly emotional and dramatized readings of the text gave him some measure of control over his audience's reception of his work.[30] Publication was another matter entirely, particularly in literature, a field that was already claimed and had been dominated by contemporaries such as Chateaubriand and, more significantly, Staël, with whom Constant had finally broken five years earlier to marry another woman. In this new arena, Constant, erstwhile politician and essayist, was an outsider who needed to capitalize on his connections.

As a first-person narrative of a man held fast by his relationship to a woman, *Adolphe* flirts with the promise of an autobiographical revelation about Constant's stormy affair with Staël. Indeed, in publishing his work, Constant did not hide his identity through anonymity, nor did any preface by Constant stave off the inevitable assumptions that in the novel, art had imitated life. Predictably, such rumors surfaced, and Constant publicly pleaded not guilty in a letter to a London newspaper. As a sincere disavowal, his statement failed to convince; as a publicity gambit, however, it helped generate a rebuttal from the editors that served as an advertisement: "from the moment one remembers the author's friendship with *the celebrated Mme de Staël*, Ellenore's character inspires a *redoubled interest and curiosity*."[31] Even so, the novel passed almost unnoticed in the British and French press and met with little commercial success.

Perhaps in an effort to increase sales, Constant added a preface to the second "edition" of the novel soon after. His exercise in self-promotion hinges upon his class identity and his connections—particularly to Staël—in a gesture of preterition that lets him announce the autobiographical links he declares it is his intention to deny. Constant asserts that he is bound by an aristocratic covenant of discretion to defend himself against the prurient interest of the general public. Indeed, the allegations against his work allow Constant to include himself among the literary elite. "Writers more celebrated than I am," he writes, "have experienced the same fate. It has been pretended that M. de Chateaubriand has described himself in René; and the woman, who in our times, is at once the most intellectual and the best, Madame de Staël, has been suspected, not only of having depicted herself in Delphine and in Corinne, but of having traced severe portraits of some of her acquaintances" (26). Constant was, of course, himself among these acquaintances, but not one of those in question in the novel. A lengthy panegyric, which pays homage to his former lover's literary genius and her personal integrity, allows Constant to play the ultimate blameless insider: the magnanimous former lover. Denied access to the literary pantheon through the front door of acclaimed genius open to Staël, Constant seeks to gain entrance through the back door of his connection to her.

The second preface, which appeared with the third edition in 1824, follows a similar strategy. Constant couches his decision to authorize a new edition of his novel as an offensive move to thwart a counterfeit edition which, he claims, will soon be published in Belgium.[32] According to Constant's remark, a proliferation of texts masquerading as the original threatens to undermine his identity as sole proprietor of the text, guarantor of its truth, and, not incidentally, principal beneficiary of its success. Constant's clear statement of intent fixes his signature irrevocably to the work and disavows all responsibility for any textual impostures.

Even as the novel's "father" asserts his paternity in no uncertain terms, he goes through the motions of abandonment. In both of his prefaces, Constant's rhetorical strategy consists in denigrating his work and playing down the significance of this unassuming "anecdote." "Everything to do with *Adolphe* has become a matter of supreme indifference to me," he writes. "I set

no store by this novel [je n'attache aucun prix à ce roman]" (31).
Nevertheless, as we have seen, the text with "no value" obviously has market value, and Constant belies his own assertions
of its worthlessness not only through his insistent and repeated
declarations of the work's intention and meaning in the prefaces, but through his attempt to influence the work's reception.
Overdetermining its moral, he gives an elaborate and over-
blown frame to his story: the publisher's note reveals Adolphe's
unhappy fate from the beginning, and not one but two evalua-
tions of it appear at the end.

The double male coda in *Adolphe* offers, as do Chactas and
Father Souel in *René*, the contrast between indulgent sympathy
for Adolphe as a victim of society on the one hand, and uncom-
promising severity toward the hero's self-serving self-presentation on the other.[33] Whereas the "Letter to the Publisher"
blames society for Adolphe's predicament, the publisher's "Re-
ply" charges Adolphe with sole responsibility for his actions.
Thus, in a move typical of Adolphe's own narrative, the text
states its moral only to assert the opposite as well. This double
discourse calls into question any single point of view and even
sketches out a position of ethical ambiguity, but this openness
is also, I would argue, an illusion. Even though these two dia-
metrically opposed interpretations seem to account for an entire range of ethical valuations of the novel, and even though
they both castigate Adolphe's treatment of Ellenore, they share
an androcentric bias. For both of these readers of the text, as
for most liberal thinkers in the early nineteenth century, the
problem of the individual's liberty and responsibility is a problem for and about men. Their rhetoric of fairness and reason,
the common coin of liberal discourse, allows them to talk a
good line, but it can also work to obscure the reality that those
who do not enjoy the rights of "Man" are precisely those who
have been excluded from this "open" debate.

So too in Adolphe's narrative. The hero as narrator does indeed present both sides of his case, but he does so in order to
have it both ways. In any case, the woman's voice and her point
of view are missing.[34] The final pages of Adolphe's text are the
most extreme but telling example of the way in which even

when Ellenore is most present, it is Adolphe who controls her discourse from behind the scenes.

Before dying, Ellenore makes Adolphe promise that he will burn a letter she has written to him but has not sent. He admits, however, that after her death he "could not resist the temptation to read it" (121), and compounds that betrayal by copying out long passages from the letter to close his text. While Adolphe thus seems to give Ellenore the last, accusatory word, it is he who has selected which words will appear and in what order. The man who makes public a woman's text, enabling her to be heard from beyond the tomb, is also her editor.

Adolphe's paratext thus features three male writers—the publisher, the reader quoted in the coda, and the author himself—whose texts range from the apparently objective to the obviously self-serving and defensive. In all three cases, however, these male figures use their discursive prerogative—the *freedom* and opportunity to speak to which they are entitled as men and men of means—to affirm their connection to the text (so that they may pass judgment on it), only to deny that such a tie might be self-incriminating. These writers' anxiety about reception, their presumption of their own guilt, and their ability to see both sides of a problem (though they want to have it both ways), signifies an important new discursive mode, not only for men as they are represented in literature, but also for Constant and other men of literature.

In his writings about *Armance*, Constant's contemporary and fellow liberal, Stendhal, makes it clear that his own anxious double talk, which takes the form of ironic posturing and transparent imposture, derives from his choice of the novel as genre. What this man of bourgeois origins knows is that he is an outsider in a domain where aristocratic women long dead have a special claim and those still alive have special privileges. Stendhal therefore goes beyond merely sympathizing with women, as Constant had done, to present his fiction of impotence as if it were written by one.

5

Taking the Woman's Part
Stendhal's *Armance*

BY THE 1820s, the mal du siècle was no longer primarily a phenomenon to which a certain number of writers alluded in the prefaces to their novels. The male malady, a literary commonplace, had become a recognized social phenomenon. In the salons of Restoration France, young noblemen had begun to bear their aristocratic privilege as a burden and wear their melancholic dissatisfaction as a badge of honor, which, for some observers, such as the bourgeois and liberal Stendhal, made them an object of ridicule. Writing from Paris as a correspondent for several English magazines in 1825, Stendhal attributed the "vague, melancholic feelings, which many rich young men of our time share" to their "idleness."[1] Under Napoleon, he notes in another article, "these young people *worked*, they gained at an early age some personal experience, and they became *Men*. . . . Now they don't know what to do with themselves: they read novels, or *sentimental philosophy* and fall rapidly into a complete disgust with everything; in a word, they have spleen." These well-off young men, he scoffs, "don't have enough strength of character, nor enough good sense to get themselves hired in a business or set sail for America. They prefer reading or writing bad verse in Paris."[2]

When, just two years later, Stendhal, still living and writing in Paris, sought a subject for his first novel, which he finally called *Armance, or Scenes from a Parisian Salon in 1827*, he chose the aristocracy of Restoration France and a young man subject to its emasculating idleness. Unlike Chateaubriand and Constant, who used their own privileged but unhappy lives as a prime source for their fiction, the bourgeois Stendhal chose the son of a marquis as his novel's hero, and rejected the first-person confessional form common to his predecessors' works. While Stendhal's narrator distances the hero from the reader with amused irony—an unprecedented phenomenon in the humorless mal du siècle tradition—the primary targets of his genuinely satiric barbs are the hypocrites, prudes, and social climbers in the hero's aristocratic milieu who exhibit none of the refined sentiments, fierce pride, or scorn for material wealth that make Octave de Malivert an old-fashioned yet fundamentally admirable embodiment of age-old noble ideals in a degraded, increasingly bourgeois era.

Like its hero and despite its very modern irony and anti-aristocratic bias, the novel itself harks back to an earlier, aristocratic golden age. According to Stendhal in the self-justificatory notes he wrote after the novel's publication, "the only works to which [Armance] bears resemblance are those that were in fashion a very long time ago, [Madame de Lafayette's] *Princess of Clèves* and the novels of Madame de Tencin."[3] Indeed, in the author's view, *Armance*'s classical style and its refined depiction of noble sentiment put it in league with Lafayette's seventeenth-century novel, the work he judges to be the "summit" of novelistic achievement. His own novel, he declares not once but twice and with obvious self-satisfaction, "seems to me delicate like *The Princess of Clèves*."[4] Thus, in sharp contrast with the silence Chateaubriand observes on the women writers who paved the way for his own novel with their attention to sentiment over plot, Stendhal openly (although privately) states his admiration for earlier women's writing and acknowledges his work's indebtedness to the feminocentric sentimental tradition. Indeed, in his version of the mal du siècle novel, Stendhal moderates Chateaubriand and Constant's blatant androcentrism by naming his novel after the heroine and by offering, albeit within the framework of the hero's story, a sympathetic portrayal of Armance, who appears as a subject in her own right, not merely as the hero's object and victim.

While Stendhal gave explicit and implicit homage in his

novel to women writers long gone, his attitude toward the female authors who were his contemporaries and rivals was problematic at best. Nowhere is Stendhal's ambivalence more apparent than in the comments he made about Claire de Kersaint, the duchess of Duras, in his chronicles of contemporary Parisian life and culture in the English press. Though appreciative of Duras's talents, Stendhal resented the success and social privilege that made her, rather than himself, the heir apparent to Lafayette's literary mantle. Indeed, and as we shall see, when he wrote his first novel, Stendhal stole from Duras the premise of *Armance* and sought to make his own name as a novelist by capitalizing on her fame.

What's a Male Writer to Do?

Throughout his multifaceted writing career, Henri Beyle (who adopted the pseudonym Stendhal a decade or so before penning *Armance*) was, by his own account, an author in search of a genre and an audience. When, in his mid-forties, this bourgeois of modest means began to write his first novel, he had already tried his hand at a wide variety of prose genres. His biography of Rossini had enjoyed some topical success just a few years before, in 1823, and the two versions of his pamphlet on Romanticism, *Racine et Shakespeare* (1823 and 1825), had recently gained him a certain notoriety. But *De l'amour* (1822) had been a dismal failure and, most important, he had given up on the idea of writing comedies for the stage. Beyle, who had always dreamed of becoming the modern-day Molière, was coming to the conclusion that the secret to earlier dramatists' triumph—the audience's shared sense of who and what should be subjected to ridicule—no longer obtained in the divided postrevolutionary age. Instead, the genre that seemed most suited to social critique in modern times and therefore most appropriate for a man of Beyle's literary ambition and political persuasion was the novel, where the writer need reach only one reader at a time.[5]

Meanwhile, it was as a novelist that Duras was making a

name for herself during this same period. Encouraged by the enthusiasm of her friends for her work, Duras had her novel about a freed black slave's unrequited love for her white benefactor's son printed in a very limited, deluxe edition for private circulation in 1824. Those who were present at the readings of *Ourika* in Duras's influential salon, or who were privy to one of these private copies, lauded it. Succumbing to the increasing demand, Duras then had her novel published anonymously (though her identity was generally known) and sold publicly. One year later, her next work, *Edouard*, a novel of love thwarted by class difference, was made public in a similar fashion. Both novels enjoyed considerable success and garnered high praise. Beyle, too, joined in the acclaim—but not without serious reservations.

In need of income to supplement his military pension, Beyle had begun in the 1820s to contribute regularly to several English periodicals. Writing for this foreign audience, he set himself up—anonymously—as an arbiter of French literary taste and a watchdog of aristocratic advantage. Even though Duras herself, unlike most of her class, shared some of the liberal beliefs that he himself professed, Beyle always tempered his praise of her work and of her social role with criticism. While his articles praised the delicacy and modesty of her work, for example, he noted its silly novelistic conventions, and warned that her stilted style "betrayed her caste," just as its subject revealed her aristocratic prejudices.[6]

Neither an aristocrat nor a bourgeois industrialist during a time of aristocratic rule and expanding capitalism, Beyle saw himself as an outsider, one of a marginalized minority of bourgeois liberals whom he dubbed the "thinking class."[7] For Beyle, Duras represented the elite whose rights and privileges could and often did impinge upon the increasingly tenuous prerogatives of such bourgeois literary men as himself. In one of his articles in the English press, for example, Beyle accused Duras of "abusing her power" and influence as wife of the "premier gentilhomme" of Louis XVIII by having a successful melodrama she found offensive censured, thus ruining the career of the playwright.[8] Moreover, for Stendhal, Duras was both agent and symptom of a worrisome new trend. He claimed, for

example, that bourgeois liberals had been so decisively co-
opted by the mid-1820s that they no longer criticized the nobility, for fear of being thought déclassé. Instead, they were
drawn to the salons of the enemy camp by the talents of noblewomen such as Duras, where they sought to make a sensation
in order to further their careers.[9]

Although Beyle admitted that Duras had talent, her status as
exception merely proved for him a sex- and class-stereotyped
rule. He drew the line at taking most other aristocratic women's
literary production seriously. "Here's another work of vanity,
disguised as a novel and inspired by the success of *Ourika*,"
he writes in one of many articles on the numerous novels
produced by noblewomen following Duras's example. "What a
waste of paper, pens, ink, and time—the duchess of Duras is
responsible!"[10] While he treats few of Duras's successors as serious rivals, his comments suggest that their number and social
advantages threaten to tip the literary balance of power decisively in their favor at a time when bourgeois literary men,
such as himself, were attempting to make the genre their own.
Women writers' long held (but always tenuous) dominance of
the novel and their recent successes made a woman's signature
an asset to be coveted in the mid-1820s and set the stage for the
circumstances that led Beyle to write his first novel.

In 1825, Duras again read her unpublished work aloud. Although *Olivier, ou le secret* was thoroughly decorous, its audacious premise—the hero's impotence—was cause for scandal in
Restoration society, which was known for its ostentatious sexual
propriety and religious piety. The nature of Olivier's secret cir-
culated by word of mouth to those outside Duras's inner circle.
One of those outsiders, Henri de Latouche, a friend of Beyle,
had already made a name for himself with several literary
spoofs and decided to capitalize on the interest generated in
Duras's unpublished novel.[11] In 1826 he published his own
Olivier and passed it off as hers by adopting the features that
had become a kind of signature for Duras's previous published
work: anonymity, luxurious paper, elegant typography, an epigraph from Byron, and even the notice, which was false in his
case, that all profits from the sale of the work would be contrib-
uted to charity. Beyle, who was in on the hoax, and other critics,

fueled public interest in the new novel with articles that attributed Latouche's novel to Duras.[12]

The scandal that Latouche orchestrated around the publication of his *Olivier* not only ensured his success, it also silenced Duras. Rhymed verse ridiculing her talent and criticizing her pretentions to literary seriousness had already been making the rounds in Paris circles after the publication of her two previous works.[13] Once she read aloud her third novel, *Olivier*, however, factors such as Latouche's appropriation of her name and fame, and Beyle's imputations against her in his journalistic writing, seemed to have made the stakes of publication too high for a woman already very modest about her literary talents and uncertain about whether she should act on any kind of ambitious wish.[14] Duras never published *Olivier*, nor did she ever publish anything again. Thus did two male writers help eliminate their literary competition, making Duras's fate an admonitory example, perhaps, for other would-be women writers.

It was in this context that Beyle wrote *Armance*, his own variation on the *Olivier* theme of male impotence, which he published, a year after Latouche's, in 1827. Like Latouche, he chose to cloak his fiction in the guise of female authorship. Unlike his predecessor, however, his anonymity was not total, nor was his female disguise complete. Instead, Beyle splits the sexual difference into two roles: in his foreword to the novel, he identifies himself, under his pseudonym, Stendhal, as the novel's editor and announces that the text's anonymous author is a woman. In his portrait of the artist as a woman, Stendhal creates a contemporary woman author as he would like to see her—one who is more like himself and who, unlike Duras, poses neither a literary nor a social threat.

Stendhal's Literary Woman

Though Stendhal calls the female author of this text "a woman of intelligence," he claims that she has "no very fixed ideas upon literary merit."[15] What she is missing, the editor states with tongue in cheek, is the good literary sense to know that he, the "unworthy" man whom she has asked to correct her style, does not have what it takes. Stendhal thus hides his authorship behind female skirts only to pull them off and expose the fictive female author's lack as he facetiously reveals his own. Rather than assert categorically his own authority, he engages instead in a form of double talk reminiscent of Constant in his prefaces to *Adolphe* and the three male writers who figure in Constant's novel. Stendhal's duplicity, however, is far more elaborate and effective, for it makes him a moving target, very difficult to pin down.

Splitting himself in two—as a female author and a male editor—allows Stendhal to make claims as one persona only to retract them as the other. Stendhal announces that as the editor he has corrected the novel's style, for example, but then denies responsibility for it by leaving untouched certain of the author's "naivetés of expression." In this, the editor cedes authority to the "author" and "quotes" her reasoning: "'Too much striving after noble turns of phrase in the end leads to deference and to dryness; they encourage the reading of a page with pleasure, but such *dulcet preciosity* makes people shut the book at the end of a chapter, and we want [readers] to read goodness knows how many chapters'" (7). Thus, Stendhal uses the female author as the spokesperson for his own views. "She" finds fault with the stilted quality that he had mocked in his own criticism of Duras's prose, and she derides the "'Germanic, Romantic grandiloquence'," typical of Stendhal's mal du siècle predecessors, Chateaubriand and Staël, which Stendhal had criticized elsewhere.[16] "'Allow me,'" Stendhal's female author concludes, "'my rustic or bourgeois simplicity'" (7).

Unlike Duras, Stendhal's fictional woman writer is not part of the reigning aristocracy, nor does she follow the lead of the bourgeois men of letters Stendhal had criticized in the English press, whose ignoble lust for advancement has them plotting in "the Ministers' antechambers for a position as the head of some office, or any other lucrative job."[17] Instead, she recalls Stendhal's own presentation of self as one of the few writers who can still claim his integrity.[18] "The author has not since 1814 been up to the first floor of the Palais des Tuileries," he writes, "she has such pride that she does not even know the names of those persons who no doubt attract notice in certain circles" (5).

Stendhal states in the foreword that he shares with the author a distaste for romans à clef, since they are based on an envy of those in power. He goes on, however, to claim that her novel makes a satire of "manufacturers and members of the privileged class" (5). Moreover, it is on the question of politics that Stendhal underscores from the first the author's sole responsibility for the text's content: "I am far from sharing certain political views which seem to run through the narrative; this is what I wanted to tell the reader" (5). In a move characteristic of the entire foreword, and of the novel itself, Stendhal's ambiguous disclaimer never states its own claims. His writing nevertheless betrays his prejudices.[19]

Despite his earlier expression of disdain for romans à clef, the editor's parting shot plays up the fiction of a mysterious, "real" female author whose identity cannot be revealed. According to him, the woman as author must, at all costs, remain anonymous: "There is an infinity of proud spirit in that heart of hers. It is the heart of a woman who would think herself older by ten years if her name were known. Besides, a subject such as this . . . !" (7). Clichés of female vanity and prudishness combine to raise the stakes of publication to a fate presumably worse than death, aging. Hence, the fictitious woman author's name is silenced and elided. Only the male "editor"'s (pseudo)name—Stendhal—remains.

Stendhal's facetious use of female anonymity as a figure of derision and a mask for his own authorship not only allows him to pretend to write *as* a woman in the novel, it also permits him to speak *through* her in order to supplant her in the foreword. Like the mal du siècle hero of earlier works, Stendhal takes the woman's part in order to have it both ways. In his first novel, *Armance*, his hero does the same. Like Stendhal, who found himself focusing his literary ambition in the novel—women's genre—Octave is required to channel his ambitious wish exclusively within the private sphere, which was associated with women. As in the foreword, however, Stendhal's novel uses those restrictions to further male advantage. Within the confining realm of salon and family, Octave reigns supreme.

His Majesty the Ego

Stendhal's novel, like Constant's *Adolphe*, introduces Octave as a young man who, having finished his education, is poised to make his debut in the world.[20] Although he had wanted to enter the military, the hero's first act in the novel is to bow to his parents' wishes that he remain at home. The narrator explains that although he is "master of himself and of his fortune" (17) and has not only the rights but the means to do whatever he will, Octave "always devoted himself unhesitatingly to what he considered the dictates of duty" (9). On the threshold of a masculine coming of age, and despite his liberal values and bourgeois ambitiousness, the aristocratic hero, caught in the anachronistic customs of his class, is thus tethered to woman's place—the home.[21] Despite these feminizing circumstances, or perhaps precisely because of them, the text, like Octave himself, emphasizes his masculinity and asserts his power over himself and others.

Determined to embody absolute self-control, Octave fashions himself as the product of cold reason and "inexorable logic" (95). The hero exaggerates these traditionally masculine attributes to such an extent that he seems to have neither desires nor emotions. "If he had felt a desire to talk," the narrator states, "he would have made a great sensation, but Octave had no desires; nothing seemed to cause him either pain or pleasure" (9). Although condemned to impotent reverie and forced to keep the company of people he despises, Octave is a figure of power, reminiscent of the Byronic *homme fatal*, who frightens and disturbs those around him. The Commandeur de Soubirane claims to be afraid of his nephew, calling him "the very *incarnation* of duty." He adds, "If you are not the Messiah awaited by the Hebrews you must be Lucifer in person. . . . What the devil are you?" (10). While the Commandeur's tendency toward hyperbole might account for this apparently excessive claim, even Octave's level-headed mother notes "something *superhuman*" in her son. "Everything about him, even his noble features, *alarmed* his mother; his beautiful, gentle eyes inspired her with *terror*. Sometimes they seemed to scan the heavens and to reflect the happiness they saw there. A moment later they were filled with the torment of hell" (17; emphasis added). She wonders whether her son's eccentricity is due to some physical malady, but the doctors she consults insist that Octave's problem is all in his mind. Echoing Stendhal's own mocking remarks in his journalism, these "intelligent men" (11) dismiss Octave's extraordinary malady as a contemporary commonplace.[22] They "told Mme de Malivert that her son was suffering from no other disease than that kind of dissatisfied and censorious sadness characteristic of the young men of his time and rank" (11). The mother already knows, however, that her son's problem only appears to be an absence of emotion. His affection for her, like hers for him, knows no bounds.[23]

Though written in the third person, *Armance* reads like a son's Oedipal fantasy come true. The mother, for example, merits nothing but praise from the "objective" narrator who declares that she had an "extremely original and piquant mind . . . [and] was untouched by affectation" (10–11). Almost fifty, Mme de Malivert had neverthless "stayed young" and was "still beautiful" (10). The mother's identification with her son is so strong that it is she who bears the physical symptoms of his psychological malady. The doctors warn the mother, who suspects a pulmonary illness in her son, "that she herself should take the greatest care of her chest" (11).[24] The father, by contrast, is shown as an inane albeit well-intentioned third wheel to the mother-son dyad: "Thoroughly dunder-headed and very rich before the Revolution, the Marquis de Malivert had returned to France only in 1814 in the wake of the king, to find his fortunes reduced by confiscation to twenty or thirty thousand francs a year. He considered himself a beggar" (11). The narrator's derogatory portrait of the father figure is just a mild version of a pattern that is even more striking in later Stendhalian texts. As Leo Bersani argues in *Balzac to Beckett*, there is only one good father in Stendhal's texts: the narrator.[25] In *Armance* the narrative voice is also that of a *son*. Although the narrator underscores his class difference from his protagonist and his ironic distance, he also identifies strongly with the young hero in whom he has a high emotional investment.

In this respect, Stendhal's *Armance* strikingly recalls Freud's analysis of the wish-fulfilling fantasies that are the basis for creativity, not in "the writers most highly esteemed by the critics, but the less pretentious authors of novels, romances and short stories."[26] Each of these "egocentric stories" has a hero, he writes, "His Majesty the Ego" (150), "who is the centre of interest, [and] for whom the writer tries to win our sympathy by every possible means" (149). In *Armance*, as in these works, all the male characters who might rival the hero for the narrator's attention or the reader's affection are portrayed as figures of derision—whether they are benevolent but ludicrous, such as M. de Malivert, or malevolently villainous, such as the Commandeur de Soubirane and Octave's nemesis, the Chevalier de Bonnivet. The only characters portrayed sympathetically are the ones who truly love Octave, that is, his mother and Armance.

While the hero and his female admirers should by all rights inhabit the "paradisical world of mothers and children" typical of Stendhal's fiction,[27] *Armance* shows trouble even in this would-be paradise. Although Octave remains at home and by his mother's side, the son bridles under his own self-imposed restraint, zealously guarding his unspeakable secret.[28]

Staying In, Acting Out

The hero adheres to such a narrow definition of filial responsibility that his self-denial goes far beyond the call of duty. When his mother sacrifices two of her family diamonds to buy him a horse, Octave refuses this symbol of aristocratic prestige and masculine mobility. Instead, he insists on staying by her side. "In vain she had urged him to venture into society, or at least to the theatre. 'I stay where I am happiest,' said Octave" (16). The hero's facility at dissimulation makes all his statements suspect, but the fact remains that this male protagonist chooses to stay at home, within the narrow confines of the living death that characterizes the *maison paternelle*. In the garden, "stood a row of lime-trees, regularly trimmed thrice a year, whose motionless shapes seemed a living symbol of the way the family lived" (12).

Whereas in Constant's *Adolphe*, the hero's frustration with the ties that bind him takes a passive form of aggression, Octave is fully capable of "extraordinary malevolence" (28) and explodes at several moments in blind fury. Octave's violent encounters with other men occur, his mother notes, "exactly at those moments when he seemed most forgetful of the sombre reverie which she habitually read in his expression" (29). Thus, in Stendhal's novel, the melancholy docility and feminine passivity typical of the mal du siècle hero merely disguises what it cannot completely repress, the violent masculine contentiousness that stems from deep-seated rage.[29]

Octave's frustration is due in large part to his elevated social station, for the privilege of his birth puts a severe constraint on his actions. Instead of delighting in his privileged position as one of the masters, Octave would like to be (or at least play) the servant. He tells Armance the fanciful plans that would allow him to leave home, family, and Paris itself to enjoy the physical and social mobility that his noble parentage does not allow: "I should take the name of Pierre Gerlat, and, starting off in Geneva or Lyon I should arrange to become the manservant of some young man destined to play more or less the same role as myself in the world" (105). In Stendhal's version, the Restoration aristocrat's family romance is thus not to imagine himself the son and heir of a nobleman, which he already is, but to fantasize, for example, a life as "the son of the senior foreman at M. de Liancourt's carding factory" (106).

If Octave dreams about becoming downwardly mobile, it is because in Restoration society, the bourgeois, unlike the nobleman, has a part to play in France's future and in its increasingly industrialized means of production.[30] For Octave, nobility itself is a moribund anachronism in the contemporary era. "Since the steam engine became queen of the world, a title has been an absurdity," Octave states, "but when all's said and done, here am I all tricked out in that absurdity" (98). Indeed, early in the novel an outside event from the pages of history forces the fictional hero to abandon his dreams of production and face up to the sole remaining duty his aristocratic title still requires, that is, *re*production.[31]

=====

The Ladies' Man, Part 1

At the beginning of the second chapter, the Malivert household is abruptly shaken out of its moribund inertia with the news that the law of indemnity, which would compensate aristocrats for the losses they had suffered when their property was confiscated during the Revolution, will soon be passed. For M. de Malivert, this promise of financial restitution represents his family's regeneration. "I can now seek a suitable match for you without having to beg for it" (21), he tells Octave and weeps at the thought of seeing his future grandchildren.

Much like a heroine whose primary function is to be married off, Octave's new wealth forces him into circulation as a commodity on the marriage market. "He was treated in an entirely new way, especially by very great ladies who could regard him as a potential husband for their daughters" (45). Although traditionally women are the objects in this economy of exchange, in *Armance* the noble and handsome Octave becomes the means to women's ambitious ends: "This mania of the mothers in this century to be for ever husband-hunting shocked Octave almost beyond words" (45). Although Octave hypocritically plays along with this new audience of admirers, that his newfound wealth has made him the object of sudden interest merely reinforces the hero's misanthropy and his scorn for the "'envy, malice, and the abject veneration of rank and wealth'" that the members of his class show.[32] Octave remarks that the only person who "was not a party to the redoubling of attentions which he owed to the money," is his cousin Armance de Zolihoff. "She alone there had some nobility of soul" (22). With her high ideals, devotion to duty, fierce pride, and noble disdain for money, Armance is not only Octave's counterpart, she is his equal.

Despite Octave's solemn vow that he will not fall in love, he succumbs to the charms of his soul sister and, with the introduction of the heroine as love interest, the mal du siècle text

shifts, once again, from the atemporal thematics of repetition
to the traditional exigencies of plot.[33] Having learned that Armance believes that his restituted fortune has turned his head,
Octave and his life take on "new purpose" (42) as he seeks to
regain the heroine's esteem. The heroine, meanwhile, strives to
retain Octave's respect by pretending not to love him, for fear
he or others will think that her interest in him is due to his
wealth.

For the heroine, and even for the other aristocratic women
in his company, it is not just Octave's fortune that makes him so
desirable. In *Armance*, Stendhal endows his "impotent" hero
with all kinds of power, including a "remarkable beauty" (23),
which exerts a special fascination over women. One of the keys
to his ability to attract the opposite sex is the way the feminine
qualities of his looks and his character soften his obvious masculinity. The narrator notes that "the set of his features . . . were
strong and gentle, and not at all strong and hard as is the case
among the common run of men handsome enough to attract
notice" (28; emphasis added). Despite the cold masculine exte-
rior he cultivates, Armance senses underneath a feminine gentleness: "Octave's eyes expressed so great a possibility of love,
and sometimes they were so tender!" (32) The loving heroine
forgives Octave his flagrant egotism because his vulnerability
interests her. "She felt, without being really clear about it, that
Octave was the *victim* of that kind of *irrational sensibility which
makes men unhappy and worthy to be loved*" (32; emphasis added).
Thus, despite his exacerbated feminine sensibility and his exaggerated self-centeredness, the hero gets his reward, the admiration of women in general and of the woman he loves in
particular. Indeed, the given in *Armance*, as in all the mal du
siècle novels, with the exception of Sand's *Lélia*, is the heroine's
unconditional love for the hero.[34]

Through the love of the heroine, Stendhal's *Armance* reveals
Octave's mal du siècle as an exacerbated but not incurable case
of egocentrism. Armance's affection and friendship have a
calming, domesticating influence on the hero, which tames his
masculine aggressivity and makes him increasingly capable of
social assimilation and personal happiness. "My pride sets a wall
of diamond between me and the rest of mankind [les autres

hommes]," he tells her. "Your presence, my dear cousin, causes this diamond wall to vanish" (106). Because of Armance, Octave believes he will no longer be subject to those "crises of fury," which used to make her fear for his sanity. He begins to see his misanthropy as a form of egotism, realizing "at last that this world, which in his extravagant pride he had believed to be arranged in a manner hostile to *him*, was merely arranged badly" (73). Armance's influence even succeeds in "reforming" Octave morally. He vows never to return to the houses of gambling and prostitution he used to frequent. Abandoning that "inexorable logic, harsh and glorying in its harshness, which had directed all his actions in earlier youth" (95), Octave suddenly finds himself, for the first time, and in the presence of Armance, swept away by tender emotion; "he felt himself carried away, he was no longer thinking, he was utterly happy" (110).

Although it seems for a time as though Octave will be cured of his mal du siècle, in the end, he succeeds in unlearning all the lessons he has learned. In the name of his fatal secret and the mysterious vow he had made to himself when he was young, he reverts, though not without some regret, to his former egocentric blindness. The text arranges a series of events to confirm the hero in his belief that he cannot love and in his suspicion that he is not loved, even as it proves the contrary to the reader.

Playing Dido to His Own Aeneas

Octave's uncle, the Commandeur de Soubirane, and the Chevalier de Bonnivet forge a letter from Armance to her confidant, Méry de Tersan, in which she professes to have fallen out of love with Octave. As a result of his enemies' trickery, Octave believes the fiction of Armance's fickleness and believes himself abandoned by her. A series of implausibly contrived coincidences nevertheless forces Octave to marry Armance so as to protect her name and, to Octave's surprise, their week on honeymoon is euphoric. The narrator underscores the heroine's sexual fulfillment: "Armance [was] intoxicated with happiness and *swoon[ed]* in his arms" (208). There were even moments "in which Armance's perfect bliss finished by making [Octave] happy" (208). What the presumably impotent hero appears to learn, writes Katharine Jensen, is that "contrary to popular belief, desire exists beyond the phallus; passion is not centered on an organ and therefore it doesn't matter whether you 'have one' or you don't."[35] Nevertheless, Octave suppresses and represses that subversive knowledge by convincing himself that Armance is only feigning happiness for his benefit. His egocentrism leads him to consider his "lack" more important than her sexual fulfillment or their emotional plenitude. Overprivileging the phallus allows Octave to remain the center of his own attention and to fashion for himself a script that will refigure his self-centeredness as selfless martyrdom.

"My life is ended" the hero announces to himself, as he quotes Virgil's Dido abandoned by Aeneas, "*'Vixi et quem dederat sortem fortuna peregi,'*" a remark Stendhal glosses in a footnote—"As she dies, abandoned by Aeneas, Dido cries out: I have lived, and that destiny which fate has marked out for me, I have followed" (205). Thus, the male protagonist actively takes up a woman's fate as his own, rewriting the classic script of the abandoned woman as a man. In order to play Dido, however, he must first take his cue from Aeneas. Like Virgil's hero, he abandons the heroine and sets sail to obey what he pretends to be a heroic, military calling—joining the fight for Greek independence—while in fact he surreptitiously chooses Dido's destiny, suicide.

Octave's suicide resembles a play in which he is both the star and his own most appreciative audience. Melodramatizing his own death scene, he pretends to suffer from a grave illness and gathers around him the ship's crewmen to witness his enactment of the rituals of death. Octave repeatedly defers the final act of his drama the better to enjoy the thrill of speaking the truth in extremis. "Except for the manner of his dying, he granted himself the happiness of telling everything to his Armance" (209) in a series of letters. Octave revels in the idea of his noble self-sacrifice, which will free his true love from her vows to him; in his will he goes so far as to provide for Armance only if she marries another.

Juliet Flower MacCannell notes that when the subject of desire is male in Stendhal, its object—woman—is seen as only a "degraded substitute" or a "delaying obstacle" on the way toward an unattainable transcendental ideal.[36] The hero of *Armance* achieves that state of plenitude by dying, a deed the text exposes as self-destructive narcissism while glamorizing and romanticizing both the act and its results. Octave's death from self-administered poison comes under a moonlit night as a gentle transition from this life to the next. When he is found the next day, "there was a smile on his lips, and his rare beauty struck even the sailors who were ordered to bury him" (210).

Although Armance's name gives the text its title, Octave's death perfunctorily ends the story. The fate of Dido is not an option open to the women who loved Octave since enobling suicide in this novel is a male prerogative. Nevertheless, it would appear that a life without Octave calls for a death from the world. For Armance and Mme de Malivert, self-immolation in the convent is the only (re)solution. In the end, the reader knows what Armance can only suspect—that Octave's death was a suicide. On the other hand, having presumably received the letters from Octave in which he tells her "everything," Armance knows but the narrator does not reveal what the reader can only guess—the nature of Octave's fatal secret.

Since the very first review of Stendhal's novel, critics have called attention to the novel's remarkable ellipsis. To supply what Stendhal failed to provide, modern editors of *Armance* almost invariably include the author's infamous letter to Prosper Mérimée in which he unabashedly identifies the hero's malady as sexual impotence. Paradoxically, whereas Stendhal's contemporaries, who were for the most part not privy to this information, considered its absence one of the novel's failings, modern critics, fully aware of the letter to Mérimée, tend to hail *Armance*'s enigmatic silence about its hero's secret as a sign of its prescient modernity and thus the text's strength. In the letter itself, Stendhal too describes his decision *not* to be explicit about his hero's sexual impotence as a calculated strategy to guarantee his own authorial power.

The Ladies' Man, Part 2

Whereas in the foreword Stendhal uses a woman the better to speak as a man and in his notes to himself he values his work for its resemblance to women's fiction, Stendhal's correspondence with Mérimée reveals the ulterior motive behind this flirtation with the feminine. In his letter of 23 December 1826, Stendhal speaks man to man in a discourse in which feminine delicacy has no place. The writer adopts instead an exaggerated posture of worldly rakishness and manly cynicism to deflect the charge that his novel is too sentimental. He thus reveals what the novel's discreet ellipsis of the hero's sexual malady serves to disguise—the sexual politics that is not fit for mixed company or for print, but that informs Stendhal's strategy for seducing his imagined reader, that is, a woman alone.

In his defensive response to Mérimée's reading of his manuscript, Stendhal insists that his concern was to make the hero's impotence clear to the reader without making it explicit. Thus he explains that he decided to call his hero and his text Olivier because Duras's novel and Latouche's imitation of it had made the name synonymous with impotence. Nevertheless, on Mérimée's advice, Stendhal rechristened the hero for publication. In the change from Olivier to Octave the author seems, then, to opt for obscurity over clarity, discreet periphrasis over indecent exposure, which offers the additional advantage, perhaps, of obscuring his debt to both Duras and Latouche. On the other hand, in retaining the initial letter *O* from the original name, the hero's new baptism represents only a slight displacement on the paradigmatic axis. The *O* in Octave's name continues to connote lack as Stendhal's protagonist joins the other stories of *O* in the mal du siècle lineage: Senancour's Obermann, Staël's Oswald, Latouche's Olivier, Duras's Olivier, and even Duras's female twist on the tradition, Ourika.

In contrast with his sexually inadequate hero, Stendhal presents himself to his male addressee as a man among men, which is to say experienced in the ways of women: "My experience has taught me that a modest girl much prefers to put her letters in a hiding-place than to hand them to her lover in person" (213). His expertise allows him the satisfaction of generalizations, such as the following: "Olivier, like all Babilans [impotent men], is quite an expert on the auxiliary methods in which *le Président* glories. A deft hand and an officious tongue would have given Armance keen sensations of pleasure" (212–213). But if the hero's expertise more than compensates for his inadequacy, it is only because of the heroine's ignorance: "*I am sure* many girls *have no precise notion* what physical marriage consists of" (213; emphasis added). In this way, lack, which had been associated with the male, is suddenly shifted to the female. During their period of apprenticeship to the "true" joy of sex, women do not even miss what the impotent male assumes is essential since "the consummation of the marriage is repulsive to them for *three or four years*, particularly when they are tall, pale, slim, and blessed with a fashionable waistline" (213). Male impotence is thus not a lack, it is an advantage that, temporarily at least, ensures his lover's happiness.

Stendhal's strategy as author borrows from this insight. He cultivates the appearance of a lack, in this case, of erudition, in order to please the reader through his own "auxiliary means" which he calls "warmth." Stendhal worries that his novel is "too *erudito*, too learned. Has it enough warmth to keep a pretty French Marquise awake until two in the morning? *That is the question*" (213). The reader who counts is thus not the real (male) reader, Mérimée, but instead the ideal reader of the yet-to-be-published text, who is fantasized as noble, pretty, French—and female. To succeed, the novel must seduce this presumably solitary reader with the pleasure of Stendhal's text. "Would a young woman take an interest in Olivier?" Stendhal continues. In order to guarantee her sympathy for the hero, Stendhal explicitly rejects the culture's comedic script for the impotent male, which would make him the subject of derision or a character out of farce.[37] Unlike the cuckold, Stendhal's hero must and will remain both desirable and desired, for that is the key to success not only for the novel but also for the author. Stendhal therefore insists on making his impotent hero a tragic figure and justifies the suicide that ends his text: "The genuine Babilan must kill himself in order to avoid the embarrassment of making a confession" (214).

Yet what is tragedy for the literary hero would be comedy for the author. Stendhal goes so far as to imagine himself suffering from a similar incapacitation only to laugh off the comic consequences and offer a titillating scenario of prostitution for his male addressee. "As for me (but at the age of forty-three years eleven months), I should make a beautiful confession, and I should be told: *What of it?* I should take my wife to Rome. There a handsome countryman, at a cost of one sequin, would pay her three compliments in one night" (214). Given the era's standards of decency and the author's choice of readers, the private story of the virile substitute cannot be told in public, he writes. Therefore Stendhal's periphrasis is a necessary strategy for modestly telling what is, in essence, an immodest story: "Giving ecstasies with your hand—what an excellent euphemism to avoid the dirty word fr*g! . . . It is necessary you should know that he spent his youth frequenting wantons; it is this that I have tried modestly to convey" (215). The author's success as a novelist thus depends on a very different rhetorical posture from the cool, flippant tone he adopts in corresponding with Mérimée. He must modestly disguise the flagrantly sexual so that his novel can be published and does not shock. If it is to keep his woman reader warm and awake at night, it must, however, continue to titillate by promising more than it delivers.

For contemporary readers, *Armance* did not deliver enough. The novel was a critical and commercial flop. In his notes to himself on the text's failure, Stendhal blames the "vulgar public": "Given the way times have changed, vulgar men at the feet of [Duras's] Ourika can hardly even see the summit of *The Princess of Clèves*," (the novel Stendhal considers most like his own).[38] Even so, there are still readers, Stendhal notes, who seek in novels a clear, accurate depiction of the human heart written in a fine, classical style. Unfortunately, the aristocrats among them would be hard pressed to favor a novel like *Armance* that satirizes noble salon society. The only group that could accept the novel's political persuasion while appreciating its style is the small number of men such as Stendhal himself who comprise the "thinking class."[39]

Unfortunately for Stendhal, these "happy few" generally do not have the leisure time to read fiction. Instead, the audience for novels is primarily those whose confining, domestic existence gives them the need for escape and consolation, women. According to Stendhal, provincial women in particular, both aristocratic and bourgeois, were increasingly drawn away from the classic *romans d'analyse* to the kind of fiction known as "chambermaid novels." These stock stories of "noble and generous heroes, thwarted love, innocent victims hounded by villains, disguised identities, crimes, frenzy, madness, death, etc.," which provide emotional thrills couched in a grandiloquent prose, are anathema to Stendhal.[40] He blames the Romantics for the proliferation of this fiction and claims no interest in catering to these tastes. The women readers he has in mind are instead Parisians who find insipid the "always perfect hero, the unhappy, innocent and persecuted women" of chambermaid novels.[41] Nevertheless, given the general decline in taste, which Stendhal saw everywhere, the two social categories of women readers are not nearly so distinct. "The principal fear I had writing this novel," Stendhal declares, "was being read by chambermaids *and the marquises who resemble them.*"[42]

Refusing to cater to the degraded literary tastes of provincial women and chambermaids on the one hand, but satirizing his other probable readers, Parisian salon women, on the other, Stendhal thus found himself writing *for* such men as himself who did not have the leisure to read fiction and *against* the women who did. Thus, when Stendhal first entered the literary scene as a male author pretending to be a woman's editor, he did so as a writer alienated from his readership. Just seven years later, Aurore Dudevant, writing as George Sand, offered her own very different variation on the theme of gender identity and authorial alienation. Abandoning her own name in favor of a male pseudonym, for quite different reasons than Stendhal, she created in *Lélia* a text that ostentatiously resists the conventional expectations of its implied reader as it offers instead, and for the first time, a portrait of a woman afflicted with a very different version of the male malady.

6

Toward a Feminist Mal du Siècle
Sand's *Lélia*

I N 1831, ON THE PUBLICATION of her first novel, Aurore Dudevant née Dupin chose a name of her own: G. Sand. In their enthusiastic reviews of *Indiana*, contemporary critics, whether or not they knew or suspected Sand's real identity, noted the indeterminacy of the pseudonym and made the writer's sex an issue. While claiming that the text necessarily mirrored its author's gender, the reviewers' circular line of reasoning nevertheless led to contradictory conclusions. Most believed that the author could be only a man, or at least that there had to be a man behind the woman writer, but others asserted that the author must be a woman. In many ways, the latter supposition seemed the least likely, for *Indiana* defied so many truisms about what women could (and should) write.[1] Unlike "women's novels"—sensitive accounts of thwarted love, which critics deemed most suitable for a female readership and whose significance, they claimed, lay primarily in the light they shed on affairs of the heart—*Indiana* seemed to capture in its pages the entire age, making it, in the words of one reviewer, an enduring work that "will be read and reread" and serve "to teach one century the history of another."[2] Sand's second novel, *Valentine*, which was similarly ambitious and anchored in contem-
___y social reality, also enjoyed considerable popular success.
ear later, when Sand was finishing her third novel *Lélia*,
ntity had become fairly common knowledge. Yet in sign-
s work, she did not revert to one of her given names,

choose a female pseudonym, or continue the fiction of the sexually undecidable "G. Sand." Instead, she opted for the explicitly masculine "George Sand," which would be her nom de plume from then on.[3] Less a disguise by this time than an assertion or assumption of male authorial identity, Sand's male pseudonym also reflected her choice of genres. Unlike her mentor Latouche in his *Olivier* or Stendhal in *Armance*, both of whom sought to sell their false women's novels by pretending that they had been written by a successful woman author, Sand did not write the "romans intimes" associated with women.[4] In *Lélia*, as in her first two works, she continued to tackle weighty contemporary issues with clear social, moral, and political significance—a high ambition regarded as male.

In addition, in her third novel Sand moved sharply away from the realist tendencies that marked her first two works to take on two genres associated with male writers: the mal du siècle novel and the "philosophical tale." Drawing upon Chateaubriand's *René*, Senancour's *Obermann* and other mal du siècle fiction, Sand reduces plot in *Lélia* to the barest minimum necessary to concentrate instead on her antisocial protagonist's disillusioned reflections on the nature of life, which she ties, as the novels of Charles Nodier had done, to deep-seated philosophical pessimism and religious skepticism. At the same time, however, like Balzac's *Contes philosophiques* and *La peau de chagrin* (1831) as well as Vigny's *Stello* (1832), Sand's novel is an experiment in a far more abstract kind of fiction. Updating the theme of melancholic ennui that Chateaubriand's *René* had first made famous, *Lélia* portrays characters not so much as independent beings who have ideas and express emotions, but as the very incarnation of these ideas and emotions.[5] While this formal innovation makes Sand's mal du siècle novel revisionist, the way *Lélia* undermines mal du siècle gender politics makes her text decidedly radical. In this work the exceptional being who embodies the modern malaise is a woman not a man, and her mal du siècle, far from a crisis in male identity, is largely a symptom of her explicitly feminist discontent.

The Female Malady

Shortly after finishing the novel, Sand wrote a laudatory review of Senancour's *Obermann*, which had been recently rediscovered and was soon to be republished. In her article, she identifies the traditional mal du siècle as a male malady and accounts for the resurgence of interest in it by noting changes in the construction of masculinity. She also describes the most recent strain of the mal du siècle in terms appropriate to women and, in particular, to Lélia, her latest heroine.[6]

In her review Sand argues that during the Empire, Napoleon's aggressive militarism had promoted traditional masculine values to such an extent that when *Obermann* was first published in 1804, men were incapable of appreciating this novel of pacifist retreat and "sublime infirmity" because they failed to recognize that they were themselves infirm. Napoleonic despotism had, in her view, infantalized the male population. Incapacitating and silencing those few who had the courage and wisdom to object, the regime required men's "blind allegiance" to a master while preoccupying them with "thoughts of war and dreams of glory" (9). With the fall of the Empire and the rise of a constitutional monarchy, however, men could no longer rule by brute force and had to learn to think for themselves, Sand claims, so that they could rule by persuasion. When this new version of masculinity did not erupt in feverish personal ambition, it led men to look inward and, under the influence of German and English Romanticism, begin to be more self-reflexive. Whereas Chateaubriand and Constant had decried such tendencies as a debilitating effeminacy, Sand, like Staël before her, praises them as a sign of heightened consciousness and sensitivity, while at the same time recognizing the "feminization" of men as a source of anxiety and uncertainty for them, and thus the etiology of many modern ills.

While Chateaubriand's René, she explains, had shown "genius devoid of willpower" (3) but sublime in its proud disdain, and Senancour's Obermann had exemplified an impotent reverie that denies the value of all action and desire, Sand claims that there is one strain of the modern malaise "which has not yet been officially noticed, even though many of us have been stricken with it" (12). This new malady, she writes, is "the suffering that comes from an inability to experience sexual fulfillment. . . . It is the exhaustion and contrition of disappointed passion; in a word, it is the malady of those who have lived" (12). Unlike the defeatism of a René or an Obermann who give up on life having had almost no experience of it, this malady is born of experience and gives rise not to vague discontent but to a kind of rage: "it is the energetic, angry, impious suffering of the soul that dreams of realizing a destiny, and before whom any destiny flees like a dream" (12).

Although Sand does not specify the gender of those who are given no outlet for their talents, the words she chooses to describe them, "des plantes" (plants) and "des âmes" (souls), occasion no fewer than nine consecutive third-person feminine plural pronouns and numerous feminine modifiers. More important, when Sand embodies this sexual impotence and mental suffering in the novel she was then finishing, the body is unmistakably that of a woman. In *Lélia*, the frustration and dejection typical of the mal du siècle hero results when an exceptional woman comes face to face with the realization that she has no desire or ambition and feels no hope for the future precisely because, as a woman, she is asked to confine her desires and ambitions to loving a man.

Sand's radical revision of the mal du siècle is unique in the annals of nineteenth-century women's literature. Indeed, few women writers took up the mal du siècle at all, let alone made it a woman's malady.[7] Ellen Moers explains that "latecomers to literature as they were, and still bedazzled with the strengths of feminine self-assertion, women writers of the nineteenth century were long reluctant to succumb to the ennui, the spleen, the *tedium vitae* of the mal du siècle."[8] Staël, for example, took on the modern failure of will in her 1806 novel, but she attributed it to her hero, giving Corinne uncontestable power.

Unlike the feminization of the mal du siècle hero, which is incapacitating but also self-aggrandizing, the virilization of the heroine in *Lélia* entails an internal system of punishment as well as reward. In Sand's novel, heroism comes at the price of

impotence, frigidity, and despair, which is, perhaps, a strategy
designed to make this figure of female power palatable.[9] Indeed, *Lélia* proves Moers's rule: the heroine's impotence frees
her from the heterosexual plot and the cultural script of femininity and is a powerful form of self-assertion. This is, of course,
the paradox of the mal du siècle generally. But Sand's heroine
is distinguished from her male precursors by the extent of her
power. The depth of the female protagonist's anger and disillusionment reveals the scope of her ambition, which Sand describes in her review as "a force that desires to *seize all, possess
all*, and before which everything escapes, even desire, through
vain fatigue and useless efforts" (12; emphasis added). While
Moers argues that the emphasis on "heroinism" in nineteenth-
century women's writing, which challenges the antiheroic assumptions of the Romantic age, often consists in "physical
heroics," "risk-taking and courage-proving" (200), its hallmark
in *Lélia* is intellectual and ideological rather than physical.
Choosing steadfast resistance rather than active engagement,
Lélia wages a lucid battle against her culture's ideological commonplaces and, in particular, the destructive myth of romantic
love. The novelist, however, at least as much as the heroine,
actively takes risks and proves her courage in and through her
heroine, in and through her text. As Sand's review of *Obermann*
suggests, in many ways she was writing *Lélia against* the two novels—*Indiana* and *Valentine*—that had won her so much fame
and *against* the expectations of the readers who had made her
works such a popular success.

Teaching the Reader a Lesson

Refusing on ethical grounds to entertain her readers with
"puerile, complicated plots" and the description of outward
appearances (14), Sand explores instead the subject she had
found so laudable in her review of *Obermann*, "the intimate sufferings of the human soul" (1). In *Lélia* Sand thus rejects "the
novel of reality" or in her terms "la littérature *réelle*" (14), which
includes not only the realist novel, a genre only then coming

into existence as such, but also all mimetic fiction, including her two previous novels. At their worst, these kinds of works, she would charge in her subsequent defense of *Lélia*, appeal to "vulgar souls draped in falsehood and prudery," who want only to read that which flatters or amuses them and who therefore "place like a demi-god on a pedestal [the writer] who lets them live as they like."[10] Sand not only refuses her place on this pedestal, she makes this refusal explicitly feminist in her third work by taking to task the truisms that link the novel with romantic love and, in turn, equate romantic love with women.

Thus the distrust and denunciation of the love plot in *Lélia* recall Staël's *Corinne*, but is even more direct, intense, and far-reaching. While *Corinne* delays the love story and diverts attention from it through long digressions, *Lélia* makes romance the focus of explicit critique from the beginning. The heroine immediately condemns romantic love as an illusion, and the novel itself reveals its plausible plots and determining destinies as the cause of her mal du siècle. As in *Corinne*, Sand's novel stages the struggle between a man's desire for conventional romance and the exceptional woman's resistance to this story, which she knows will be her undoing. Sand, however, goes even further than Staël in refusing to reduce female subjectivity to the pangs of unfulfilled romantic desire by reversing traditional gender roles in the novel. Sténio, the young Romantic poet who is the hero of *Lélia* loves conventionally, and in his abject surrender to his idolatrous love for Lélia, he takes the stereotypically female role to extremes. Furthermore, Staël's Corinne, like almost all other literary heroines, finally succumbs to the standard love plot. Lélia, on the other hand, will resist to the end the hero's demands that she conform to his romantic expectations.

In its subversion of the love plot and censure of romantic love, *Lélia* risked displeasing both segments of its "natural" readership—the general public on the one hand, which had perhaps appreciated Sand's first two works to the extent that they met many traditional expectations about romance and the novel,[11] and a far more limited audience on the other, which appreciated idealism's formal iconoclasm and mal du siècle pessimism, but expected the text nevertheless to confirm cultural and literary commonplaces about men, women, and power.

While Sand's review of *Obermann* praises the readers who appreciate the sensitive portrayal of suffering souls and an elevated discussion of philosophical ideas in fiction, describing them as "deep souls prone to dreaming, or delicate and attentive minds" (1), her novel shows that insofar as these ideal, feminized readers resemble the typical Romantic poet, the mal du siècle hero, and the reader of "women's novels," they must unlearn the truisms most central to their beliefs.

For the first third of the novel, the text constructs an implied reader in the image of the naïve and conventional Sténio the better to attack this naïveté and call into question these conventions. Just as Lélia frustrates Sténio's desire for her, the text thwarts its implied reader's desire for a more conventional story that would promote a traditional ideal of romantic love. Whereas in Wayne Booth's famous model of reading pleasure the real reader must create himself in the image of the implied reader who is complicitous with the implied author,[12] in Sand's fiction the relationship between the text and the implied reader is adversarial until this reader learns, as Sténio will, the heroine's lessons. Like Sténio, the weak man who is mystified, mesmerized, and continually surprised by Lélia, the implied reader is constantly unsettled by this thoroughly unconventional text.[13]

The novel proper begins, for example, without preamble, with the point-blank interrogation of an unspecified addressee by an unidentified speaker: "Who are you? And why does your love cause so much evil?"[14] Despite the immediate intimacy this abrupt beginning establishes with the reader, the text's apparent candidness hides as much as it divulges. No mentorlike narrator guides the reader by the hand to contextualize the series of impassioned and portentous outpourings with which the novel begins. The third-person narrator who does appear twenty pages later gives only minimal indications of the historical and social setting, makes very little reference to everyday concrete details, and flaunts the text's infraction of the laws of fictional verisimilitude. In a strikingly modern mix of genres and tones, the novel shifts without warning from impassioned love letters to heady philosophical speculations on the meaning of life, from lyrical evocations of idyllic nature to farcical melodrama.

The text thus provokes in its implied reader the vertigo evoked in the epigraph: "When credulous hope risks a confident glance amidst the doubts of an isolated and desolate soul to fathom and heal them, its foot totters at the edge of the abyss, its eye is troubled, it is stricken with dizziness and death." More than a simple allegory of the struggle between Sténio's doomed hopes and Lélia's inveterate disillusionment, the epigraph figures the text as a deadly abyss that puts the implied reader at risk, forewarning those who dare to read on that the text is unshakable in its profound pessimism and that, no matter what rescue fantasies the readers of *Lélia* may entertain, "the isolated and desolate" Lélia cannot be "saved."

Feminist Idealism?

Whereas mimetic novels recount the changes characters undergo in the course of the narrative, the characters in *Lélia*, an idealist novel, represent atemporal abstractions that do not change over time. As the "Autopsy of Lélia" in Sand's *Sketches and Hints* would have it, Lélia symbolizes doubt, Trenmor represents stoic expiation, Magnus embodies superstition and repressed desire, and Pulchérie incarnates the senses.[15] Rather than individuals made even more complex by their personal histories, particular circumstances, and internal contradictions, these characters are schematized and exaggerated types. Thus *Lélia*'s idealism is both deeply pessimistic and essentializing. In these respects, the novel marks a sharp contrast with the realism that Naomi Schor has identified as characteristic of feminist literature, in which insights tend to be grounded in experience and material reality, revealing gender as a social construction and thus implying hope for change.[16] On the other hand, the text's idealism is far from absolute, for *Lélia* does turn toward realism at precisely those moments when the novel most explicitly attempts to teach its readers (feminist) lessons.

First, although most of the characters in the novel do not change fundamentally over time, Sténio is the notable exception. The hero undergoes a dramatic and traumatic transformation because, as I have suggested, it is those readers who identify with his romantic longing whom the text proposes, precisely, to change through this admonitory example. Having symbolized romantic love, poetry, and credulous hope through most of the text, Sténio is driven to despair, debauchery, and suicide by the end.

Second, while the level of abstraction in the representation of the characters would appear to make gender a matter of indifference in the novel, it is crucial in fact not only in *Lélia*'s critique of the gender hierarchy implicit in romantic love, but also in the way the work presents its heroine. While on the one hand Lélia throughout the text resists the notion that she is a woman so as not to be trapped into a limiting female role and identity, on the other, when she tells her story to her courtesan sister, Pulchérie, she reveals that her impotence comes, precisely, out of her experience as a woman in a man's world. Thus, as Schor has shown in her illuminating analysis of the novel, Sand's allegorization of woman "fails" because the feminist impulses behind her text's ethical idealism strain the boundaries of female allegory in a desire to reveal the real conditions of women under patriarchy. As a result, allegory "collapses into linear narrative and psychological realism."[17] Indeed, these more realistic passages—where the two women confide in each other, giving voice to a female experience, which is usually silenced—were found by contemporary critics of this idealist text to be all too shockingly real and by modern feminist readers often to be refreshingly so.

Third, Sand's novel does not just present its main characters as ideas, it also features characters who treat each other and themselves as embodiments of abstract principles and, in so doing, reveal idealization as a question of power. Nowhere is this clearer than when Trenmor and Sténio try to divine Lélia's essence. The men's idealization of Lélia takes the form of the demonization and idolization that are so common in the representation of woman in Western culture and so symptomatic of patriarchal sexual politics. What is different about this text is that the woman—whom the male characters worship and condemn, admire and fear—undercuts this objectification and mystification by daring to talk back.[18] As an idealized character resistant to her own idealization, Lélia replicates the split that inhabits the text itself. While on the one hand *Lélia* sets up its characters, including its heroine, as icons, on the other its iconoclastic representation of female subjectivity shows idealism as an instrument of women's oppression.

So far, I have been assuming the incompatibility between idealism and feminism, a subject first explored by Schor in her "*Lélia* and the Failures of Allegory." In her later more general study of Sand and idealism, however, Schor questions the equation of feminism with realism and reminds us that insofar as idealism is "an aspiration toward a better world" as well as a "refusal to reproduce mimetically and hence legitimate a social order inimical to the disenfranchised," it can itself be feminist.[19] In Sand's novel neither the idealism that is so central nor its key moments of realism are unproblematic, for even as they underscore the text's iconoclastic feminism, they also undermine it. Thus, while Sand's use of gender reversal constitutes a feminist revision of the androcentric mal du siècle genre, her adoption of idealism in turn calls into question the feminist status of its representation of gender. This contradiction is, as I shall show, central to the tangled question of *Lélia*'s move toward a feminist revision of the mal du siècle and Sand's own ambivalent sexual politics.[20]

Galatea Speaks

The speaker who dominates the opening pages and who we later learn is Sténio, allies himself immediately with a first-person plural pronoun to label Lélia, the unknown creature he addresses, as the Other: "There must be some terrible mystery in you, something unknown to *men*. You are certainly not formed from dust and animated with the same life *we* are! You are an angel or a demon, but you are not human" (3; emphasis added). Given the monstrousness of this inhuman figure of mystery, the implied reader identifies, initially at least, with the speaker, with "us"—with "men." While Sténio excludes the heroine from the common, human ground between other-

worldly extremes, he also attempts to "naturalize" this exceptional being by making her a real woman, the Other necessary
to his initiation into (heterosexual) love.

Reversing and undercutting the dynamics of sexual power
in a novel like *Adolphe*, the man in *Lélia* does not succeed in
seducing the woman (nor does she deliberately seduce him).
And it is the hero, not the heroine, who fears abandonment,
the man, not the woman, whose life depends on love. Sténio's
emphatic language underscores the role reversal. The hero
avows his love as an unrequited desire for romantic fusion that
verges on abject masochism: "From now on I am a part of you.
You have taken hold of me, perhaps unknowingly; but I am
enslaved. . . . Without you there is no poetry, there is no God,
there is no longer anything" (8). Sténio's anxiety is exacerbated
by his foreboding that Lélia's fierce independence will brook no
love for a man. Indeed, from the beginning the heroine draws
power from her emotional impotence: "How happy you are,"
Sténio tells Lélia, "to have your soul free and the power to
dream alone, to love alone, to live alone!" (9).

As with the mal du siècle heroes, Lélia's antisocial difference
makes her appealing to the opposite sex. Sténio finds the heroine, despite her blasphemous denial of love and defiance of social and religious conventions, an object of fatal attraction. His
liberal use of stereotypes of revolt, sublime majesty, and genius
to describe Lélia set the heroine upon a far loftier pedestal than
the one given any of the male protagonists in the French mal
du siècle tradition and recall instead the figure of superiority
cut by Byronic heroes: "Your eyes burned with a somber power
and your high forehead, from which you had brushed aside
your black hair, rose sublime with pride and genius above the
crowd, above the priest, even above God" (6). As Staël does with
Corinne, Sand creates in Lélia a heroine who is blessed with the
gifts of "male" supremacy. The exaggerated terms of Sténio's
description, however, place the heroine outside the domain of
verisimilitude in a realm that would seem to transcend gender,
a point to which I shall return. Similarly, his insistence on her
cold, rigid impenetrability makes her a figure not of life but of
stone, a statue who must, nevertheless, be made to speak.[21]

Like Chactas and Father Souël in *René*, Sténio senses that the enigmatic woman who bewitches him holds a secret, and he demands that she make her confession. The reader familiar with the mal du siècle genre would have similar expectations, met immediately and exhaustively, though hardly ingenuously, by the heroes of *René* and *Adolphe*. When, seven pages from the beginning of the text, Lélia herself finally speaks, it is as if the "pale . . . marble statue" of Sténio's creation has finally come alive. Resisting Sténio's demand and the power relationship it implies, however, Lélia makes no confession. Instead, she echoes Father Souël's final debunking of the mal du siècle hero's claim to singularity and asserts that hers is a universal, human condition: "Like you, I was born in this vale of tears; and all the unfortunate ones who creep the earth are my brothers" (7).

Although in other contexts Lélia too will declare herself an exception and an exceptional woman, her refusal to do so here is a strategic resistance to Sténio's mystification of her. In laying claim to a demeaning egalitarianism, the heroine attempts to escape idealization's trap of extremes and claim for herself a space as a subject, one who is not subject to the interlocutor who would create her in his own image. Rewriting the Pygmalion/Galatea script, Sand thus brings the female statue to life not as the perfect object of man's desire but as a self-contained and troubled subject who rebuffs his self-interested idolization of her.

Throughout part 1 of the novel, Sténio desires immediate gratification. Like an overeager and impatient reader, he demands to know the end of the story from the beginning. Lélia voices the hero's questions and with them the reader's expectations, but she refuses to reveal any answers or make any single prediction. "Whether I can love," she says, "whether I'll make you happy, whether I am good or perverse, whether you will become great through my love or destroyed through my indifference: this is all dangerous knowledge. God refuses it to a person your age, and He forbids me to enlighten you. Wait" (10). "God's will" and Lélia's refusal thus protect the story's interest by suggesting possible plot alternatives without revealing the end.

Just as Lélia defers these questions and the issue of love through an imperative of delay, so too does the text, by introducing yet another character and a different enigma. Skirting Sténio's demand for her confession, Lélia discloses the secret hidden in Trenmor's past. Although its effects on Sténio are negligible, Lélia designs her telling of Trenmor's transformation from gambler to thief to prisoner to wise man to teach the inconsolable hero stoic resignation and to show the moonstruck young man that the love women inspire in men is tame by comparison with the life-and-death drama to which Trenmor's compulsive gambling gave rise.[22] As in *Corinne*, these delaying techniques, which buy more narrative time, create a dilatory space that sidetracks the love plot but cannot completely derail it. When, after Lélia's resistance and deferral, the text opens up a realist space within the idealist struggle of ideas and values—the setting shifts suddenly to an elegant ball described in all its material detail—the two male characters bring the focus back to Lélia as enigma in their competition to define what idea this woman represents.

Woman: All or Nothing

Trenmor and Sténio watch "the large rooms full of noise and movement" (29), but most of all they fix their gaze on Lélia as she observes the same scene from above. "Dressed in a man's costume, austere but elegant, she had the serious gaze of a [poet from ages past when the age was poetic and poetry was not bandied about by the populace]" (29).[23] Trenmor notes her physical beauty and intellectual power approvingly as he attempts to read this coldly impassive woman's outer shell to determine her inner essence. This act of reading is, however, more like an act of writing. For Trenmor, Lélia is a tabula rasa, the perfect surface on which man may inscribe meaning. As he tells Sténio, "You can inscribe the greatest names of history, theater, and poetry on such a face whose expression concentrates it all" (30).

According to Trenmor's description, Lélia is the sum of disparate parts, from mythological figures to literary creations and their creators:

She is Pygmalion's Galatea, the perfect marble. She has Tasso's ethereal expression and Dante's somber smile. She has the easy, cavalier attitude of Shakespeare's young heroes: she is Romeo, the poetic lover; Hamlet, the pale, ascetic visionary; and Juliet, half-dead, hiding the poison and the memory of a broken love in her heart. . . . Corinne, dying, must have been plunged into [just such] mournful attention when she listened to her last poems being spoken at the Capitol by a young girl.   [29–30][24]

Whereas Staël gave Corinne both the poetic power associated with men as well as the need for love identified as womanly, and Octave in Stendhal's *Armance* allowed himself to take the male and female part by playing both Dido and Aeneas, Trenmor's idealizing vision seems to show a way beyond gender dimorphism. Ultimately, however, the heroine is able to signify all things for Trenmor because in the fragmented yet all-encompassing polymorphism he ascribes to her, she has no identity of her own. For him, Lélia is not an enigma—as she is for Sténio—but a symbol, the incarnation of all things poetic and heroic: "Yes, Lélia embodies all these ideals, because she embodies the genius of the poets, the grandeur of all heroisms" (30). In her ability to represent everything—even mutually contradictory elements—Trenmor regards Lélia as a female colossus, far larger than life, but for that very reason, perhaps not a woman at all.

The conflict in *Lélia* between Sténio and Trenmor is played out as a struggle between restrictive and inclusive definitions of woman within the framework of a deceptively simple question—"Is Lélia a woman?"—which hides a more ideologically loaded one—"What is a woman?" While Trenmor sees the cross-dressed Lélia as a figure of plenitude—"Can one imagine anything more complete," he asks, "than Lélia dressed, poised and dreaming as she is now?" (29)—for Sténio this phallic figure is but an empty shell.[25] He claims that without the capacity to love, Lélia is "without value, . . . a lifeless image, . . . a shade, at the most a shadow of an idea" (30). Because she cannot love, Lélia is neither a woman nor a man, for in Sténio's gesture toward egalitarianism, the capacity to love defines the new man of feeling as well as eternal woman.[26]

For his part, Trenmor does not categorize Lélia as a member of the second sex either, that is, until she shows the signs of narcissism and weakness he considers synonymous with womanhood. Shocked that the heroine seems to be leading Sténio on for her own amusement, Trenmor accuses her of being the best and worst of her sex, of being *une femme froide*. He warns Lélia that her frigidity makes her fatal: "If you surrender that young soul to the gust of corrosive passions, if you devastate him with icy despair and then abandon him, how will he find his way again to heaven?" (33) In his diatribe, Trenmor addresses the heroine as "femme," both elevating her to the grandeur of which he believes woman capable and reducing her to its frailties. "Look here, woman! . . . you must send Sténio away or flee from him" (33).

Lélia rejects Trenmor's attempt to assign her an identity on the basis of her gender and his misreading of her intentions. Instead she claims for herself a double identity—"I am a woman, an artist" (34). In a move that is characteristic of Sand's heroines and Sand herself, however, Lélia locates herself outside stereotypes of femininity even as she leaves other women securely entrenched within them. The heroine admits, for example, that she is "weak and cowardly," but insists that she is not "ungrateful or vain. I don't have those feminine vices," she asserts (34). Lélia declares, too, that she is not like those heartless *femmes froides* who can "break a man's heart, destroy a poet's soul" (34) because, in her own way, she loves Sténio. Refusing Trenmor's binary logic and defying his prediction, Lélia tries a middle road that would unite her with Sténio, but on her own asexual terms.

Like the novel, which subverts the conventions of romance as a lesson for its readers, the heroine rewrites the love story as an ideological Bildungsroman for the hero. In place of the love relationship, Lélia substitutes a structure of apprenticeship that will allow her to teach Sténio the limits of love. Like Corinne, Lélia puts love in its place as one human need among many, redefining it moreover as "the aspiration of the most ethereal part [of our soul] for the unknown," not the "violent aspiration of our entire being toward another" (36). She states that the latter, modern notion of love is a perversion of the "natural" relations between the sexes that obtained in a simpler time when pleasure—not love—was the tie that bound the couple.

In contrast with Chateaubriand's analysis in *Génie*, Lélia's history of cause and effect does not blame this contemporary decadence on the erosion of sexual difference. Instead, Lélia concludes that the desire to prostrate oneself before another in a relationship of dominance and submission is a displacement of love for God in an agnostic age.[27] "Today, with poetic souls, the feeling of adoration even enters physical love," she tells Sténio. "Strange error of a greedy, impotent generation!" (37). Despite her impassioned rhetoric, the heroine's attack on the ideology of love does not sway Sténio. Instead, it drives him to write his own death sentence.

The Cost of Living

As Sténio prepares his suicide by poison toward the end of Part 1, he writes a Wertherian farewell love letter to the woman whose love is killing him. But if his suicidal intentions are an attempt through death to claim center stage as Werther, René, and Octave had in previous novels, the peremptory way his plans are thwarted reveals in no uncertain terms the novel's interests. No sooner does a character attempt to escape the heroine's control than he is summoned to her side. As in *René*, *Adolphe*, and *Armance*, all thought and action lead to the mal du siècle protagonist. In *Lélia*, however, the narrator calls explicit attention to the text's willful feminocentrism.

To explain Sténio's precipitous cancelling of his plans for suicide by poison and his rushing out to be with Lélia at her deathbed, Trenmor's interruption of Sténio's last rites and announcement that it is Lélia who is dying would have sufficed. Nevertheless, the author not only determines that Sténio will live once again *for* the heroine, but overdetermines this crucial plot twist in a way that calls attention to the contrivance. Onto the clichés of romantic suicide—at midnight the hero writes a letter to the loved one who has spurned him as the wind whistles through the wainscoting—the narrator adds a gesture that is startling in its everyday banality. "On the table in front of Sténio was a cup filled to the brim, which Trenmor knocked

over as he brushed against it with his coat" (39). I would suggest
that this incident is not, as one critic states, Sand's "unscrupulous" and "unnecessary" recourse to chance.[28] Instead, by calling attention to the arbitrariness of this twist in the plot, the
text reminds the reader of the fiction's factitiousness and of the
author's power to stage-manage events to suit her own designs.
Just as Lélia agrees to love the hero but then resists the script
Sténio prepares for her, the text conforms to novelistic conventions even as it subtly mocks and undercuts them. The author's
controlling presence and her playful use of conventions become even more visible in Lélia's deathbed scene, when the
story shifts abruptly from high (melo)drama to social satire to
reveal that the only way to guarantee the forward movement of
plot is to submit to the logic of romance.

While Lélia lies dying on the sofa, the only treatment that
the doctor, who has been called to her side, offers his patient is
benign neglect. Equally skeptical of and open to any and all
remedies, he is convinced the real cure is psychological. He tells
the heroine, "You and I don't fear the cholera, we defy it! ∴..
Let's jeer at the cholera; it's the only way to deal with it" (40).
Exasperated yet amused by the secular miracle man who does
not believe in medicine, the moribund Lélia calls for a priest
who will, in theory, practice what he preaches. But Magnus,
"the tall, handsome Irish priest of the Chapel of Sainte-Laure,"
recoils at the sight of her. "'This woman again!' he cried, drawing back with terror" (41). Lélia taunts the priest with his inability to pray for her, but Magnus immediately acknowledges
the superiority of her power and, in an echo of the epigraph,
despairs of the fate of his soul in her presence. Through the
power of her skepticism, Lélia demonstrates her superiority
and shows science and religion as shams. "What is this century
coming to?" she asks. "The scientist denies, the priest doubts"
(44). The heroine makes her death a trial of literature as well,
as she challenges Sténio: "Take up your harp and sing me
verses from Faust, or else open your books and tell me again
about the sufferings of Obermann, the transports of Saint-
Preux. Let us see, poet, if you still understand suffering. Let us
see, young man, if you still believe in love" (44). The female

protagonist thus names the literary models for her figurative *mal* only to condemn their inability to cure her disease.

As Lélia lies dying, she mocks and pities Sténio's last wish, which is to learn about love from her lips. As a last resort, however, she ends up agreeing to a kind of Pascalian wager. "My God," she cries out, "have pity on him and spare my life so that I can save his. If You do this, *I vow to live for him*" (45; emphasis added). The heroine's contract with God pledges her own life so that they both might live. Her will alone, however, is not enough to guarantee that the story will continue. Only Sténio, playing Prince Charming, can bring her back to life and thus save the novel from premature foreclosure. "Lélia fell stiff and cold on the parquet floor. It was a last, horrible crisis. Sténio pressed her against him, crying with despair. His heart was burning, his hot tears fell on Lélia's brow. His kisses brought the blood back to her lips, and perhaps his prayer reached heaven: Lélia weakly opened her eyes . . . " (45). The text thus lays bare the novelistic mechanism for generating plot: the heroine can only live in fiction if she agrees to love. While in the traditional novel, this premise has a corollary—the cost of love for a woman is her life—in Sand's novel, it is the hero who must pay the highest price for love.

The Wages of Sex

Part 2 of *Lélia* finds the hero and heroine in the idyllic setting of the Villa Viola, sharing a moment of quiet bliss. This scene, which might, in other novels, be the prelude to a romantic consummation of passion or its coda is, in Sand's text, a brush with death. When Lélia responds to Sténio's request for a word of love or a sign of life with a caress, "this brusque, burning effusion nearly cost the life of this child who had received his first woman's kiss from Lélia's cold lips. He turned pale, his heart stopped beating; near dying, he repulsed her with all his strength, because he had never feared death so much as at this instant when life was revealing itself to him" (58). While sexual

desire in the mal du siècle tradition is almost always disembodied until it results in the heroine's death, in *Lélia* the character who links Eros with Thanatos is the hero.

The struggle between Sténio and Lélia pits a man against a
superwoman: "She enveloped him in her arms and pressed
against him with superhuman force. Sténio, who still wanted to
resist, felt himself dominated by this power which paralyzed
him with fear" (58). Despising himself for his "cowardly timidity," Sténio becomes the aggressor. Sexual desire unleashes
the beast within the feminized male: "abandoning himself to an
impulse that had something voracious and savage about it, he
in turn gripped her in his arms" (59). Lélia angrily repulses the
hero's violent attack and explains that she can only love him
when he submits to her will.

In *Lélia* sex is, quite explicitly, a question of power in which
the heroine insists on a controlling, "masculine" role. Does she
therefore conform to the stereotype of the "castrated" woman
who must in turn emasculate her would-be lover? On the one
hand, Lélia's ideal recalls the way in which male writers have
traditionally figured both their desire for women and their fear
of them by attempting, in Eileen Boyd Sivert's words, "to ren-
der women harmless by rendering them sexless."[29] The heroine desires the hero in a presexual or asexual state, when he is
her virginal child and, later, when he is dead. The novel does
not so much reject a logic of dominance and submission, so
much as it reverses its traditional gender roles.

On the other hand, perhaps there is some logic at work here
that takes the heroine beyond the privileging of the phallus,
beyond the vicious cycle of domination and submission. In her
reading of *Lélia*, Sivert argues that the heroine's desire is more
constructive than destructive:

> There may be something more positive in [Lélia's] desire to render
> [Sténio] sexless than the wish to see the other as "mutilated" as she is
> seen to be herself. In Sténio Lélia wants to love a man who is also a
> woman who is also a child, who is not a master or a slave. For, while un-
> able to realize an alternative way of loving, she does see that there is no
> answer for her in "normal" sexuality, in the "normal" role of woman,
> in any kind of accepted relationship between man and woman. [66]

While it is true that Sand's heroine is looking for some kind of relationship not yet imaginable under patriarchy, it is also true that, for the moment, her ideal of heterosexual union as a platonic, maternal bond is a fantasy of motherhood steeped in paternalism. Despite her tenderness and benevolent intentions, the heroine's fantasy is fundamentally egocentric. She constitutes herself as sole subject, with Sténio as the grateful and willing object of her overbearing maternal affection.

The heroine reimagines the family under contrary-to-fact conditions as an ideal that would have allowed her to display self-sacrificing heroism. Rejecting the infantalized status of a Werther, a René, or an Adolphe who remain their father's sons, Lélia imagines herself instead in the superior position of older sister or mother. "Oh, if I had a younger brother, I would have guided him through life," she tells Sténio. "I would have tried to spare him its suffering and its dangers. If I had children, I would have nourished them at my breast, I would have carried them in my arms and in my soul. . . . I feel clearly that I would have been a courageous, passionate, tireless mother" (157). Even when her desire takes the form of a triangle, the son she fantasizes for herself is the result of an immaculate conception, thereby obviating the need for a paterfamilias. "Trenmor will be my brother" she announces to Sténio, "and you my son" (154). Desire, in Sand's novel, thus takes on a fantasmatic form that attempts to go beyond the Oedipus or Electra complex, first, by viewing that relationship from the perspective of the mother not the child and second, by eliminating the father altogether.[30]

If the heroine locates love within a family model, it is because the incest taboo is Lélia's protection against sexuality: "So be my brother and son, and let the thought of any marriage whatsoever seem incestuous and bizarre" (157), she tells the hero and Trenmor. Theirs will be a blissfully asexual union, she promises, through which they "will perhaps reach truth, wisdom, repose" (154). According to the heroine's ideal, then, idealism has its own rewards because it frees her and her male companions as well from the trials of the flesh. Inasmuch as idealism is a denial of the body, it is a way to escape the romantic plot and

the most egregiously oppressive forms of heterosexual relations. For the hero, however, love without sex is not love.
"'Can't you love me?' asked Sténio with a trembling voice and a
torn heart" (60).

Female Impotence

In sharp contrast with other mal du siècle novels such as Duras's
Olivier, Latouche's *Olivier*, and Stendhal's *Armance*, which mys-
tify male impotence by keeping it a secret, little mystery is made
of Lélia's emotional and physical incapacity.[31] In part 2, the
heroine candidly tells Sténio that sensual love is beyond her
capacities, though the union of souls is not. Lélia herself, the
narrator, and the other characters openly call this incapacity
"impotence," a word more commonly applied to men's sexual
dysfunction. Indeed, the use of this "male" term for a female
malady invests the heroine with the power negated by the pre-
fix but implied by its association with men. The heroine herself
reveals the paradox of her situation when she describes her
heart as "rendered impotent perhaps by too much strength"
(105) and Lélia sums up her anomalous position: "The coldness
of my senses placed me beneath the most abject women. The
exaltation of my thoughts elevated me above the most passionate men" (109).

An excess of power, energy, and desire in the heroine frees
her from the narrative constraints that make love a woman's
destiny, but only to incapacitate her. Despite her resistance to
the laws of romance, the heroine remains locked within the
sexual plot because the text, a novel of ideas, puts its heroine in
a metaphysical and sexual dead end, which offers no other
arena—political, social, emotional, religious or historical—for
the exercise of her considerable powers. Even the realm of the
arts, which provided Staël's Corinne with a domain in which she
could reign supreme, offers Sand's heroine no satisfactory way
out. Early in the novel, Lélia puts a stop to Sténio's mournful
professions of undying love by voicing her rage against God

for making her a woman only to change her into stone. Unlike Staël's heroine, Corinne, whose improvisational verse is her own, Lélia states that the song of lamentation she sings is one she translated from a foreign poet. Sténio, however, suspects that she makes this claim to translation simply to disguise her own poetic voice. Enraged by her appropriation of his privileged instrument and calling, Sténio seizes the harp from the heroine to silence her and prevent her from invoking his poetic muse. Is Lélia then, like René before her, a would-be poet?

The heroine's own comments on poetry combine wistful longing for its healing, restorative power with deep-rooted suspicion. On the one hand, Lélia envies Sténio whose muse affords him consolation, catharsis, and transcendence. On the other hand, she identifies poetry as the root of her dissatisfaction: "Drunk with her [poetry's] promises, lulled by her sweet mockeries, I could never resign myself to reality," she reveals. "Poetry had created other sensitivities in me that nothing on earth could satisfy" (107). In the struggle between the real and the ideal, the latter, with its seductive illusions, has gained in her the upper hand, ill preparing her for life—or even for literature. Unlike Staël's *Corinne* or the autobiographical *Künstlerromane* often favored by Woolf, Cather, Mansfield, and other twentieth-century women writers as an alternative to the marriage plot,[32] Lélia will not "solve" her problems by becoming George Sand, novelist.

While the heroine of Sand's text has the power of discourse, it is primarily the power of rhetoric rather than narrative. If Lélia's talent is literary, then her genre of choice is a kind of poetic prose marshaled in the service of cultural criticism. Lélia debunks with impassioned eloquence the literary myths of love and demystifies society's institutions while maintaining a clear-eyed vision of her own contradictions.

The narrator describes Lélia's struggle against self-deception as an exceptional form of heroism in an age when men are vain hypocrites or mindless conformists pursuing blind ambition. Alone among men, Lélia represents an exemplary lucidity and integrity: "Blighted by the consciousness of her degradation, Lélia alone was aware enough to ascertain it, sincere enough to

avow it to herself. . . . [She] made her way through the world
without seeking pity or finding affection" (87). In *Lélia*, in other
words, heroinism is the drama of an isolated soul who has full
consciousness of her situation.

The heroine gets a chance to speak for herself and at length
in the first person. More than a third of the novel consists of
her direct discourse in conversation, letters, and, in the most
remarkable instance by far, the thirty pages of part 3 in which
she finally makes the "confession" that Sténio had demanded.
Lélia does not make it to him, however, but to her courtesan
sister Pulchérie instead.

Feminist Realism?

In these pages of confession the text pays the most explicit
homage to its mal du siècle precursors, all the while rewriting
them in the feminine and criticizing their grandiose assertions.
At the outset of her narrative, Lélia, like Chateaubriand's René,
establishes the parameters of her discourse by excluding events
and weaving a narrative almost exclusively out of inner experience. No sooner has Lélia made her sententious pronouncement than Pulchérie undercuts her solemn self-importance by
calling her "deplorably vulgar" (105). For Pulchérie, "pitiless in
her good sense" (105), Lélia's particular brand of unhappiness
is far from a sign of her uniqueness and superiority. It is merely
a literary cliché. Much like Father Souël's in *René*, Pulchérie's
remarks function as a critical counterpoint to Lélia's own. To
appreciate the vast difference between Chateaubriand's novella
and Sand's *Lélia*, however, one need only imagine the "moral"
of *René* coming in part from the hero's sister and alter ego—a
courtesan.

While the novel as a whole is ahistorical and idealist, the
heroine in her own narrative historicizes the ideas she relates
by revealing them as the result of her lived experience. While
Sand's novel generally attempts to "defy the rules of logic and
time to put effects before causes or, more often, skip causes

entirely, asserting themselves without motivation or justification,"[33] its heroine offers a linear and chronological narrative that operates according to a logic of intersubjective, historical cause and psychological effect. In her confession the heroine identifies her seemingly immutable essence as the product of a particular experience, which nevertheless unites her to others—to her generation on the one hand and to her sex on the other.[34]

Lélia describes her childhood as an exhilarating time in which her "power of love and admiration" (106) seemed to increase with every passing day to such an extent that her "feeling of well-being bordered on delirium" (107). "I gave my love to everything as if it were an inexhaustible source of life," she explains to Pulchérie. "The least object of esteem or amusement inspired me. . . . I reached adolescence in a fullness of sensitivity that could go no further without breaking its mortal envelope." Up to this point, the heroine has self-consciously identified herself with the mal du siècle generation: "When I entered active life, I was naive in the ways of the world, but I had no new emotion to feel. This is the story of an entire generation" (106–107). But when Lélia meets a man and begins to focus all of her emotion on him, her experience and disillusionment are distinctly female.

Lélia herself describes her love as destiny dictated by the constraints of gender: "Had I been a man, I would have loved combat, the odor of blood, the pressures of danger. Perhaps in my youth I might have sought to reign by intelligence and to dominate others by powerful speeches. As a woman I had only one noble destiny on earth, which was to love. I loved *valiantly*" (110). The heroine's "emphasis added" makes woman's only outlet for her ambitious wish an act of bravery and courage, a "manly" exercise of the will. Indeed, Lélia tells Pulchérie that she found pleasure in the illusion of love to the extent that it charged her with energy and tested her power: "I enjoyed the expansion of my mind and feelings. . . . My afflicted soul . . . demanded obstacles, fatigues, devouring jealousies to repress, cruel ingratitudes to pardon, great works to pursue, great misfortunes to endure" (109–110). In this sense, she gets her wish:

the man had other desires, which the heroine whose "body had grown impoverished as a result of austere mystical contemplations" (107), does not share.

Despite her disillusionment and sensual frigidity, Lélia goes through the motions of desire, playing woman's submissive role to the hilt. As she explains, "my heart was outliving my senses. [Growing pale and closing my eyes I sacrificed myself]" (107).[35] According to Lélia, love, which is woman's only outlet for action, effaces her as a separate and equal subject and makes her instead man's self-abnegating Other in a kind of voluntary slavery. Unwilling and unable to sustain this self-immolation, Lélia suddenly sees her idol for what he is, "a man like the others. And when I was weary of prostrating myself, I broke the pedestal. Then I saw him reduced to his true height" (109).[36]

The heroine's destruction of her idol adumbrates her iconoclastic telling of this story, which, like the novel of which her narrative is a part, both reverses traditional gender roles and short-circuits the seduction premise entirely, thus undercutting the very basis of the libertine novel as well as the liberal variation on the same theme in *Adolphe*. In telling her story, the heroine presents her choice of love object as pure chance and the man himself as nameless and faceless, "Then a man came, and I loved him" (107). Here, man is only a category; individual existence is reserved for woman. The termination of this first love affair is just as abrupt as its beginnings. Lélia reduces the minute psychological dissection of a moribund relationship that constitutes the entire novel in *Adolphe* to a single throwaway line: "One day I felt so worn out with loving that I stopped suddenly" (113). Despite the relationship's devastating effects on her, the heroine refuses to make the dissolution of the ties that bind more of a story. She dismisses and demystifies them with a shrug: "When I saw how easily this bond was broken, I was astonished at having believed in its eternal duration for so long" (113).

Whereas in *Adolphe* the heroine has everything to lose—family, friends, fortune, and finally her life—if the hero breaks their bond, in Sand's novel Lélia herself makes the break, and with far fewer risks. In the rarefied atmosphere of Sand's ide-

alist novel, the privileged heroine is free from the fear of
economic sanction and apparently unconcerned about social
ostracism. Lélia may thus expose women's dependence on the
love plot with relative emotional impunity. Having broken with
female plot, she is largely liberated from the myriad social pressures to conform to cultural stereotypes of proper femininity
which beleaguer the heroines of mimetic texts. The invulner-
ability she enjoys as a result of the novel's idealism makes her
an ideal ideologue.

In Sand's other early novels, enlightened men must rescue
the heroine, who is still in a state of passivity and ignorance,
from herself and from society.[37] In *Lélia*, however, Lélia and
Pulchérie, each in her own way, are the spokespersons for an
explicit feminist critique. Both heroines have the insight to see
their own past in terms that transcend the strictly personal, as
well as the ability to put their perceptions into impassioned
rhetoric. Throughout the novel, the heroine and her courtesan
sister wage a clear-eyed ideological battle against both the idol
of romantic love and its all-too-frequent corollary, the subordination of women. Lélia refuses to have woman reduced to her
sexuality and affectivity. "Does a woman's role really confine
itself to the transports of passion?" she asks. "Are men just
when they accuse a woman of departing from the attributes of
her sex if she responds badly to their raptures?" (157). Pulchérie takes an even harder line on the paucity of women's options: "Under what mountains of injustices [a woman] must
accustom herself to sleep, to walk, to be lover, courtesan, and
mother! These are three conditions of woman's fate that no
woman escapes whether she sells herself in a market of prostitution or by a marriage contract" (100).

Whereas the novel as a whole might be termed a fiction of
lamentation, the heroine's narrative with its retrospective sum-
mation of her life, resembles a novel of formation which carries
a definite ideological message. Unlike René, the heroine herself draws the moral of her tale; others must learn its lesson.
The addressee of her narrative, Pulchérie, however, has chosen
prostitution over love, pleasure over pain, and resignation over
rebellion; she is thus already freed, if not from a version of

female plot, then at least from the self-deceptive illusions that bear the brunt of Lélia's attack. It is the implied reader, then, who stands to learn or be persuaded by Lélia's ideological critique, knowledge that will begin to separate that reader from Sténio who has remained deaf to Lélia's message and who must learn what Lélia teaches through experience.

L'Ecole des hommes

Part 4 of the novel offers to Sténio, who has not been privy to Lélia's confession, his moment of truth. The heroine takes Pulchérie aside for a moment, then leaves her sister amid the revelers at the gala orchestrated by the prince dei Bambucci so that she may lead the ever-faithful hero to one of the boudoirs in the pavilion of Aphrodite. Throughout this scene, Sténio is literally and figuratively left in the dark. In the postcoital bliss of the next chapter, oblivious to the machinations that have transpired behind the scene, he believes he has made love to Lélia. Although the attentive reader may suspect the deception, the text does not immediately confirm this suspicion. In fact, throughout this scene the heretofore reliable though sometimes uncommunicative narrator corroborates Sténio's mistaken assumption: "'Come,' *said Lélia* in a softened voice. 'I pity you, child. Come, lie by me and forget your pain'" (143; emphasis added). It is not until the hero himself learns otherwise that the text stops calling his seductress "Lélia." Just as Pulchérie and Lélia entrap Sténio and then taunt him with his gullibility, the narrator baits the readers' hook and leads us on. While the price of Sténio's knowledge will be his precipitous decline into debauchery and eventual death, the text spares the implied reader, who has been persuaded of the error of Sténio's ways, from this vicarious punishment.

    In Sténio, Sand has created a man who, in the culture's terms, is like a woman. Indeed, unlike Stendhal's Octave—the feminized mal du siècle hero who gets to have it both ways—Sand's hero, as he admits to Lélia, thinks he wants to be a heroine and let Lélia play the man. "Lélia, this is why I love you," he tells her. "You have taken on my role, which men refused you. Far from repudiating your role, I beg that you play it out" (150). The woman's part, which Sténio embraces so willingly in turn, constrains him with a vengeance. Thus, as with the innocent eighteenth-century heroine, Sténio's first step into sexuality leads inexorably to his moral and physical downfall.

Toward the end of the novel, Sténio, drunk with wine and despair, turns away the innocent Claudia who loves him with denunciations of love's illusions that could be direct quotes from Lélia. Later, addressing the figure of Don Juan, which had served him as a model in his decadent days, Sténio decries the egotistical belief in female subservience and masochism which underlies romantic love and its vile counterpart, a kind of psychological sadism known as seduction:

> Did you read somewhere in the Counsels of God that woman is a thing made for man's pleasure, incapable of resistance or change? Did you think that this ideal womanly perfection of renunciation existed on earth and would assure the inexhaustible renewal of your joys? Did you believe that one day delirium would tear from your victim's lips an impious promise and that she would cry out: "I love you because I suffer. . . . I am devoted to you because you despise me?" [203]

As in the *romans à thèse* studied by Susan Suleiman, Sand's novel establishes a structure of apprenticeship in which "the hero himself explicitly proclaims the 'truth' at the end of his story, . . . he becomes . . . the spokesman and possibly a theorist of the doctrine whose validity the novel seeks to demonstrate."[38] Although *Lélia* is much too complex and paradoxical to be categorized a pure *roman à thèse*, it does aim its ideological messages at the reader. Sténio's reassessment of his life and his love operates, as do similar moments in thesis novels, as "one of the means by which the reader is led to a 'correct' understanding, both of the story and of what it is designed to demonstrate" (79).

In his despair Sténio blames Trenmor and Lélia whom he calls the "authors" of his fate. The hero presents himself as a victim of their crime of abandonment and accuses his would-be mentors of failing to rescue him from his dysphoric plot. Nevertheless, it would take far more than the intervention of mere mortals to prevent the hero's death for, as the novel's epigraph implies, the real author of Sténio's destiny, Sand, has already sealed his fate. Indeed, in the denouement the author makes little attempt to mask the end as anything but the conclusion she had foreordained, just as, throughout the text, she explicitly highlights the implausibility of the novel's plot.

God the Author

During most of the moments of high drama in *Lélia*, a mysterious figure, previously unknown to the reader or temporarily unidentified, suddenly materializes to save a character in dire need of help. Rather than mask these interventions, which are necessary for the continuation of plot, the narrator calls attention to their artificiality. In each case, it is a rescue that is manqué. Trenmor's timely arrival at the end of Part 1 and then again midway through the novel saves Sténio not once but twice from suicide. His intervention, however, merely defers a foreordained conclusion. Similarly, although Magnus rides up on his horse and whisks Lélia away from the ruins of a toppling monastery, the heroine is a very reluctant damsel in distress since she had welcomed death as an escape from pain. In this fictional universe, knights in shining armor are doomed to failure. Rescue is only a fantasy—a temporary postponement of the hero's tragic fate or a prolongation of the heroine's unhappy life, as in Sténio's kiss, which brings the heroine back to life at the end of Part 1.

The last pages of the novel follow suit by recording a final series of miscarried rescue attempts and their irreversible consequences. Trenmor arrives to save Sténio from his life of debauchery and lead him to the calm of the Camaldules monastery, where he leaves him in the company of Magnus. On the day before Trenmor's promised return, Sténio, despondent over Lélia, leaves little doubt as to his suicidal intentions, but his rivalry with Magnus over Lélia dooms the possibility of salutory male bonding. The priest—weak-willed, jealous, and deranged—fails to intervene.

While the text records in elaborate detail Magnus's seesaw of doubts and self-justifications throughout the long, tragic night, in the final—and fatal—drama of misconnections, the cause is not psychology but happenstance, and is given no long explanation. In a scene of fast-paced action and adventure out of keeping with the slow, continually arrested movement of the novel, Lélia and Trenmor rush to rejoin Sténio at the monastery. "Suddenly a horse fell. The carriage rolled over it and overturned violently. Trenmor was severely injured" (218). Calling attention to the accident, the narrator labels it a key element in a far greater design, one that makes the twist of fate, literally, a deus ex machina: "Lélia was spared all harm. Perhaps God had his designs" (218). The text thus attempts to naturalize the sudden plot twist by assigning responsibility to God in a perfunctory "explanation" that presumably constitutes its own justification. Hours later, when Lélia arrives at the monastery, Sténio has already committed suicide. In a soliloquy over his dead body going on for many pages, the heroine mourns his death while asserting that "God did not wish" Sténio to be saved (224).

Like the generalizations in *René* or the maxims in *Adolphe*, the many references to God in *Lélia* work to make the events in this implausible fiction seem not just necessary but inevitable. Thus, "God" allows the writer to pursue her own designs in the guise of acting under higher orders. Paradoxically, however, these attempts at naturalization call attention to their own artificiality. Indeed, given that "God's law" in the novel parallels the social and cultural conventions of fiction, the text itself points out the literary expectations and ideological assumptions at work even as it obeys these "God-given" laws of gender and genre. For example, *Lélia* has shown that as a novel it must conform to one or another variation on the love plot. Similarly, to qualify as fiction rather than fact, the novel must have a beginning, a middle, and a conclusive—whether beatific or tragic—end. Despite the text's unconventional plurality of voices, experimentation with literary form, and dilation of narrative time, *Lélia*'s minimalist plot moves in traditional ways and nowhere more so than in its titillating finale, Lélia's death at the hands of a madman.

Just as Sténio's suicide is foreordained and overdetermined,

so is Lélia's own demise. Trenmor, detained by an act of God
(the carriage accident), will arrive too late to save her. As Lélia
keeps vigil over Sténio's corpse, Magnus, who has been listening
to her meditative outpouring of grief, confuses her in his
twisted mind with the devil. In a jealous rage, he strangles the
innocent heroine as a desperate gesture of exorcism. "'Yes, yes,'
he cried out, 'when you are dead, I will no longer be afraid
of you! I will forget you, and then I will be able to pray.'
He choked her until there was only a faint breath of life left
within her" (229).[39] Lélia revives long enough to drag herself to
Sténio's side and praise God for her deliverance: "Blessed be
God, . . . everything passes, everything dies . . . everything returns to God" (230). Again, God's will parallels the author's
designs and the story's interest, which needs to do away with
the heroine while rescuing her from moral and religious
opprobrium.

Unlike Sténio, Goethe's Werther, or Stendhal's Octave, Lélia
does not succumb to despair, nor does she claim the "right" to
take her own life. While the heroine's murder punishes her for
her power, it also makes her a blameless victim of a madman's
rage.[40] Because she does not kill herself, the heroine remains a
rebel without becoming a criminal. Lélia, the outcast and here-
tic, is buried in hallowed ground, while Sténio, the conformist
who ended up a suicide, is not. Just as in life the hero and heroine did not share the same literary plot, the position of their
burial plots seems to suggest that they will not be joined even
in death.

Dysphoria thus reigns supreme in this novel of ideas in
which references to God both underscore and justify the text's
pessimism. Lélia explains to Sténio that it is God's design that
man should always be lacking: "God has placed invisible but
insurmountable obstacles between the soul and the vague objects of its anticipation so that the fire of sacred desires will not
be extinguished by examination and possession" (153). Lélia
epitomizes the impossible fulfillment of desire, as does Sténio
in his choice of love object, and it is these two characters who
occupy the novel's center. Trenmor, by contrast, who has freed
himself of desire altogether, provides an illustrative counter-
example but is relegated to the status of mere subplot. Simi-

larly, the jaded but commonsensical Pulchérie, who has learned to desire only what she may in fact enjoy—physical pleasure—offers a crucial satiric counterpoint to Lélia's story, but finally is rooted too much in the real and not enough in the ideal to merit center stage in this novel of profound discontent.

Given the text's dysphoric premise, Sand's choice of idealism is a conservative one. Whereas realism might allow a character to escape through history, idealism overdetermines the unhappy ending of *Lélia* by assuming a world that does not change. In the novel society cannot make any significant, positive intervention in the plot, nor can Lélia affect society. The heroine's malady is incurable, and the patriarchal order against which she rebels is here to stay. Indeed, in Lélia, Sand creates a heroine whose revolt is always already contained by her metaphysical and pessimistic resignation.[41] Her superiority resides in accepting that she can do little to secure her own happiness. To a certain extent, then, *Lélia* mythologizes woman's powerlessness by making her impotence the source of her power, a tactic similar to the one used for the hero in the androcentric mal du siècle novel. The heroine's impotence would seem to justify the novel's pessimism, just as the text's pessimism in turn naturalizes this impotence and the heroine's impasse. Nevertheless, the idealism that had served the novel's pessimism throughout the text provides in its conclusion a note of guarded optimism. *Lélia* comes to a dead end, but, as in Sand's previous novels, the full stop is then followed by a coda that unites the lovers, but in a far different and nonrealist mode.

In the protorealist *Indiana,* the conclusion turns toward a pastoral ideal, but this better world is, even in the terms of the novel, problematic. As Sandy Petrey points out in his analysis of *Indiana,* while the ending's idealism gives the novel an apparently happy end, it also marks a return to conventional gender relations, romance, and the kind of subordination of women to men that the heroine herself had earlier attacked. In *Valentine,* too, the lovers who are separated by the constraints of realism are nevertheless joined in the end by death. While *Valentine* closes with an image of the hero and heroine's double tomb, romantic fusion remains a tantalizing *im*possibility for Lélia and Sténio, even beyond the tomb.[42]

The final scene of *Lélia* transcends the strictures of physical topography through an otherworldly flight of metaphors. Trenmor goes down to the lake that separates the tombs of Sténio and Lélia. Looking up into the night sky, he "noticed two [meteors] which, coming from the opposite shores, joined, mutually pursued each other, and remained together the entire night, whether they played amid the reeds, whether they let themselves glide over the tranquil waves, or whether they embraced tremblingly in the fog like two lanterns ready to go out" (230). In this symbolic passage, the text thus realizes Sténio's desire for coupling and Lélia's confident assertion of union in death.

The narrator, however, attenuates the veracity of the reunion by presenting it not as fact but as Trenmor's fancy, "a sweet and superstitious idea" (230). The reader who follows Trenmor's interpretation and sees the two meteors as the star-crossed lovers reads too much into mimesis while also interpreting the description accurately as allegory: "When day appeared . . . the two mysterious flames held each other for some time in the middle of the lake, *as if* it caused them pain to separate" (231; emphasis added). Furthermore, the union that is described proves ever renewable but never final. "Then they were each driven in contrary directions, as if they were each going to return to the tombs they inhabited" (231). This scene, which remythologizes love as a transcendant union, also refuses both the notion of a perfect fusion in which two would become one, as in *Valentine*, and the subordination of the woman implicit in the regressive pastoral sketched out in *Indiana*.

Despite *Lélia*'s far more radical and subversive message, or perhaps because of it, almost no contemporary reviewer of the novel made any mention of its feminist implications. For Sand's more realist works—*Indiana* and *Valentine*—critics, even those who disagreed with her progressive views, were quick to recognize them as pleas for women's rights and a critique of romantic love, and the literary merits of these novels were far more universally acknowledged. For *Lélia*, the reviews were decidedly polarized but all pronounced this roman de femme by a woman writer as a work not for women, but for men to admire or condemn, in ways that effectively silenced its oppositional meaning.

The Wrong Readers

In their enthusiasm for *Lélia*'s formal iconoclasm and the way it highlighted ideas, Sand's champions, most notably Gustave Planche, passed over the novel's radical politics in silence. Indeed, for such men, the novel's elevated plane of ideas meant that it was a book intended for an elite, male audience. *Lélia*, one critic wrote, will appeal "to all those who are in the habit of thinking and reflecting," and perhaps not, therefore, "to women or the common reader."[43] The majority of reviewers, however, condemned the novel for its scandalous evocation of women's sexual desire (or lack thereof). They too made no mention of the feminist dimensions of Sand's work, even to condemn them, and declared, but for different reasons, that the book was fit only for men. In the scathing review that launched the controversy in the press about the novel, Capo de Feuillide advises his male readers to send their wives and daughters out of the house or even out to a ball rather than risk exposing them to the pages of Sand's scabrous novel.[44] Even so, Feuillide claims that were a woman to read the novel, she could not identify with the heroine, for "what woman would consent to pose or look at herself in a mirror to be painted, or paint herself as Lélia!" (71).

Inasmuch as readers believed Lélia to be Sand's self-portrait, the insult to the author was obvious. In his review of the novel, Sainte-Beuve defended Sand against attacks by those who had adopted his own truism that a woman writer's fictions almost inevitably record her (love) life in the form he called the *roman intime*. "People have reproached the writer for having taken the intimate genre too far, as if there were the least connection between it and the almost constantly dithyrambic, grandiose, and so-called symbolic tone of this poem."[45] If poetic excess is a bulwark against accusations of confessional self-portraiture,

perhaps the novel's idealism—its high tone and pointedly alle-
gorical meaning—may be understood as an attempt to steer the
fiction away from the charges of autobiography so commonly
leveled against women's texts, and against the mal du siècle authors as well. In this, however, *Lélia* fails. The limited success
the novel enjoyed was primarily a succès de scandale.

In her preface to an 1834 edition of the novel, published
together with *Valentine* and several of her short stories, Sand
acknowledges that *Lélia*'s lesson may be lost on some readers
because of a fundamental failure of recognition. After all, she
admits, there are, "among French women, those who are lucky
enough or blind enough to draw from each new disillusionment and every new betrayal, an increasingly confident and
childish credulousness."[46] In other words, some women readers
resemble the young Sténio or the young Lélia before the disappointment in love that changed them forever, and thus may
resist the novel and fail to hear its message. Nevertheless, Sand
implies, *Lélia* gives voice to the vast majority, whom experience
has taught or will teach to be wary of (romantic) illusions and
society's treatment of women. Her novel gives voice to their
vague metaphysical discontent, just as it discloses their feminist
anger.

Of all the critics who reviewed the novel when it was first
published, only Sainte-Beuve saw that the premise from which
Sand started was one common to many women's experience
and one with which they could *identify*. Not only did Sainte-
Beuve describe Lélia's malady as "the boredom, death, and inability to love or believe" typical of women in their thirties who
have been disillusioned and deceived, he also related Sand's audacious novel to a more generalized spirit of feminist protest
and independence in women writers beginning in the 1830s and
saw "the spirit of revolt against society" that animated it (2:66).
In his view, however, Sand's decision to translate women's discontent with their lot into metaphysical terms, thus turning realism into idealism, alienates most readers who, like himself,
fail to find in the novel the pleasures of verisimilitude and recognition. Moreover, for Sainte-Beuve, because *Lélia* combines
idealism with pessimism, Sand represents the malady that afflicts her character as incurable and portrays it not as the result

of "certain social circumstances relative to the fate of particular individuals" (70), but as a general predicament of all creation. Sand's text thereby loses much of its potential impact.

While on the one hand Sainte-Beuve's reading of the novel reveals a surprising degree of insight into the work's feminist problematic and a sympathy with the cause of women's emancipation, on the other his review defends *Lélia* because he believes Sand will not make this same kind of "mistake" again. For Sainte-Beuve, it is precisely Sand's idealism, the way it tends toward generalized, metaphysical abstractions that makes her text too overwhelming to be laudable. "A work so full of *power* and often grace," he writes, "seemed *extraordinary* rather than *beautiful*, and *frightened rather than charmed* those who admire on the strength of what their heart feels" (2:70; emphasis added). Like Sténio, then, who stands in awe and in fear of Lélia's power, Sainte-Beuve declares himself frightened by this all-too-powerful text and the "infinite resources" of this woman "who had begun to write only eighteen months before" (2:71).

Unlike the "charming" *Valentine*, Sand's *Lélia* refuses to indulge the reader by using "feminine" wiles in its rhetoric of persuasion. "I would even find fault with its style," Sainte-Beuve writes, "which is too studied" and lacks those "gratuitous weaknesses and careless irregularities," which betray the author's "delicate inner recesses of thought" (2:71–72). In the literary gospel according to Sainte-Beuve, writers should conform to the cultural codes of femininity. Their writing should seem natural not artificial, casual conversation rather than conscious craft, closer to feeling than to thought, even though he argues that for Sand, whose talent is natural, this would mean being even more conscious of her craft. Sand's style, by contrast, fails the litmus test of artistry and femininity. Inasmuch as her text is polished and faultless, it is also hard and impenetrable—Sainte-Beuve's own private phantasm of the writer's power and, particularly the exceptional woman writer's power, as a form of virility.

While Sand's all-too-idealist text evidences phallic qualities, for Sainte-Beuve, its intellectual depth also gives it a more conventionally "female" form, that is, the gaping abyss. This image, which Sand chose as her epigraph, is a representation not only of the text but also, Sainte-Beuve would have us believe, of its author. In *Mes Poisons*, he recounts the cooling of his friendship with Sand: "For a long time, I found myself at the side of the woman who wrote *Lélia* as if I were next to an abyss." He notes that what makes the unfathomable chasm so deadly was its attractive environs: "the edge was covered with magnificent, cheerful vegetation and, asleep in the high grass, I admired it. But one day, finally, I leaned over and I saw! *O quanta Charybdis!*" (2:308). In a familiar male phantasm, the woman writer, like her heroine and her text, threatens to pull the (male) reader into a deadly abyss.

Rescue Fantasies Revisited: Modern Critics on *Lélia*

For Sainte-Beuve, the seductive powers of Sand and her novel are cause for alarm. In the recent resurgence of interest in *Lélia*, they are reason for rejoicing, and nowhere more so than in two of the first modern studies of the novel, published in the early 1980s, which, in their similarities and differences, offer a kind of paradigm of contemporary critical response. Both Temchin in "Straining the Structures of Romanticism" and Sivert in "*Lélia* and Feminism" seek to rescue the novel from the margins of the literary canon. Though the former rereads Sand under the aegis of formalist modernism and the latter through the insights of French feminism as well, both critics use modern critical approaches to reinterpret the text's apparent "flaws" as its saving—and subversive—grace. Both laud the heterogeneity of the novel as its transformative power, for example. "By sharing the place of the narrator with other characters and with disembodied narrative voices," Sivert writes, "Lélia (and George Sand) undoes exclusive, appropriating narrative authority, but she admits the 'other' into a kind of shared writing without losing control over the recounting of herself. Having no voice in society, Lélia can be heard in narration."[47] The text, in other words, is feminocentric, yet the proliferation of centers undermines the authority of any one single voice.

Unlike the other mal du siècle texts, Sand's discourse does not frame and contain its embedded narrative(s) as a way to stifle the Other in the interest of the Same.

Nevertheless, despite its multivocal pluralism, the text evinces a remarkable coherence. Temchin notes that "Sand has given [all the characters] acute powers of observation and a penchant for lyrical, metaphorical expression."[48] They all speak "that eloquent declamatory language that Pulchérie deprecates as 'their luxuriant manner of expression, which has become the ordinary language of our time'" (105). Moreover, "disregarding the illusion of realism and blurring the formal distinctions among letters, the spoken word, and narration, Sand has imposed upon them instead the coherence of her language and vision" (88–89). My own analysis underscores Temchin's point by showing that this coherence is an expression of the work's idealism. To overemphasize *Lélia*'s resemblance to an *oeuvre ouverte* is to obscure the other and equally powerful counterforce in the novel that insists on absolutes, control, and endings. Similarly, excessive attention to *Lélia*'s dialogical multiplicity hides its equally notable perlocutionary force. The text does not do a modernist disappearing act, which leaves meaning floundering in the undecidable. Far from abandoning control, the text corroborates the views of its ideological spokesperson and wields its powers of persuasion over the reader with a heavy hand. As I have shown, *Lélia* is an assertive attempt at moral suasion and ideological persuasion.

While Sivert's reading of *Lélia* through and with Luce Irigaray and Hélène Cixous is illuminating, it also casts a modern feminist shadow over Sand's nineteenth-century difference. First and foremost, the profound pessimism of Sand's text gives the lie to the hortatory formulations of modern advocates of *l'écriture féminine*. In "The Laugh of the Medusa," by Hélène Cixous for example, a simple gender reversal and act of resistance brings about a radical revision of the world. "Women . . . have only to stop listening to the Sirens (for the Sirens were men) for history to change its meaning. You only have to look at the Medusa straight on to see her. And she's not deadly. She's beautiful and she's laughing."[49] While *Lélia* also features gender reversal and the heroine's resistance, Sand's Medusa-like heroine may be beautiful, but she is still deadly, and she is not laughing.

Although Sand's novel dramatizes the high cost of being a woman who is the exception to society's rules, the text attempts, as I have shown, to transcend gender through allegory and deny it through idealism. Moers argues that in *Lélia* "George Sand created the Romantic hero as a woman," that is, the heroine adopts the hero's attributes and yet "remains all Woman."[50] But Sand has created in Lélia a protagonist who is both a woman and the personification of an idea. Gender is extrinsic as well as intrinsic to the characterization of the heroine, and this double identity allows the author to hide a potentially radical feminism while bypassing the question of gender altogether. Given Lélia's "masculine" attributes and her adoption of the male role, to assign the heroine unequivocally to the female sex perhaps begs the question. Except for Lélia and Pulchérie's lucid and sympathetic analysis of social constraints on the female sex, women in general are given almost no attention in the novel. Furthermore, these heroines and the text itself lock other women into the inferior position society assigns them and makes room only for the exceptions.

While the text's feminism has limits, its most important revision of assumptions about gender remains its exceptional heroine who is not a passive object of male desire, but a strong, self-reflexive subject. This notion of woman as subject, which was radical in the fiction of the early nineteenth century, is still viewed as exceptional even today. Diane Johnson notes that "consciousness and the power of reflection are more usually the properties of male protagonists and gamblers" and that "there are few female gamblers in modern fiction—there are more victims."[51]

Mal du siècle novels give ample demonstration that the fascination with female vulnerability and victimization is hardly a new phenomenon. Chateaubriand's *René* and Constant's *Adolphe*, for example, present the spectacle of the heroine's victimization from the voyeuristic perspective of the male. On the other hand, the heroes in these novels are themselves far more like victims than like gamblers. Sand's heroine differs from her male predecessors' female protagonists in that she is a subject; she contrasts with their heroes as well in that she refuses to see herself as victim. She is, instead, like her creator, a gambler, who in Johnson's words "claims for woman the rank of person, differently preoccupied but as worthy as men to attract the notice of fortune, to be in the game and to be dealt a hand, good or bad" (26). Thus, in *Lélia*, Sand attempts to secure literary space and time for the exceptional heroine: a female protagonist who is and is not a "woman," a woman who is "like a man," and a heroine whose "male" malady unveils the sexual politics of the fictions of impotence in the French Romantic novel.

Epilogue

The parameters of this book might be mapped out as the distance and difference between two similes. In the three androcentric fictions by male authors, the hero is "like a woman." In the feminocentric novels by Staël and Sand, the heroine is "like a man." Although the figure establishes resemblance, it does not abolish difference. Despite the symmetry of the chiasmus, a man who is like a woman is not the male equivalent of a woman who is like a man. I have attempted to show that in the mal du siècle novel, male feminization and female virilization have a different status and are played for different stakes. In schematic and overreaching summary, one might say that in the male-authored fictions, the hero's feminine traits are the sign of his disempowerment, whereas in *Corinne* and *Lélia*, the heroine's virile attributes are the mark of her power. Nevertheless, Chateaubriand, Constant, and Stendhal use the feminine in the male to shore up male power, while Staël and Sand figure the heroine's power as the transcendence of the social constraints on her gender. The androcentric fictions evidence a nostalgia for older forms of patriarchy and an anxiety about the loss of old certainties of sexual difference. The feminocentric novels, by contrast, use the loss of absolutes to criticize the gender and power arrangements of the old and new orders.

Despite the profound pessimism of Sand's *Lélia*, the 1830s has been called the "golden age of the women writer." In her study of nineteenth-century French attitudes toward women and women writers, Christine Planté tells us that after over forty years of legal oppression and social repression, the enormous success of Sand's novels, the emerging importance of numerous other women writers, the beginnings of a first collective movement of women's liberation, and the significance of "the woman question" in social and political debates gave indications that women were moving toward some kind of emancipation.[1] Unfortunately, Planté continues, this exhilarating historical moment was short-lived. Talk of women's entrance into men's domains and examples of their success aggravated men's fear that male power and masculine identity were in serious jeopardy. The antifeminist backlash that resulted condemned this new version of women with their "virile" aspirations as a menace to the entire social order (44).

In response to these new threats to male rule, two important new twists in the literary representation of gender appeared in the late 1820s and the 1830s. On the one hand, as Naomi Schor notes, the period saw a "multiplication of borderline cases: androgynes and castrati," as in Gautier's *Mademoiselle de Maupin* (1836) and Balzac's "Sarrasine" (1830).[2] On the other hand, and even more commonly, literary texts whose politics were far from feminist, featured not only a "proliferation of effeminate characters," as had been the case in the earlier mal du siècle works, but also a corresponding preponderance of "viriloid female characters" whose "masculine" superiority, unlike that of a Corinne or a Lélia, took a decidedly sadistic turn.[3] While the first pattern would seem to represent a "breakdown of gender distinctions,"[4] the second reinforces these differences and the power relations they imply even though it seems to reverse them.

In the past fifteen years, some of the best criticism in the field of nineteenth-century French studies has turned attention to works from the 1820s and 1830s such as Balzac's "Sarrasine" or *La Fille aux yeux d'or*, which clearly thematize gender difference as a question or exhibit a sustained and perverse fascination with a woman's maleficent power. As a result of this emphasis on "modern" or "sexy" nineteenth-century texts, which are not ostensibly "about" men (although of course they are), critics have tended to neglect the contemporary Romantic novels, written in some cases by the same authors, which focus, as their mal du siècle predecessors had, on the troubled subjectivity of disempowered men. Indeed, between 1831 and 1838, the mal du siècle enjoyed a sharp resurgence of popularity. Along with *Lélia* and the reedition of Senancour's *Obermann*, there appeared at least fourteen novels, all of them by men, offering variations on the mal du siècle theme that had begun with *René*.[5] If we are to understand the many and varied literary responses to a perceived rise in women's power and the apparent disempowerment of some men, especially literary men, this second phase of the mal du siècle, along with the first, may provide valuable lessons about the crisis of gender in the 1830s, not to mention the even more famous gender crises that took place at the end of the nineteenth century in Europe and trouble us now in our own fin du siècle.

The three most famous mal du siècle works of the July Monarchy—*Volupté* by Sainte-Beuve (1834), *Le Lys dans la vallée* by Balzac (1836), and *La Confession d'un enfant du siècle* by Musset (1836)—follow the traditional androcentric pattern: a first-person male narrator makes his confession of debilitation a surreptitious self-aggrandizement and reveals himself as a feminized man. In *Volupté*, shy, sensitive Amaury prefers a domestic interior of women and games to the world of men and politics. Balzac's Félix divides his time between the two worlds but, like Amaury, enters into an emasculating "contract" with the pious object of his desires. Musset's Octave, like Adolphe, is both drawn to seduction and guilt ridden about abandoning his victim. In a world dominated by father figures, the heroes fail to become fathers themselves. Sainte-Beuve's Amaury and Balzac's Félix pine away for the faithful wives of other men, while Musset's Octave, who mourns his exemplary father, fails at debauchery and stumbles at virtue. As a result, Amaury and Octave exclude themselves from the fatherland. Renouncing his physical desires, the hero of Sainte-Beuve's *Volupté* joins the priesthood and sets sail for America. Musset's Octave bids farewell to the town of his birth so that the mistress he has mistreated may be with another man.

As in most fiction of the 1830s, in these mal du siècle novels woman is more the object of a male gaze and his desires than she is a subject in her own right. Unlike many of the heroines of the now more famous works by Balzac, Gautier, and others, however, in the second mal du siècle phase she has almost no existence outside the hero's representation of her and does not enjoy any obvious virilization. Indeed, despite Sand's notoriety, none of the three writers, even Sainte-Beuve, who had become her friend and confidant, and Musset, who was her former lover and claimed to be writing "their story" in *La confession*, featured in their novels a Sand-like heroine who dared arrogate male privileges. Nor did any of them take up in any sustained way *Lélia*'s formal or feminist challenge to received ideas about the novel and the place of man and woman in it. Eschewing Sand's audacious subversion of literary and cultural commonplaces, her rhetorical pyrotechnics, and her idealism, they favored instead the traditional mal du siècle form—a first-person confession written in a lyrical but essentially conventional style—with occasional attention to the material details of everyday life or to the specifics of contemporary political events more typical of realism than of the "roman personnel."[6] In this way, the authors conjured away the threat represented by *Lélia* the novel, Lélia the heroine, and Sand the woman author. At the same time, however, other aspects of their texts, which distinguish them as a distinct, second phase of the mal du siècle suggest that these authors did in fact come under the influence of Sand and that their works registered women's growing social power.

To put the difference between the two phases of the mal du siècle in its simplest formulation, in *Volupté, Le Lys dans la vallée*, and *La Confession d'un enfant du siècle*, the novel of male narcissism characteristic of previous androcentric mal du siècle fictions becomes a semirealist novel of adultery. In these later, decidedly Oedipal texts of homosocial and triangular desire, the hero, who considers himself a child, falls in love with an idealized mother figure involved with another man. In contrast with the classic mal du siècle texts of male solipsism, however, the female protagonist in these July Monarchy texts is not the man's narcissistic double, a woman whose unshakable and boundless love confirms his desirability. Instead, like Lélia, though with far less force, the heroine resists the hero's desires. In *Volupté*, Mme de Couaën sublimates with relative ease her amorous feelings for Amaury in the name of moral purity and wifely devotion. Similarly, in *Le Lys dans la vallée*, which consists almost entirely of Félix's attempt to seduce Lady Dudley by confessing his impossible love for another woman, the hero and his narrative fail miserably. Toward the end of *La Confession*, an event occurs that would have been unthinkable in previous texts: the hero's main love interest falls in love with another man.

In this second phase of the mal du siècle, the hero, like his predecessors, still cannot join the world of men. On the other hand, in these later works that world is decidedly *there*. Indeed, through the theme of adultery, the later works refigure the impediments to the hero's sexual success and to his social assimilation not as a psychological block that comes almost exclusively from within the mal du siècle protagonist, but as moral, social, and legal obstacles that lie outside him. In *Volupté* and *La Confession*, the world is embodied in the hero's idol and/or rival, a "real man" whom the hero can never be. When Musset's Octave, who is in mourning for his father, puts on the dead man's dressing gown and sits in his chair, he cannot even fool himself into thinking he is his father. The soft voice of reproach he imagines hearing asks: "'Where has the father gone? It is obvious this is his orphaned son.'"[7] Sainte-Beuve's Amaury admits that, unlike his hero, the counterrevolutionary conspirator Georges, and despite his own dreams of public glory, he is a man consumed by the pleasures of the flesh and the pain of solitary reflection. Like their predecessors, all three works reveal that these heroes, despite their marginalization, do not call into question the patriarchal order; instead, they regret their inability to play a more central role in it.

Although Amaury, Félix, and Octave all admit that it is something in themselves that makes them unfit men,[8] the heroes also insist that they are victims of fate, and place the blame on historical circumstances that are clearly beyond their own control. Thus, early on in *Volupté*, Amaury makes a personal claim on behalf of his entire generation: "What I need is a chance to act, some exploit by which I would know what I am worth and demonstrate it to others." But the moment of counterrevolutionary heroism is past: "We who are too young by a few years, full of vigor, what are we to do? . . . In place of the rolling thunder of battles, all we have are spider webs and whispered conspiracies" (54). This grand statement of historical impossibilities is both a general truth and a particular lie, for

Amaury uses this historical argument to extricate himself from the ties that would bind him to a woman.

The second chapter of *La Confession* expresses a similar nostalgia for an earlier, military age as Musset elevates the sense of belatedness that haunts all of the mal du siècle heroes into a long soliloquy on the entire second generation. He explains that the sons of Napoleon's soldiers grew up dreaming that they would, as their fathers had, prove their manhood through military valor. Instead, after the Reign of Terror and the fall of Napoleon, all they know is disenchantment, doubt, and despair. And, in a remark that recalls Chateaubriand's *René*, he condemns the era as a no-man's-land between the past and the future: "All that was is no longer; all that will be is not yet" (20).

Though similarly haunted by the image of a lost, virile age, the historical explanations given in this second stage mal du siècle text do not, as Chateaubriand had done in his preface, blame women—the other victims of historical circumstance and social constraints—for the feminization that has befallen men. Indeed, in their historical fictions of causality, Chateaubriand and Musset present a curious chiasmus. Chateaubriand, who was writing at a time of great social and political upheaval, makes no mention of these desperately tragic or dangerously exhilarating circumstances in his preface. Instead, in explaining man's "feminization," he focuses attention on the general influence of women at a time when in fact women had lost a great deal of political power and social influence. In the 1830s, by contrast, women were making some gains in the public perception of their rights and abilities, but in his history of the (male) generation, Musset fixes the reader's attention instead on the political reasons that explain why men are no longer "men."[9]

Although woman remains peripheral to the historical metalanguage of the July Monarchy texts, within the story itself and in the representation of the hero's psychology, the novel nevertheless follows the familiar logic of cherchez la femme. Amaury states from the beginning that once he reached puberty, the "idea of woman . . . stayed with me, invaded my being, and broke off all trace of previous impressions" (43). From the very first line of *Le Lys dans la vallée,* Félix declares that a woman's wishes are his command even if it means, as it does here, revealing to her how another, previous lover had been his raison d'être. Despite the attention to larger political and social circumstances in the second chapter of *La confession,* Octave's narrative proper begins with his abandonment by one woman, and his eventual loss of a second woman to another man brings his story to an end.

Moreover, when these fictions of causality turn away from causes to concentrate on effects, the narrating hero enjoys, as his predecessors had, a privileged position: in all three texts, the male protagonist's restrospective narrative memorializes the unobtainable heroine as the dead or absent woman over whom he now exercises power. In *Volupté,* the heroine's demise is a long, drawn-out affair, sanctimonious in the extreme, which gives the newly ordained hero the chance to show that he has transcended the imperious need for her and for women in general which had motivated his actions his whole life long. Of all the mal du siècle novels, *Le Lys dans la vallée* gives by far the most sensational representation of a woman ravaged by her love for the hero. Félix depicts Henriette on her deathbed, emaciated by jealousy and feverish with the violent unleashing of her repressed desires for him. As for the heroine of *La Confession d'un enfant du siècle,* "whatever Brigitte does," writes Naomi Segal, and "in this she is exactly like Amélie and Ellénore, . . . she is never seen as acting on her own will: both her long-suffering and her final 'betrayal' are [the hero] Octave's doing, not hers." [10] Although Brigitte does not die in the melodramatic climax of the novel, Octave, mad with jealousy and the violent anger that her hold on him inspires, almost kills her as she sleeps, thus demonstrating the life-and-death power he has over her but does not choose to wield.

In other words, while the heroines in this second phase of the mal du siècle do not fulfill to nearly the same degree the self-aggrandizing fantasies of the heroes as the women in earlier texts had, a man's response to a woman's power over him is once again to reassert his power over her by telling her story his way. Indeed, if in the first phase of the mal du siècle the feminization of men gives them a story to tell, by the second phase it allows these heroes, who are semiautobiographical re-presentations of the author, to come to writing. For Sainte-Beuve and Musset, who gave fictional form in these works to their own emotional frustrations and social marginalization, the traditional mal du siècle format offered distinct advantages; it gave the hero control over his narrative and made writing a similarly compensatory empowerment for the author.

In later decades of the nineteenth century, however, the no-tion of the artist and writer as a feminized man will become even more explicit and commonplace, and the question of his virility or lack thereof will take center stage. In her analysis of the "rhetoric of sickness" in decadent texts from Baudelaire to D'Annunzio, Barbara Spackman shows that according to these works, "a man becomes a woman when he writes" through a process of ventriloquism.[11] The poet or writer takes on femi-nine qualities as his own not in order to praise women but to expel them from the scene of his "convalescence." It is as if, in these texts, the authors cannot be both artists and men; in any case they cannot be a man among women. In Huysmans's *A Rebours*, according to Spackman, Des Esseintes "commemorates the death of his virility, . . . [which] here refers explicitly to sexual potency" so that he "can devote himself to aesthetic matters. . . . In the *Journaux intimes* Baudelaire vividly charac-terizes the relationship between [male] sexual potency and the arts: 'The more man cultivates the arts, the fewer erections he has'" (67).

Annelise Mauge's research on the "crisis of masculinity" at the turn of the century and Elaine Showalter's analysis of "sex-ual anarchy" during this period allow us to see the decadents' obsession with feminization and impotence as part of a virulent antifeminist backlash.[12] My own work here suggests as well that these decadent male writers, who mark the beginning of "our" modernity, are latter-day avatars of the mal du siècle, who make disabled subjectivity an integral part of an empowering (au-thorial) male identity. Showalter's study of "the female malady" in England from 1830 to 1980, Sandra Gilbert and Susan Gubar's exploration of the "no-man's-land" in modernist litera-

ture in America and England, and Kaja Silverman's analysis of
the crisis in male subjectivity recorded in post–World War II
cinema suggest that the male malady did not end with the nineteenth century, nor is it only in France that literary men use
fictions of impotence as an "authorizing" empowerment.[13] What
remains to be seen, however, is what we will do about it.

Notes

Prologue

1 Susan Faludi argues that premature declarations of the end of feminism are part of an "undeclared war against American women" and cites many studies about women's status (*Backlash: The Undeclared War against American Women* [New York: Crown, 1991]).

2 See Faludi, *Backlash*, 281–312.

3 For an early analysis of this phenomenon, see Elaine Showalter, "Critical Cross-Dressing: Male Feminists and the Woman of the Year," *Raritan* 2, no. 2 (Fall 1983): 130–149. Throughout this book, I use such terms as "feminine," "masculine," "feminized," and "virilized" to refer to the social construction of gender differences at particular historical moments.

4 Susan Jeffords, "Performative Masculinities, or, 'After a Few Times You Won't Be Afraid of Rape at All,'" *Discourse* 13 (Spring–Summer 1991): 102–118.

5 I borrow this concept from Elizabeth Janeway, "On the Power of the Weak," *Signs* 1 (Autumn 1981): 103–109. See also, Jean-François Lyotard, "Sur la force des faibles," *L'Arc* 64 (1976): 4–12.

6 Tania Modleski, *Feminism without Women: Culture and Criticism in a "Post-feminist" Age* (New York: Routledge, Chapman and Hall, 1991).

7 For an excellent discussion of the "aporia of gender" in nineteenth-century realist fiction, see Dorothy Kelly, *Fictional Genders: Role and Representation in Nineteenth-Century French Narrative* (Lincoln: University of Nebraska Press, 1989).

1. Rereading the Mal du Siècle

1 Mario Praz, "The Lady with the Lyre," in *On Neoclassicism*, trans. Angus Davidson (Evanston: Northwestern University Press, 1969), 261–262.

2 *Mémoires d'outre-tombe*, 2 vols. (Paris: Gallimard, 1946), 1: 462.

3 For documentation and examples, see the critical introduction to *René* by Armand Weil (Paris: Droz, 1935), xl–lxv; Pierre Barbéris, *A la recherche d'une écriture: Chateaubriand* (Paris: Mame, 1974), esp. 665–692; and Pierre Barbéris, *"René" de Chateaubriand: Un nouveau roman* (Paris: Larousse, 1973).

4 On this phenomenon, see Margaret Waller, "Being René, Buying Atala," in *Rebel Daughters: Women and the French Revolution*, ed. Sara Melzer

and Leslie Rabine (New York: Oxford University Press, 1992), 157–177; and "The Melancholy Man and the Lady with the Lyre: The Sexual Politics of Genius in Early Romantic Fiction and Painting," in *Selected Proceedings of the Sixteenth Annual Nineteenth-Century French Studies Colloquium* (Amsterdam: Rodopi, forthcoming).

5 Duras read her manuscript aloud in her salon, but *Olivier ou le secret* remained unpublished until a modern edition by Denise Virieux appeared in 1971.

6 For a detailed comparative study of the thematics of this phenomenon in a wide range of canonical and noncanonical works, including some of those studied here, see Glyn Holmes, *The Adolphe Type in French Fiction of the First Half of the Nineteenth Century* (Sherbrooke, Quebec: Editions Naaman, 1977).

7 Stendhal, *Armance*, trans. Gilbert and Suzanne Sale (London: Merlin Press, 1960), 11.

8 Michael J. Call sketches out the contemporary critics' reaction to this phenomenon in *Back to the Garden: Chateaubriand, Senancour and Constant* (Saratoga: Anma Libri, 1988), 3–13. For the history of the term, see also Armand Hoog, "Who Invented the 'Mal du Siècle'?" *Yale French Studies* 13 (1954): 42–51.

9 Pierre Barbéris analyzes this phenomenon in *"René" de Chateaubriand*.

10 The single exceptions—the heroines of Duras's *Ourika* and George Sand's *Lélia*—will prove this rule, a point I will explain below.

11 Joan DeJean, "Staël's *Corinne*: The Novel's Other Dilemma," *Stanford French Review* 11 (Spring 1987): 77–87.

12 In addition to *René, Adolphe, Armance,* and *La Confession d'un enfant du siècle*, the classic examples of the genre include Senancour's *Obermann* (1804), Sainte-Beuve's *Volupté* (1834), and Balzac's *Le Lys dans la vallée* (1835). Although Senancour's novel was first published as *Oberman*, in the 1833 edition the title and protagonist gained the more Germanic double *n*. I have used this later designation throughout.

13 Claude-Prosper de Crébillon, *Oeuvres complètes*, 2 vols. (Geneva: Slatkine, 1968), 2: 362.

14 Nancy K. Miller, "The Exquisite Cadavers," *Diacritics* 5 (Winter 1975): 40.

15 See, for example, the chapter on Françoise de Grafigny's *Lettres d'une Péruvienne* in Nancy K. Miller, *Subject to Change* (New York: Columbia University Press, 1988), and her "Men's Reading, Women's Writing: Gender and the Rise of the Novel," *Yale French Studies* 75 (1988): 40–55.

16 I take this insight from Melinda Sansone, *"Lettres d'une Péruvienne:* The New Sentimental Plot and Its Feminist Implications," and "Possessing the Sentimental Tradition," unpublished essays.

17 For a summary of the eighteenth-century sentimental tradition in England, see Janet Todd, *Sensibility: An Introduction* (London: Methuen, 1986).

18 Only Staël's Oswald obeys the call of the father by marrying a woman other than the heroine, but even he is left to mourn the heroine and regret his abandonment of her.

19 Nancy K. Miller, *The Heroine's Text: Readings in the French and English Novel, 1722–1782* (New York: Columbia University Press, 1980).

20 Naomi Schor, *Breaking the Chain: Women, Theory and French Realist Fiction* (New York: Columbia University Press, 1985), 144, 142.

21 The question of incest makes *René* an exception, however.

22 Miller, *Subject to Change*, 8. *Corinne* is one of the four novels Miller analyzes.

23 While I see and make connections here between literature, history, and biography, I do not mean to reduce any one of them to the other nor describe these connections as causal in any simple sense. The vexed question of their interconnections is beyond the purview of this work.

24 See Pierre Barbéris, *Balzac et le mal du siècle: Contribution à une physiologie du monde moderne*, 2 vols. (Paris: Gallimard, 1970); *"René" de Chateaubriand*; and "Mal du siècle ou d'un romantisme de droite à un romantisme de gauche," *Romantisme et politique, 1815–1841*, Colloque de l'Ecole Normale Supérieure de Saint-Cloud (Paris: Armand Colin, 1969), 164–182.

25 On gender relations during this period see, for example, Joan Landes, *Women and the Public Sphere in the Age of the French Revolution* (Ithaca: Cornell University Press, 1988); Sara Melzer and Leslie Rabine, eds., *Rebel Daughters: Women and the French Revolution* (Oxford: Oxford University Press, 1992); Geneviève Fraisse, *Muse de la raison: La Démocratie exclusive et la différence des sexes* (Aix-en-Provence: Alinéa, 1989); and Christine Planté, *La Petite Soeur de Balzac* (Paris: Seuil, 1989).

26 Barbéris views the work of Staël and Chateaubriand (and Stendhal as well) in this light in "Mme de Staël: Du romantisme, de la littérature et de la France nouvelle," *Europe* 64 (Jan.–Feb. 1987): 6–22.

27 See, for example, Fraisse on Sylvain Maréchal's 1801 "Proposal for a law forbidding women to be taught to read," in *Muse de la raison*, 13–36.

28 Marlon B. Ross, "Romantic Quest and Conquest: Troping Masculine Power in the Crisis of Poetic Identity," in *Romanticism and Feminism*, ed. Anne K. Mellor (Bloomington: Indiana University Press, 1988), 40, 41. See also his excellent full-length treatment of this subject in *The Contours of Masculine Desire: Romanticism and the Rise of Women's Poetry* (New York: Oxford University Press, 1989).

29 See, for example, John Lough, *Writer and Public in France: From the Middle Ages to the Present Day* (Oxford: Clarendon Press, 1978); Priscilla Parkhurst Clark, *Literary France: The Making of a Culture* (Berkeley: University of California Press, 1987); and Rachel Bowlby, *Just Looking: Consumer Culture in Dreiser, Gissing and Zola* (New York: Methuen, 1985).

30 On this contrast, see also Madelyn Gutwirth, "*Corinne* et l'esthétique du camée," in *Le Préromantisme: Hypothèque ou hypothèse*, ed. Paul Vialleneix (Paris: Klincksieck, 1975), 237–245; Waller, "Melancholy Man and the Lady with the Lyre"; and Marie-Claire Vallois, "Old Idols, New Subject: Germaine de Staël and Romanticism," in *Germaine de Staël: Crossing the Borders*, ed. Madelyn Gutwirth, Avriel Goldberger, and Karyna Szmurlo (New Brunswick: Rutgers University Press, 1991), 82–97.

31 In her study of this distinct narrative form, Naomi Segal notes that such works "have often been grouped . . . under a variety of rubrics: as the 'personal' or 'autobiographical novel' or the 'novel of the individual,' the work of 'French introspectives,' instances of 'short fiction in France,' contexts for 'the hero in French Romantic literature' or 'the "Adolphe" type'" (*Narcissus and Echo: Women in the French 'Récit'* [Manchester: Manchester University Press, 1988], 16).

32 Chateaubriand, *Atala, René* (Paris: Garnier-Flammarion, 1964), 64.

33 Sainte-Beuve, *Volupté*, ed. André Guyaux (Paris: Gallimard, 1986), 86–87.

34 On this formalist level, Duras's spare, restrained work resembles theirs. Her novels fall, as theirs do, into recognizable, established sentimental genres: *Edouard* and *Ourika* are, like most mal du siècle fictions, first-person framed narratives and her *Olivier* is reminiscent of the epistolary genre that had been especially popular in the eighteenth century.

35 Susan Kirkpatrick argues that women writers' "innovative openness in representing the subject of writing" and their tendency "to explode notions of the self as coherent and self-contained" stem from the women writers' experience of self-division in the conflict between their "own socialization according to the norms of domestic womanhood" and the audacious act of self-representation. See *Las Románticas: Women Writers and Subjectivity in Spain, 1835–1850* (Berkeley: University of California Press, 1989), 34. While male authors may also stress the contradictory, alienated, self-divided self (see *René* and *Adolphe* particularly), their works are not nearly so innovative or multivocal. Though this difference separates the audacious feminist writers from the tradition, it does not distinguish all women's writing from men's.

36 David Rollo, "The Phryné and the Muse: Onanism and Creativity in Chateaubriand's *Mémoires d'Outre-Tombe* and *René*," *Nineteenth-Century French Studies* 18 (Fall–Winter 1989–1990): 25.

37 Naomi Schor notes the need for critics to begin looking at the representation of men in women's writing in "The Portrait of a Gentleman: Representing Men in (French) Women's Writing," *Representations* 20 (Fall 1987): 113–133.

38 Given the audacity of Sand's novel, these works are appear almost as afterthoughts to the tradition and are discussed here in the Epilogue.

2. *Fictions of the Feminine in Chateaubriand's* René

1 Chateaubriand's comments, originally published in *Genius of Christianity*, were later republished in the 1805 preface to *Atala, René* 64. Future references to these comments, as well as to *Atala* and *René*, are to this edition.

2 I have argued that the marked contrast in the reception of Chateaubriand's two fictions—the public bought representations of Atala but readers wanted to be René—exemplifies the new ideologies of gender which were central to the formation of bourgeois culture. See Margaret Waller, "Being René, Buying Atala."

3 For references, see Chapter 1, note 25.

4 *Atala* and *René* were published together in a separate edition in 1805. My discussion of *René* is based on this edition, which has become the standard.

5 Denis Diderot et Jean Le Rond d'Alembert, eds., *L'encyclopédie*, and Pierre Larousse, *Grand dictionnaire du XIXe siècle*, s.v. *Tendre*.

6 Other mal du siècle novels work in similarly doubled ways to praise and deplore the reign of sentiment in men. In the preface to the second edition of *Adolphe*, for example, Constant describes "feminine" sentiment as ennobling, but the tale he tells belies his approbation by showing the way such feelings debilitate the hero and traumatize the heroine.

7 Many of the comments quoted here from Chateaubriand's preface were first published in his *Défense du Génie du christianisme* (1803), a response to contemporary critics' attacks on his morals and methods.

8 Chateaubriand, *Génie du christianisme*, 2 vols., ed. Pierre Reboul (Paris: Garnier-Flammarion, 1966), 1: 56.

9 Nevertheless, in 1805, just three years after its publication, Chateaubriand expunged *Atala* and *René* from *Genius of Christianity* to publish them together in a separate edition and left the latter work to its own rhetorical devices.

10 Although I consulted Irving Putter's translation of *René* (1957), my own translations, which attempt to convey the original text upon which my close readings are based, often differ markedly from his.

11 Ross Chambers, *Story and Situation: Narrative Seduction and the Power of Fiction* (Minneapolis: University of Minnesota Press, 1984), 214.

12 Roland Barthes, *S/Z*, trans. Richard Miller (New York: Farrar, Straus and Giroux, 1974), 135; emphasis added.

13 "The story's interest" is "the 'interest' of its producer (or its consumer)" in protecting "an article of merchandise (the narrative) which has not yet been put on the reading market" (Barthes, *S/Z*, 136, 135).

14 I borrow the concept from Eve Sedgwick's *Between Men: English Literature and Male Homosocial Desire* (New York: Columbia University Press, 1985).

15 Stendhal's *Armance*, the only mal du siècle novel by a male author which is exclusively in the third person, neverthless turns on a *confession manquée*. Only two texts explicitly eschew the male frame of reference or structure of address: Stendhal claims his novel was written by a woman and Balzac's Félix addresses his narrative to Natalie de Manerville, the new object of his affections.

16 Michel Foucault, *The History of Sexuality*, trans. Robert Hurley (New York: Random House, 1980), 61–62.

17 In his statement, René echoes both the words and the sentiment of Rousseau, his pre-Romantic precursor and the paradigm for autobiographical confession: "I cost my mother her life, and my birth was the first of my misfortunes" (*Les Confessions* [Paris: Flammarion, 1968], 45).

18 See Terry Eagleton, *The Rape of Clarissa: Writing, Sexuality, and Class*

Struggle in Samuel Richardson (Minneapolis: University of Minnesota Press, 1982), 95–100.

19 Showalter, "Critical Cross-Dressing," 146.

20 Kirkpatrick, *Las Románticas*, 10.

21 Later Romantic texts follow *René*'s lead by turning attention from the hero's secrets to the heroine's—in *Adolphe* to Ellénore's letter from beyond the grave, in *Le Lys dans la vallée* to the heroine's deathbed confession of her desire, in *La Confession d'un enfant du siècle* to Brigitte's enigmatic behavior and Octave's doubts about her fidelity.

22 Lettre à M. de Fontanes sur la deuxième édition de l'ouvrage de Madame de Staël (quoted in Gilbert Chinard, "Quelques origines littéraires de *René*," *PMLA* 43, no. 1 (Mar. 1928): 301.

23 I borrow the term from Peter Brooks whose work is less concerned with the theatrical subgenre than with melodrama "as a mode of conception and expression, as a certain fictional system for making sense of experience" (*The Melodramatic Imagination: Balzac, Henry James, Melodrama, and the Mode of Excess* [New Haven: Yale University Press, 1976], xiii).

24 Barbara Johnson, *The Critical Difference* (Baltimore: Johns Hopkins University Press, 1980), 9.

25 This tradition dates back much further than the eighteenth century, of course. The epigraph to Rousseau's *La Nouvelle Héloïse*, for example, cites Petrarch as its authorizing intertext: "Non la connobe il mondo, mentre l'ebbe: / Connobill'io ch'a pianger qui rimasi" ("The world possessed her without knowing her / And me, I knew her, I remain here below to mourn her"). For a discussion of the role of female death in fiction see Elizabeth Ermarth, "Fictional Consensus and Female Casualties," in *The Representation of Women in Fiction*, Selected Papers from the English Institute, 1981, ed. Carolyn G. Heilbrun and Margaret R. Higonnet (Baltimore: Johns Hopkins University Press, 1983), 1–18. The obverse—male death and female survival—also occurs but is markedly more rare; see Godelieve Mercken-Spaas, "Death and the Romantic Heroine: Chateaubriand and de Staël," in *Pre-Text/Text/Context: Essays in Nineteenth-Century French Literature*, ed. Robert L. Mitchell (Columbus: Ohio State University Press, 1980), 79–86.

26 A dead woman is the sine qua non in almost every one of the mal du siècle works by men. *Armance*, with its hero's elaborately staged suicide, is one of the few exceptions. Nevertheless, Octave's absence in death does not allow the heroine, Armance, to speak. Despite the novel's title, the third-person narrator, who is left with the task of telling this tale, makes it the hero's story rather than the heroine's.

27 In the eighteenth century, the word "intéressant" was often applied to beautiful (female) victims. See Jacques Truchet's introduction to *Théâtre du XVIIIᵉ siècle* (Paris: Gallimard, 1972), 1: li. The fascination with female victimization was, of course, taken to an extreme in Sade. His first description of Justine, for example, links interest and tears: "Tears ran abundantly from the eyes of that interesting maid" (*Justine ou les malheurs de la vertu* [Paris: Union

Générale d'Editions, 1969], 25). In what is perhaps not an unrelated vein, "situation intéressante" is the euphemism for pregnancy.

28 In the letter announcing her death, René learned that "Sister Amélie of Mercy died a victim of her zeal and charity, while caring for her companions, who had been stricken with a contagious illness. The entire community was inconsolable, and Amélie was regarded as a saint" (174).

29 On the role of the interlocutor in ferreting out the truth of sex from confession through analysis, see Foucault, *History of Sexuality*, 66–67.

30 On the *René* craze in literature and in popular culture, see Chateaubriand, *Mémoires d'outre-tombe*, ed. Pierre Clarac (Paris: Gallimard, 1946), 1: 462; Barbéris, *"René" de Chateaubriand*; and Waller, "Being René, Buying Atala."

31 For Gérard Genette, writing about Flaubert, the whole of modern literature seems to have begun with the *"dedramatization*, one would almost like to say *denovelization* of the novel" (*Figures of Literary Discourse* [New York: Columbia University Press, 1982], 200).

32 Here again, the single exception proves the mal du siècle rule. The 1804 edition of *Obermann* alludes only obliquely to the hero's failed relationship with a woman. In the 1833 "supplement" to the text, however, Senancour added a kind of dream sequence in which the hero explicitly confesses his passion for "Mme Del***" and identifies this fatal weakness as the origin of all the uncertainties that make up the text. The shadowy female figure thus emerges as first cause.

33 For the eighteenth-century sentimental novel in England, according to Janet Todd in *Sensibility: An Introduction*, male sensibility poses a narrative problem: "what to do with the man of feeling who has, in an unfeeling world, avoided manly power" (88–89). Because he is a man, "he cannot be raped and abandoned." Because of his "womanly qualities of tenderness and susceptibility," he will not seduce. These twin impossibilities desexualize his plot (100). The mal du siècle authors, by contrast, resexualize the hero's story by borrowing the sensational demonstration of female vulnerability from what Miller (*The Heroine's Text*) calls "the dysphoric plot" of the eighteenth-century heroine's text.

34 Doris Kadish argues to the contrary that Amélie is, if not virilized, symbolically empowered. See *Politicizing Gender: Narrative Strategies in the Aftermath of the French Revolution* (New Brunswick: Rutgers University Press, 1991), 68–76.

3. *What's Wrong with Mr. Right: Staël's* Corinne, or Italy

1 These and other contradictions complicate analyses of Staël's life and works in modern feminist terms. For an excellent discussion of Staël's views on women to which the following remarks are indebted, see Susan Tenenbaum, "Liberal Heroines: Mme de Staël on the 'Woman Question' and the Modern State," *Annales Benjamin Constant* 5 (1985): 37–52.

2 Despite the glowing description of the brave new private sphere in her essays, in *Corinne* Staël shows the English version of this life, which was already in place, as a living death that serves the paternal order and cripples the spirit of both sexes, a point to which I return.

3 On the importance of liberty in Staël's philosophy see Simone Balayé, *Lumières et liberté* (Paris: Klincksieck, 1978); and Enzo Caramaschi, "Le Point de vue féministe dans la pensée de Mme de Staël," *Voltaire, Mme de Staël, Balzac* (Padua: Liviane, 1977), 137–198.

4 In "*Corinne* et la presse parisienne de 1807," in *Approches des lumières: Mélanges offerts à Jean Fabre* (Paris: Klincksieck, 1974), 1–16, Simone Balayé summarizes some of the articles I analyze at length here. For other readers' responses to the novel, I am indebted to her article, "*Corinne* et les amis de Madame de Staël," *Revue d'histoire littéraire de la France* 66 (Jan. 1966): 139–149.

5 Letters from Audibert (letter dated 1 June 1807) and from Elzéar de Sabran, quoted in Balayé, "Corinne et les amis de Mme de Staël," 140.

6 Corinne served as a model and inspiration for women writers in later years as well, from the French poet Delphine Gay to the American writer Margaret Fuller. See Helen O. Borowitz, "Two Nineteenth-Century Muse Portraits," *Bulletin of the Cleveland Museum of Art* 66, no. 6 (Sept. 1979): 247–267; and Madelyn Gutwirth, *Madame de Staël, Novelist* (Urbana: University of Illinois Press, 1978), 281–285.

7 L'abbé de Féletz, *Journal de l'Empire* (12 May 1807): 3.

8 *Gazette de France* (27 May 1807): 592; the second emphasis is added.

9 See the malicious innuendoes about Staël's sexual identity cited in Gutwirth, *Madame de Staël*, 287.

10 *Mercure de France* (16 May 1807): 323; emphasis added.

11 See Julia Epstein, "Either/Or—Neither/Both: Sexual Ambiguity and the Ideology of Gender," *Genders* 7 (Spring 1990): 99–142.

12 *Mercure de France*, 323.

13 *Gazette de France* (23 May 1807): 574.

14 Miller, *Subject to Change*, 163.

15 *Le Courrier français* (31 May 1807): 2.

16 The essay was never published but has been reproduced, with variants, in Germaine de Staël, *De l'Allemagne*, ed. La comtesse de Pange and Simone Balayé, 2 vols. (Paris: Hachette, 1958), 1: 93–94. In earlier drafts of this essay, Staël acknowledged that the inferiority of the hero was also a problem in her previous novel, *Delphine* (1802).

17 Miller notes that in creating an inadequate hero, Staël joins Isabelle de Charrière in her novels *Caliste* (1788) and *Mistress Henley* (1784), which also build "on a line of problematic men in the novels of eighteenth-century women writers. Oswald joins Riccoboni's Alfred, Ossery and Marquis de Cressy, Tencin's Barbasan and Comminge, as a man insufficiently aware of the superiority of the woman in love with him; and blind to his own flaws" (*Subject to Change*, 198). Staël, however, radically refashions the commonplace

first, by contextualizing and politicizing the hero's failure to measure up, and second, by making the heroine's superiority intellectual and artistic as well as moral.

18 Germaine de Staël, *Corinne, or Italy*, trans. and ed. Avriel H. Goldberger (New Brunswick: Rutgers University Press, 1987), 4. All references to *Corinne* are to this edition.

19 Only Octave in Stendhal's *Armance* is an exception. He is far from heroic or selfless, however. His violent demonstrations of manliness are the risible outbursts of a young man stuck at home in a new industrial age that requires entrepreneurial drive rather than physical prowess from its ruling-class men.

20 Benjamin Constant, "De Madame de Staël et de ses ouvrages," in *Mélanges de littérature et de politique* in *Oeuvres* (Paris: Gallimard, 1957), 869–870. Like Staël, Constant refers to Oswald, a Scotsman, as if he were English and often uses the word "English" loosely to mean "British." Critics do the same and I follow that practice here.

21 The main action of the novel is set in the years from 1794 to 1803 and thus precludes any reference to Bonaparte's coronation in Milan in 1805. Contemporary readers and Napoleon himself perceived the implicit critique and the extent of Staël's ambitious wish for her heroine, however. On the political import of Staël's novel in the Napoleonic context, see Balayé, *Madame de Staël;* and Joan DeJean, *Fictions of Sappho, 1546–1937* (Chicago: University of Chicago Press, 1989), 176–186. On Staël's using her father's triumphant return to Paris in 1789 as a model for her celebration of female genius in fiction, see Jean-Claude Bonnet, "Le musée staëlien," *Littérature* 42 (May 1981): 4–19.

22 See Claudine Herrmann, "Corinne, femme de génie," *Cahiers staëliens,* n.s. 35 (1984): 60–64.

23 Miller, *Subject to Change,* 166–167.

24 Gutwirth, *Madame de Staël,* 230.

25 Miller shows this construction of a place out of time as "a form of resistance to the plausibilities of patriarchal plot." This "desire to control story by refusing its plots . . . constitutes the trope of the woman writer in France par excellence" (*Subject to Change,* 9).

26 Marie-Claire Vallois, *Fictions féminines: Mme de Staël et les voix de la Sibylle* (Saratoga: Anma Libri, 1978), 172.

27 Gutwirth, "*Corinne* et l'esthétique du camée," 243.

28 Miller, *Subject to Change,* 186.

29 Joan DeJean shows this Italian idyll as an homage to the seventeenth century, "the Golden Age of salon activity," and argues that this tension in the novel is between the oral, digressive conversational tradition of the seventeenth-century salon ruled by women and "novelistic development within a fixed, linear chronology" that would dominate the later nineteenth-century novel ("Staël's *Corinne*" 78, 81).

30 See, for example, the blurred distinctions between direct and indirect

discourse, between information and opinion, between heroine and narrator in the passage on Saint Peter's, 57–59. See also Vallois's excellent study of the problems of voice in *Corinne* in *Fictions féminines*, 165–182.

31 *Corinne, ou l'Italie*, ed. Claudine Herrmann, 2 vols. (Paris: des femmes, 1979), 1: 271.

32 Marlene LeGates, "The Cult of Womanhood in Eighteenth-Century Thought," *Eighteenth-Century Studies* 10 (1976): 31. There is only one short scene in *Corinne* (bk. 12, chap. 1) in which the hero's desire threatens to get the better of him. The heroine's strategy is to declare herself ready to submit to Oswald as an indirect—and successful—appeal to his sense of guilt. Thus, in this traditional reenactment of sexual mores, a woman has no sexual desires of her own and is dependent on a man's honor for her sexual protection.

33 For an excellent discussion of Staël's revision of Rousseau's philosophical and fictional premises, see Gutwirth's "Woman as Mediatrix: From Jean-Jacques Rousseau to Germaine de Staël," in *Woman as Mediatrix: Essays on 19th-Century European Women Writers*, ed. Avriel H. Goldberger (New York: Greenwood Press, 1987), 13–29, and her "Madame de Staël, Rousseau, and the Woman Question," *PMLA* 86, no. 1 (1971): 100–109.

34 Janine Rossard, *Pudeur et romantisme* (Paris: Nizet, 1982), 50. She associates this movement with Mme Cottin, Chateaubriand, Mme de Krudener, Balzac, Musset, and Sand as well as Staël.

35 Mercken-Spaas, "Death and the Romantic Heroine."

36 Gérard Gengembre and Jean Goldzink, "L'Opinion dans *Corinne*," *Europe* 64 (Jan.–Feb. 1987), 53.

37 Tony Tanner, *Adultery in the Novel: Contract and Transgression* (Baltimore: Johns Hopkins University Press, 1979), 101–102.

38 Staël's hero worship of her own father, who had died in 1804, three years before *Corinne* was published, complicates any understanding of her critique of the paternal. See Charlotte Hogsett, *The Literary Existence of Germaine de Staël* (Carbondale: Southern Illinois University Press, 1987), 33–35 and Bonnet, "Le musée staëlien," 4–10.

39 *La Revue philosophique* (11 June 1807): 474.

40 *Le Courrier français* (31 May 1807): 2.

41 In *Refiguring the Father: New Feminist Readings of Patriarchy* (Carbondale: Southern Illinois University Press, 1989), Patricia Yaeger and Beth Kowaleski-Wallace argue that contemporary feminist critics would do well to "reconcile a Lacanian view of a disembodied, 'dead' father with a historical view that is reflective of psychic experiences and configurations and yet, at the same time, . . . rooted in history" (xv). In reaction to the univocal and ahistorical vision of patriarchy in some feminist criticism, the contributors to the volume stress its particular psychological and historical configuration within specific texts. It is precisely through its representation of "a disembodied, 'dead' father," I am arguing, that Staël's novel gives riveting fictional form to both sides of this "new" feminist critical coin.

42 *Le Courrier français* (29 May 1807): 3.

43 On love and passion in Staël, see Gutwirth, "Forging a Vocation"; Jean

Starobinski, "Suicide et mélancolie chez Mme de Staël," in *Mme de Staël et l'Europe* (Paris: Klincksieck, 1970), 242–252; and Caramaschi, "Le Point de vue féministe."

44 The critique of idolatry will be a common theme in Sand's *Lélia* as well. There, it is a lesson the heroine must teach the hero.

45 See Anne Louis Anton Mooij, *Caractères principaux et tendances des romans psychologiques chez quelques femmes auteurs de Mme Riccoboni à Mme de Souza, 1757–1826* (Groningen: Drukkerij de Waal, 1949), 11–12.

46 Hermann, "Corinne, femme de gènie," 75.

47 For example, in his defense of Staël's novel, Constant stresses the terrible loneliness of the genius in a hostile society. He is forced to "learn how to live alone, suffer alone, be scornful alone" ("De Madame de Staël," 868). He downplays the *other* side of the equation to which Staël gives so much emphasis in the first half of the novel: the exhilarating empowerment that comes with the exercise of exceptional talent in a supportive community.

48 Kirkpatrick, *Las Románticas*, 31.

49 Whereas I stress Corinne's (and Staël's) control over discourse, Vallois offers a very different and persuasive interpretation of these moments of aphasia, which she sees as typical of all of Staël's female protagonists. See especially "Les Voi(es) de la Sibylle," *Stanford French Review* 6 (1982), 35–48.

50 See Rogers, "Wasting Away."

51 *Mercure de France* (16 May 1807): 324; emphasis added.

52 *Gazette de France* (27 May 1807): 592.

53 Lawrence Lipking, "Aristotle's Sister: A Poetics of Abandonment," in *Canons*, ed. Robert von Hallberg (Chicago: University of Chicago Press, 1983), 98.

54 Letter from Adrien de Mun (12 May 1807), quoted in Balayé, "*Corinne* et les amis de Madame de Staël," 144. As I have mentioned, however, later readers, primarily women, made Corinne an empowering model for their own ambitious and artistic wishes.

55 *Journal du commerce* (30 May 1807): 595; emphasis added.

56 Balayé, "*Corinne* et les amis de Madame de Staël," 145.

57 *Gazette de France* (23 May 1807): 575.

4. The Double Bind of Liberalism in Constant's Adolphe

1 Benjamin Constant, *Oeuvres*, ed. A. Roulin (Paris: Gallimard, 1957), 1596.

2 See Guy Howard Dodge, *Benjamin Constant's Philosophy of Liberalism: A Study in Politics and Religion* (Chapel Hill: University of North Carolina Press, 1980). For a critical assessment of Dodge's book and other works, see George Armstrong Kelly, "Constant and His Interpreters: A Second Visit," *Annales Benjamin Constant* 6 (1986): 81–89.

3 Nevertheless, Norman King reads the novel politically and shows the novel as a failed attempt to find a liberal alternative to aristocratic reaction and bourgeois self-interest in "Structures et stratégies d'*Adolphe*," in *Benjamin*

Constant, Madame de Staël, et le groupe de Coppet, ed. Etienne Hofmann (Oxford: The Voltaire Foundation, 1982), 275–283. See also Michèle Vialet, "*Adolphe*: Echec en amour ou temporisation politique," *Annales Benjamin Constant* 5 (1985): 53–73.

4 The heroine's death, however, is the coup de grâce the text saves for its dramatic end.

5 Benjamin Constant, *Adolphe,* trans. L. W. Tancock (Harmondsworth, Middlesex: Penguin Books, 1964), 64. References to *Adolphe,* unless otherwise indicated, are to this edition.

6 Benjamin Constant, *Adolphe,* ed. Paul Delbouille (Paris: "Les Belles Lettres," 1977), 246.

7 *Adolphe,* ed. Delbouille, 103. On libertinism and determinism, see Nancy K. Miller's analysis of the famous libertine trope, "Il n'y a que le premier pas qui coûte," in "*Les Liaisons dangereuses*: Pas à pas," *Modern Language Studies* 12 (1982): 45–46.

8 See the discussion of this paradox in Theodora Zemek, "Benjamin Constant, Adam Smith and the 'moule universel': The Impartial Spectator and His Social Framework," *Annales Benjamin Constant* 7 (1987): 49–63. On mechanistic inevitability in Constant's work, see Frank Paul Bowman, "Benjamin Constant et l'histoire," in *Benjamin Constant,* ed. Etienne Hofmann, 129–150.

9 *Adolphe,* ed. Delbouille, 103; emphasis added.

10 Constant insisted on the cliché of woman's exclusive dependence on love despite his relationship with the century's most salient exception to this rule. For a discussion of this and other contradictions in Constant's writings on love, see Tzvetan Todorov, "Benjamin Constant: Politique et amour," *Poétique* 14, no. 56 (1983): 485–510.

11 Comments such as these reveal the male bias inherent in the "universal" man invoked in Constant's political writings (see *Collection complète des ouvrages publiés sur le gouvernement représentatif et la constitution actuelle de la France, formant une espèce de Cours de politique constitutionnelle,* 4 vols. [Paris: 1818–1820], 1: 317), quoted in Kurt Mueller-Vollmer, "Politique et esthétique: L'idéalisme concret de Benjamin Constant, Guillaume de Humboldt et Madame de Staël," in *Benjamin Constant, Madame de Staël, et le groupe de Coppet,* ed. Etienne Hofmann (Oxford: Voltaire Foundation, 1982), 455.

12 J.-K. Huysmans thus ridicules novels of seduction in his preface to *A Rebours* (Paris: 10/18, 1975), 26.

13 See Michel Gilot and Jean Sgard, "La Vie intérieure et les mots," 509–528; and Pierre Deguise, "Benjamin Constant, romantique froid?" 182–195, both in *Le Préromantisme: Hypothèse ou hypothèque,* ed. Paul Vialleneix (Paris: Klincksieck, 1975).

14 The novel, she maintains, is a practice of the ambivalent sign rather than the univocal symbol and, as such, marks the advent of psychology in literature (Julia Kristeva, "The Bounded Text," in *Desire in Language: A Semiotic Approach to Literature and Art,* trans. Thomas Gora, Alice Jardine, and

Leon S. Roudiez; ed. Leon S. Roudiez [New York: Columbia University Press, 1980], 48–49).

15 Chateaubriand, *Génie du christianisme*, cited in the preface to *René* (Paris: Garnier-Flammarion, 1964), 63.

16 For an excellent analysis of the maxim as self-justification disguised as neutrality, see Colette Coman, "Le Paradoxe de la maxime dans *Adolphe*," *Romanic Review* 73 (1982): 195–208.

17 Diary entry, 28 Nov. 1806, quoted in Delbouille, introduction to *Adolphe*, 15; emphasis added. This abandonment of one woman for another is precisely what Staël's hero would do in *Corinne*.

18 Diary entries, 24 Feb. 1807 and 28 May 1807, quoted in Delbouille, introduction to *Adolphe*, 16; emphasis added.

19 Peter Brooks, "Freud's Masterplot," *Reading for the Plot: Design and Intention in Narrative* (New York: Knopf, 1984), 97–98.

20 As in the libertine text, "the master is he who speaks" (Roland Barthes, *Sade/Fourier/Loyola*, trans. Richard Miller [New York: Hill and Wang, 1976], 31).

21 See George Moskos, "Editing Ellénore: The Disappearing Feminine in Constant's *Adolphe*," unpublished essay.

22 See Marian Hobson, "Theme and Structure in *Adolphe*," *Modern Language Review* 66 (1971): 312.

23 The most notable examples from the pre-*Adolphe* repertoire are *Manon Lescaut, La Nouvelle Héloïse, Atala*, and *Corinne*.

24 Brooks, "Freud's Masterplot," 109.

25 Perhaps we have yet to take the full measure of the fact that a man's death, by contrast, rarely is the premise for a woman's text.

26 For a critique of the male bias implicit in "sexual" theories of narrative and notions of reading pleasure, see Susan Winnett, "Coming Unstrung: Women, Men, Narrative, and Principles of Pleasure," *PMLA* 105 (May 1990): 505–518.

27 Terry Eagleton, "Text, Ideology, Realism," in *Literature and Society*, Selected Papers from the English Institute, 1978, ed. Edward W. Said (Baltimore: Johns Hopkins University Press, 1980), 161.

28 According to Kristeva, this process of inclusion as exclusion characterizes the role of woman in the novel from its beginnings ("The Bounded Text," 49–50).

29 Martha Noel Evans, "*Adolphe*'s Appeal to the Reader, " *Romanic Review* 73 (May 1982): 312.

30 See Georges Pholien, "*Adolphe* et son public," *Revue d'histoire littéraire de la France* 85 (Jan.–Feb. 1985): 18–25. See also Evans, "*Adolphe*'s Appeal," 302–303.

31 *Morning Chronicle* (23 June 1816), rpt. in *Adolphe*, ed. Delbouille, 265; emphasis added.

32 To add one more level of doubt to an already duplicitous discourse, no extant evidence corroborates his claim. See *Adolphe*, ed. Delbouille, 217.

33 Alison Fairlie, "Framework as a Suggestive Art in Constant's *Adolphe*," *Australian Journal of French Studies* 16 (1979): 12, 16.

34 On the "missing woman" in *Adolphe* as well as in critical interpretations of the novel, see Eve Gonin's rewriting of it, *Le Point de vue d'Ellénore: Une réécriture d' "Adolphe"* (Paris: Corti, 1981). See also Moskos, "Editing Ellénore."

5. *Taking the Woman's Part: Stendhal's* Armance

1 Dated 20 June 1825, *Courrier anglais*, ed. Henri Martineau, 5 vols. (Paris: Le Divan, 1935–1936), 1: 164.

2 Dated 18 Mar. 1825, *Courrier anglais*, 5: 29–30.

3 Stendhal, *Armance, ou quelques scènes d'un salon de Paris en 1827*, ed. Henri Martineau (Paris: Garnier, 1962), 261.

4 *Armance*, 262 and 263.

5 See Stendhal, *La Comédie est impossible en 1836*, in *Mélanges* II: *Journalisme* (Genève: Cercle du Bibliophile, 1972), 256ff, and Jean-Jacques Labia, "Le Recours au roman, ou l'impossibilité de la comédie au dix-neuvième siècle: L'Expérience inaugurale de Stendhal," in *Proceedings of the Xth Congress of the International Comparative Literature Association*, ed. Anna Balakian (New York: Garland, 1985), 1: 11–15.

6 Dated 1 Dec. 1825, *Courrier anglais*, 2: 333.

7 See Stendhal, *D'un nouveau complot contre les industriels* (Paris: Sautelet, 1825).

8 Dated 18 Dec. 1825, pub. Jan. 1826, *Courrier anglais*, 2: 396.

9 Dated 1 June 1825, *Courrier anglais* 2: 352. See also his remarks, 18 Jan. 1826, pub. Feb. 1826, *Courrier anglais* 2: 426–427.

10 Dated 1 July 1824, *Courrier anglais* 2: 182.

11 On the publishing history, see for example Henri Martineau's introduction to *Armance*, iii.

12 In a February 1826 review of Latouche's novel in *New Monthly Magazine*, *Courrier anglais* 2: 421–428.

13 For examples, see E. A. Férard. "*Olivier* par Mme la duchesse de Duras," *Le Figaro* (25 Jan., 1 Feb. 1930), n.p. Beyle's assertion that Duras in fact wrote Latouche's 1826 *Olivier* was disproved by the discovery of her own *Olivier* manuscript, published by Denise Virieux (Paris: Corti, 1971) who gives an informative history of the controversy.

14 On Duras, see Claudine Herrmann's introduction to *Ourika* (Paris: des femmes, 1979); Chantal Bertrand-Jennings, "Condition féminine et impuissance sociale: Les romans de la duchesse de Duras," *Romantisme* 63 (1989), 39–50, and G. Pailhès, *La Duchesse de Duras et Chateaubriand, d'après des documents inédits* (Paris: Perrin, 1910).

15 Stendhal, *Armance, or Scenes from a Parisian Salon in 1827*, trans. Gilbert and Suzanne Sale (London: Merlin, 1960), 5. References to *Armance* are to this edition.

16 See Jean-Jacques Hamm, "Stendhal et Chateaubriand: Analyse d'une

influence," in *Stendhal et le romantisme*, ed. V. del Litto et al. (Aran, Switz.: Editions du Grand Chêne, 1984), 103–112.

17 Dated 1 June 1825, *Courrier anglais* 2: 352.

18 See Yves Ancel, "Stendhal et l'invention des 'Happy Few,'" *Elséneur: Cahiers de la modernité* 2 (Dec. 1983): 110–132.

19 See Norbert Sclippa, *Texte et idéologie: Images de la noblesse et de la bourgeoisie dans le roman français des années 1750 à 1830* (New York: Peter Lang, 1987), 201–223.

20 For a detailed comparison of *Armance*'s opening lines with those in *Manon Lescaut, Les Egarements du coeur et de l'esprit*, and *Adolphe*, see Michel Crouzet, "Le Réel dans *Armance*: Passions et société, ou le cas d'Octave: Etude et essai d'interprétation," in *Le Réel et le texte* (Paris: Armand Colin, 1974), 31 ff.

21 In other words, he foregoes his male prerogative of mobility for a feminizing immobility. In the nineteenth-century literary representation of sexual difference, immobility characterizes the female lot. See Schor, *Breaking the Chain*, esp. chap. 8, "Unwriting *Lamiel*."

22 Though in his journalism, Stendhal makes claims for the widespread nature of the mal du siècle phenomenon, none of the other characters in the novel, including Armance who otherwise resembles him closely, suffer from this malady. The novel as genre thus continues to explore the individual male as exception even as it implies a more general sociopolitical rule.

23 Unlike the previous texts of the mal du siècle, where the mother was a missing link in the son's failed bonding with the father, in *Armance*, the primary bond is that between mother and son.

24 For a short moment in the text, the ideal mother's marital fidelity is in question, but the men she brings home on the sly soon prove to be the doctors she will hire to diagnose her son. In what will be a pattern throughout the novel, all secrets, all desires, return to the son, who maintains his place as center of attention and object of concern.

25 Leo Bersani, *Balzac to Beckett: Center and Circumference in French Fiction* (New York: Oxford University Press, 1970), 102–103. Lucien Leuwen's father is a notable exception.

26 Sigmund Freud, "Creative Writers and Day-Dreaming," in *The Standard Edition of the Complete Psychological Works of Sigmund Freud*, trans. James Strachey, 24 vols. (London: Hogarth Press, 1957), 9: 149.

27 Bersani, *Balzac to Beckett*, 100.

28 For Pierre Bayard, *Armance* is the story of a son's resistance to his mother's paranoid desire that he tell her all. The power struggle between them is merely repeated when the hero falls in love with the mother substitute, Armance. See *Symptôme de Stendhal: Armance et l'aveu* (Paris: Lettres Modernes, 1979), 37, 42.

29 Sand will give a feminist twist to this rage in *Lélia*.

30 On Stendhal's *Armance* as a critique of emerging capitalism and an outmoded aristocracy, see Pierre Barbéris, "Mal du siècle," 172–173.

31 Barbéris argues that reproduction is a duty that Octave, for political reasons, decides he will not perform. See Pierre Barbéris, "*Armance*, Armance: Quelle impuissance?" in *Stendhal*, ed. Philippe Berthier (Paris: Aux Amateurs de Livres, 1984), 67–86.

32 George M. Rosa, "Writing the World: *Armance* and Byron's *Don Juan*," *Studi francesi* 31 (May–Aug. 1987): 219.

33 Eric Gans notes, "'Duty' imposes on Octave an experience of the moment that is detemporalized and 'thematic'; his forbidden desire for Armance privileges despite his intentions the narrative present" ("Le Secret d'Octave: Secret de Stendhal, secret du roman," *Revue des Sciences Humaines* 40, no. 157 [Jan.-Mar., 1975]: 87).

34 On a similar note, in his letter to Mérimée about *Armance*, Stendhal regrets all the "true things [that] are beyond the reach of art! For instance the love inspired by a man without arms or legs" (214). Stendhal's example underscores the fantasy underlying not only his own fiction of the male malady but mal du siècle literature as a whole. No matter what the man's problem, which is usually not a physical disability but an emotionally crippling self-centeredness, there is one certainty upon which he can depend: the love of a woman. A similar pattern holds true for Byron's heroes as well. Man can do no wrong that will make him unattractive to woman. See George M. Rosa, "Byronism and 'Babilanisme' in *Armance*," *Modern Language Review* 77 (1982): 804.

35 Katharine Jensen, "Sex and Sensibility in *Armance*," unpublished essay.

36 Juliet Flower MacCannell, "Stendhal's Woman," *Semiotica* 48 (1984): 160.

37 In Larousse's *Grand dictionnaire du XIXe siècle*, a discussion of the physiology of sexual impotence is followed by no less than six "anecdotes" recording the comical situations and witticisms to which male impotence is said to give rise. The comedic temptation is also evident, as we have seen, in Stendhal's ribald (re)writing of the untellable impotence plot in his letter to Mérimée; it appears as well in the "detachable" chapter on impotence in *De l'amour* entitled "Des fiascos," which Stendhal planned to censure in the 150 copies destined for his female readers and the general public. See *De l'amour*, ed. Henri Martineau (Paris: Garnier Frères, 1959), xxiv-xxvi.

38 *Armance* (*Romans et nouvelles*, ed. Henri Martineau, [Paris: Gallimard, 1952], 1429).

39 For an excellent discussion of Stendhal's vexed search for a public responsive to his work, to which my own discussion here is indebted, see Ellen Constans, "Stendhal et le public impossible," in *Stendhal: L'Écrivain, la société et le pouvoir*, ed. Philippe Berthier (Grenoble: Presses Universitaires de Grenoble, 1984), 33–55.

40 Constans thus summarizes Stendhal's mocking rendition of the genre in his English journalism ("Stendhal," 44). Stendhal's remarks come from an 1832 letter he wrote to Count Salvagnoli about his next novel, *Le Rouge et le noir*.

41 *Romans et nouvelles*, 702, 703.

42 *Romans et nouvelles*, 1428; emphasis added.

6. Toward a Feminist Mal du Siècle: Sand's Lélia

1 A year later, when Sand's identity became known, one of the critics rehearses the stereotypes of femininity while he attempts to get over the shock: "Having read and reread [the novel], I am absolutely speechless with amazement to think that a woman wrote it, a delicate and frail woman prey to the admirable gift for writing, that a simple woman, with tears in her voice and heart, was able to cast this steady gaze on society," *Journal des débats* (21 July 1832), quoted in Françoise Van Rossum-Guyon, "A propos d'*Indiana*: La Préface de 1832, problèmes du métadiscours," in *George Sand*, Colloque de Cerisy, ed. Simone Vierne (Paris: SEDES, 1983), 76. Sandy Petrey notes that for some critics, Sand's novel and her choice of pseudonym allowed them to begin thinking of gender as a social construction, which is also, he argues, the lesson of Sand's realist text ("George and Georgina Sand: Realist Gender in *Indiana*," in *Sexuality and Textuality*, eds. Judith Still and Michael Worten [Manchester: Manchester University Press, forthcoming]).

2 H. Boussuge, review of *Indiana, Cabinet de lecture* (24 June 1832), 13.

3 For her short story "La Marquise" (1832), Sand had chosen Georges, the French version of this masculine given name.

4 "Roman intime" is a term coined by Sainte-Beuve in 1832 in his "Du roman intime ou Mademoiselle de Liron," *Oeuvres* (Paris: Gallimard, 1960) 2: 1007–1024. In "George Sand et le roman intime: Tradition and Innovation in 'Women's Literature,'" in *George Sand: Collected Essays*, ed. Janis Glasgow [Troy, N.Y.: Whitston, 1985], 220–226), Lucy McCallum Schwartz argues that while Sand owes much to this tradition, she nevertheless transforms both its means and its ends.

5 On similarities between *Lélia* and the works of Senancour, Nodier, and Balzac, see Pierre Reboul, introduction to *Lélia* (Paris: Garnier, 1960), lviii–lxv, who makes much of the novel's debt to the works of Sand's contemporaries without taking enough account of its significant differences from them. For an excellent discussion of *Lélia* and the genre question, see Isabelle Hoog Naginski, *George Sand: Writing for Her Life* (New Brunswick: Rutgers University Press, 1991), 107–114, which appeared after I completed this book.

6 First published in *Revue des Deux Mondes* (15 June 1833), then printed as a preface to the novel in 1840; see George Sand, preface to Senancour, *Obermann* (Paris: Charpentier, 1874), 3. When Sand refers to the general reading public, she does not ever say explicitly that she means men; nevertheless, the experiences she attributes to this "universal" reader—service in the military and the government—were in nineteenth-century France exclusively male.

7 Duras's *Ourika* is an exception. See the discussion in Chapter 1.

8 Ellen Moers, *Literary Women: The Great Writers* (Garden City, N.Y.: Anchor, 1977), 200.

9 It is perhaps this need to counterbalance a woman's clear superiority with inferiority that explains one aspect of a continuing cultlike fascination for Sand and, in particular, her life. Biographers and critics alike stand in awe of Sand's emotional strength, sexual appetite, and prolific productivity. And yet they read *Lélia* as both a flimsily disguised account of the severe depression she suffered in the early 1830s and an adequate metaphor for her life as a whole. André Maurois consecrated this reductive parallel when he entitled his biography *Lélia, ou la vie de George Sand*. This equation opts for the metaphor of severe emotional and sexual debilitation over a more complicated figure that would combine pain with power and productivity. As Sand did for Lélia, her biographers have done for her: the powerful woman must be rendered impotent if she is to retain her status as an awesome yet reassuring cult figure.

10 Sand, "A propos de *Lélia* et de *Valentine*," preface to *Romans et nouvelles* (1834); rpt. in Sand, *Questions d'art et de littérature* (Paris: Calmann-Lévy, 1878), 51.

11 While Sand's first two novels are in many ways daring revisions of these traditions, the radical formal iconoclasm and subversive critique in *Lélia* shows the degree to which they were nevertheless fundamentally conventional.

12 See Wayne Booth, *The Rhetoric of Fiction* (Chicago: University of Chicago Press, 1961), 138. I borrow the term "implied reader" in order to distinguish between this construct, the actual reader of the text, and what Susan Suleiman and Inge Crosman, in their anthology of modern theories of audience and interpretation, call the "reader in the text" (Susan Suleiman and Inge Crosman, eds., *The Reader in the Text* [Princeton: Princeton University Press, 1980]).

13 My use of the terms alludes to Courtivron's article "Weak Men and Fatal Women." Courtivron argues that the image of George Sand was partially responsible for the notion of woman as an exotic and satanic femme fatale in nineteenth-century literature and the popular imagination. Inasmuch as contemporary readers saw *Lélia* as the author's own personal confession, Sand's third novel played a key role in this mythology.

14 George Sand, *Lélia*, trans. Maria Espinosa (Bloomington: Indiana University Press, 1978), 3. References to *Lélia* are to this edition.

15 Quoted in Reboul's introduction to *Lélia*,, xxvii.

16 On the question of idealism, realism, and feminism, I am indebted to Naomi Schor's two essays on the subject, "*Lélia* and the Failures of Allegory," *L'Esprit Créateur* 29 (Fall 1989), 76–83, and "Idealism in the Novel: Recanonizing Sand," *Yale French Studies* 75 (1988): 56–73. See also her latest work, *George Sand and Idealism*, forthcoming from Columbia University Press.

17 Schor, "*Lélia*," 80.

18 While many of the other characters in the novel resist their mystifica-

tion in one way or another, none of them make idealization anywhere near as problematic as the heroine does.

19 Schor, "Idealism in the Novel," 73.

20 On this ambiguity, see Naomi Schor, "The Scandal of Realism," in *A New History of French Literature*, ed. Denis Hollier (Cambridge: Harvard University Press, 1989), 656–661.

21 On woman as statue in the work of male novelists, see Schor who notes that in mid-nineteenth-century French literature, "woman's literariness seems to be bound up with her being turned into marble, her enigmatization" (*Breaking the Chain*, 45).

22 Refusing woman's usual role as object of male desire in male bonding, Lélia nevertheless acts as an intermediary in an attempt at this process, telling one man's story for and to another. She does so, however, as we shall see, in her own desire to create an asexual ménage à trois.

23 The passage in brackets does not appear in Espinosa's translation of *Lélia*; I have included it in my translation, a practice I shall follow throughout this chapter.

24 Miller sees Sand's "transposition of the recital from the academy in Florence to the Capitol in Rome" as a tribute to "the power of the female poet Staël created" and "a tribute to the public authority of the precursor's text" in *Subject to Change*, 195.

25 On Lélia as a phallic figure, see Naomi Schor, "Female Fetishism: The Case of George Sand," *Poetics Today* 6, nos. 1–2 (1985): 306.

26 The following discussion shows how the hero's definition of love becomes more and more restrictive until, finally, it denotes heterosexual love at its most incurably romantic and explicitly sexual.

27 The condemnation of love as idolatry was already a leitmotif of nineteenth-century French literature; for examples from Senancour, Nodier, and Balzac, see notes to the Garnier edition of *Lélia*, 56. I am contending, however, that Sand gives a feminist twist to this critique of idolatrous love. See also Mireille Bossis, "L'homme dieu ou l'idole brisée dans les romans de G. Sand," 179–187; and Nadine Dormoy-Savage, "Identité et mimétisme dans quelques romans de George Sand," 159–169, both in *George Sand*, Colloque de Cerisy, ed. Simone Vierne (Paris: SEDES, 1983).

28 Reboul, notes to *Lélia*, 60.

29 Eileen Boyd Sivert, "*Lélia* and Feminism," *Yale French Studies* 62 (1981): 55.

30 For a different, biographical interpretation of Sand's female Oedipus complex see Kathryn J. Crecelius, introduction to *Family Romances: George Sand's Early Novels* (Bloomington: Indiana University Press, 1987), 1–22.

31 We do not learn its causes, however, until Lélia's narrative within a narrative in part 3.

32 See Susan Gubar, "The Birth of the Artist as Heroine: (Re)Production, the *Künstlerroman* Tradition, and the Fiction of Katherine Mansfield," in *The Representation of Women in Fiction*, Selected Papers from the English Institute,

1981, ed. Carolyn G. Heilbrun and Margaret R. Higonnet (Baltimore: Johns Hopkins University Press, 1983), 19–59, and Grace Stewart, *A New Mythos: The Novel of the Artist as Heroine, 1877–1977* (St. Albans, Vt.: Eden Press, 1979).

33 Shelley I. Temchin, "Straining the Structures of Romanticism: George Sand's *Lélia* Reconsidered" (Ph.D. diss., Tufts University, 1981), 24.

34 I am grateful to Rachel Kranz for this insight.

35 Unlike Balzac's Foedora in *La Peau de chagrin* whose coldness is a wall she consciously interposes between herself and others, we learn from Lélia's confession to Pulchérie that her frigidity is an infirmity suffered from within. Through Lélia's first-person narrative Sand turns the *femme froide* paradigm inside out. She presents the heroine not as a stereotyped enigmatic object but as a unique and tormented subject. To explain Lélia's incapacity through a narrative of cause and effect is to create sympathy for an otherwise unsympathetic travesty on the culture's definition of womanhood as the capacity for loving a man. For a comparison of Lélia and Foedora, see Nadine Lemoine-Guéry, "La femme froide chez Honoré de Balzac et George Sand," *Présence de George Sand* 14 (June 1982): 46–52.

36 The criticism of love as idolatry is a recurring motif in Sand's novels. Mireille Bossis notes that Sand uses the metaphor of the broken idol fourteen times in *Lélia* alone. ("L'homme dieu," 179).

37 See Regina Bochenek-Franczakowa, "Quelques Aspects du 'féminisme' dans les premiers romans de George Sand (1832–1834)," *Romanica Wratislaviensia* 10 (1975): 88.

38 Susan Suleiman, *Authoritarian Fictions: The Ideological Novel as a Literary Genre* (New York: Columbia University Press, 1983), 74–75.

39 Once again in the novel, sexual desire is linked with a deathly violence. Inasmuch as Lélia is less a body than a voice, she must not only be wrested from life but above all be silenced.

40 Nancy Rogers notes that unlike the angelic Romantic heroines who waste away "in a quiet, lingering fashion," "more assertive, aggressive women such as Lélia in *Lélia*, Valérie Marneffe in *La Cousine Bette*, and Flore in *La Rabouilleuse*, tend to be assigned more violent, exotic deaths" ("Wasting Away," 252–253).

41 Leslie Rabine makes this point about *Indiana* in "George Sand and the Myth of Femininity," *Women and Literature* 4, no. 2 (Fall 1976): 14.

42 For a feminist analysis of the ending of *Valentine*, see Miller, *Subject to Change*, 219–223.

43 *Le Journal général de la littérature de France*, (1833), quoted in Reboul *Lélia* (Garnier ed.), 586.

44 C. Feuillide, *L'Europe littéraire* (22 Aug. 1833), 70.

45 Charles Augustin Sainte-Beuve, *Les Grands Ecrivains français, XIXe siècle, Les Romanciers*, 2 vols., ed. Maurice Allem (Paris: Garnier, 1927), 2: 68. References to Sainte-Beuve are to this edition.

46 George Sand, "A propos de *Lélia* et de *Valentine*," 48.

47 Sivert, "*Lélia*," 48.

48 Temchin, "Straining the Structures," 87.

49 Hélène Cixous, "The Laugh of the Medusa," trans. Keith Cohen and Paula Cohen, *Signs* (Summer 1976): 885.

50 Ellen Moers, foreword to *Lélia*, trans. Maria Espinosa, vii.

51 Diane Johnson, "The I as Female: Elizabeth Hardwick," *Terrorists and Novelists* (New York: Knopf, 1982), 26. According to Sainte-Beuve, Sand herself was exceptional for similar reasons. "No one ever gambled more candidly in this perilous game of life," he writes. The male critic lauds the woman writer for playing life straight and taking it like a man. He notes "the audacity of her undertaking," and praises the work's daring as a compensation for its flaws: "*Lélia*, with its defects and excesses, is a book that richly deserved the risk" (2: 73).

Epilogue

1 Christine Planté, *La Petite Soeur de Balzac: Essai sur la femme auteur* (Paris: Seuil, 1989), 17.

2 Naomi Schor, *Breaking the Chain*, 30.

3 Isabelle de Courtivron studies this phenomenon in "Weak Men and Fatal Women." She cites, among others, the amazon Marie de Verneuil in *Les Chouans* by Balzac (1829), the hermaphroditic Camille of Latouche's *Fragoletta* (1829), Mathilde de la Môle in *Le Rouge et le noir* (1830), and Mariquita in *La Fille aux yeux d'or* by Balzac (1834–1835).

4 Schor, *Breaking the Chain*, 30.

5 *Maladies du siècle* (1835), a collection of three novellas by Edouard Alletz, took the phenomenon as its theme and title. For a thorough survey of these works, see Glyn Holmes, who considers them in light of Constant's *Adolphe* rather than Chateaubriand's *René* in *The Adolphe Type in French Fiction*.

6 See Joachim Merlant, *Le Roman personnel de Rousseau à Fromentin* (Paris: Hachette, 1905).

7 Alfred de Musset, *La Confession d'un enfant du siècle*, ed. Maurice Allem (Paris: Garnier, 1968), 129. References are to this edition.

8 Amaury explicitly identifies his problem as an anxiety about his own masculinity and virility. His fear that his penis was deformed was, he claims, the "reason for my errors and the all too lengthy deviation that was my life" (Sainte-Beuve, *Volupté*, 45). The three lines of ellipses that mark the revelation of this secret in Sainte-Beuve's text call attention to that which cannot be said about men and their bodies even as they recall the figurative ellipsis of the hero's presumed sexual impotence in Stendhal's *Armance*.

9 This is not to say that Musset's reading of history in chapter 2 completely ignores the woman question, but he sees women's attitudes and the relations between men and women as one symptom or consequence among many, not a primary cause. See *La Confession*, 11–12.

10 Naomi Segal, *Narcissus and Echo*, 109.

11 Barbara Spackman, *Decadent Genealogies: The Rhetoric of Sickness from Baudelaire to D'Annunzio* (Ithaca: Cornell University Press, 1989), 80.

12 See Annelise Maugue, *L'identité masculine en crise au tournant du siècle* (Paris: Rivages, 1987); Elaine Showalter, *Sexual Anarchy: Gender and Culture at the Fin de Siècle* (New York: Viking, 1990).

13 See Elaine Showalter, *The Female Malady: Women, Madness, and English Culture, 1830–1980* (New York: Penguin, 1987); Sandra Gilbert and Susan Gubar, *No Man's Land: The Place of the Woman Writer in the Twentieth Century*, vol. 1: *The War of the Words* (New Haven: Yale University Press, 1988); and Kaja Silverman, "Historical Trauma and Male Subjectivity," *Psychoanalysis and Cinema*, ed. E. Ann Kaplan (New York: Routledge, 1990), 110–127. Frank Lentricchia's recent criticism of Gilbert and Gubar's work on male writers and impotence suggests that some contemporary male critics fear that the presence of women and the influence of feminism has feminized them and "their" domain (Lentricchia, "Patriarchy against Itself—The Young Manhood of Wallace Stevens," *Critical Inquiry* 13 [Summer 1987]: 742–786). If, as Gilbert and Gubar's response would contend, the complaint of this new masculinist criticism is that women have failed "to attend to the sufferings of men," then this uncanny echo of the mal du siècle refrain suggests that the critical backlash may have only just begun. See "The Man on the Dump versus the United Dames of America; or, What Does Frank Lentricchia Want?" *Critical Inquiry* 14 (Winter 1988), 404.

Works Cited

Alletz, Edouard. *Maladies du siècle*. Paris: Gosselin, 1835.

Ancel, Yves. "Stendhal et l'invention des 'Happy Few.'" *Elséneur: Cahiers de la modernité* 2 (Dec. 1983): 110–132.

Balayé, Simone. "*Corinne* et les amis de Madame de Staël." *Revue d'histoire littéraire de la France* 66 (Jan. 1966): 139–149.

———. "*Corinne* et la presse parisienne de 1807." In *Approches des lumières: Mélanges offerts à Jean Fabre*. Paris: Klincksieck, 1974. 1–16.

———. *Madame de Staël: Lumières et liberté*. Paris: Klincksieck, 1978.

Barbéris, Pierre. *A la recherche d'une écriture: Chateaubriand*. Paris: Mame, 1974.

———. "*Armance*, Armance: Quelle impuissance?" *Stendhal*. Ed. Philippe Berthier. Paris: Aux Amateurs de Livres, 1984. 67–86.

———. *Balzac et le mal du siècle: Contribution à une physiologie du monde moderne*. 2 vols. Paris: Gallimard, 1970.

———. "Mal du siècle ou d'un romantisme de droite à un romantisme de gauche." *Romantisme et politique, 1815–1841*. Colloque de l'Ecole Normale Supérieure de Saint-Cloud. Paris: Armand Colin, 1969. 164–82.

———. "Mme de Staël: Du romantisme, de la littérature et de la France nouvelle." *Europe* 64 (Jan.–Feb. 1987): 6–22.

———. "*René*" de Chateaubriand: Un nouveau roman*. Paris: Larousse, 1973.

Barthes, Roland. *Sade/Fourier/Loyola*. Trans. Richard Miller. New York: Hill and Wang, 1976.

———. *S/Z*. Trans. Richard Miller. New York: Farrar, Straus and Giroux, 1974.

Bayard, Pierre. *Symptôme de Stendhal: Armance et l'aveu*. Paris: Lettres Modernes, 1979.

Bersani, Leo. *Balzac to Beckett: Center and Circumference in French Fiction.* New York: Oxford University Press, 1970.

Bertrand-Jennings, Chantal. "Condition féminine et impuissance sociale: Les romans de la duchesse de Duras." *Romantisme* 63 (1989): 39–50.

Bochenek-Franczakowa, Regina. "Quelques Aspects du 'féminisme' dans les premiers romans de George Sand (1832–1834)." *Romanica Wratislaviensia* 10 (1975): 77–90.

Bonnet, Jean-Claude. "Le Musée staëlien." *Littérature* 42 (May 1981): 4–19.

Booth, Wayne. *The Rhetoric of Fiction*. Chicago: University of Chicago Press, 1961.

Borowitz, Helen O. "Two Nineteenth-Century Muse Portraits." *The Bulletin of the Cleveland Museum of Art* 66, no. 6 (Sept. 1979): 247–267.

Bossis, Mireille. "L'Homme dieu ou l'idole brisée dans les romans de G. Sand." *George Sand.* Colloque de Cerisy. Ed. Simone Vierne. Paris: SEDES, 1983. 179–187.

Bowlby, Rachel. *Just Looking: Consumer Culture in Dreiser, Gissing and Zola.* New York: Methuen, 1985.

Bowman, Frank Paul. "Benjamin Constant et l'histoire." In *Benjamin Constant.* Ed. Etienne Hofmann. Oxford: Voltaire Foundation, 1982. 129–150.

Brooks, Peter. "Freud's Masterplot." *Reading for the Plot: Design and Intention in Narrative.* New York: Knopf, 1984. 90–112.

————. *The Melodramatic Imagination: Balzac, Henry James, Melodrama, and the Mode of Excess.* New Haven: Yale University Press, 1976.

Call, Michael J. *Back to the Garden: Chateaubriand, Senancour and Constant.* Saratoga: Anma Libri, 1988.

Caramaschi, Enzo. "Le Point de vue féministe dans la pensée de Mme de Staël." *Voltaire, Mme de Staël, Balzac.* Padua: Liviane, 1977. 137–198.

Chambers, Ross. *Story and Situation: Narrative Seduction and the Power of Fiction.* Minneapolis: University of Minnesota Press, 1984.

Chateaubriand, François-René de. *Atala, René.* Paris: Garnier-Flammarion, 1964.

————. *Atala, René.* Trans. Irving Putter. Berkeley: University of California Press, 1957.

————. *Génie du christianisme.* Ed. Pierre Reboul. 2 vols. Paris: Garnier-Flammarion, 1966.

————. *Mémoires d'outre-tombe.* Ed. Pierre Clarac. 2 vols. Paris: Gallimard, 1946.

Chinard, Gilbert. "Quelques Origines littéraires de *René*," *PMLA* 43, no. 1 (Mar. 1928): 288–302.

Cixous, Hélène. "The Laugh of the Medusa." Trans. Keith Cohen and Paula Cohen. *Signs* (Summer 1976): 875–893.

Clark, Priscilla Parkhurst. *Literary France: The Making of a Culture.* Berkeley: University of California Press, 1987.

Coman, Colette. "Le Paradoxe de la maxime dans *Adolphe.*" *Romanic Review* 73 (1982): 195–208.

Constans, Ellen. "Stendhal et le public impossible." In *Stendhal: L'Ecrivain, la société et le pouvoir.* Ed. Philippe Berthier. Grenoble: Presses Universitaires de Grenoble, 1984. 33–55.

Constant, Benjamin. *Adolphe.* Ed. Paul Delbouille. Paris: "Les Belles Lettres," 1977.

————. *Adolphe.* Trans. L. W. Tancock. Harmondsworth, Middlesex: Penguin Books, 1964.

————. "De Madame de Staël et de ses ouvrages." In *Mélanges de littérature et de politique.* In *Oeuvres.* 869–870.

————. *Oeuvres.* Ed. A. Roulin. Paris: Gallimard, 1957.

Courtivron, Isabelle de. "Weak Men and Fatal Women: The Sand Image." In *Homosexualities and French Literature.* Ed. George Stambolian and Elaine Marks. Ithaca: Cornell University Press, 1980. 210–227.

Crébillon, Claude Jolyot de. *Oeuvres complètes.* 2 vols. Geneva: Slatkine, 1968.

Crecelius, Kathryn J. *Family Romances: George Sand's Early Novels.* Blooming-ton: Indiana University Press, 1987.

Crouzet, Michel. "Le Réel dans *Armance*: Passions et société, ou le cas d'Oc-tave—Etude et essai d'interprétation." In *Le Réel et le texte.* Paris: Ar-mand Colin, 1974. 31–110.

Deguise, Pierre. "Benjamin Constant, romantique froid?" In *Le Préroman-tisme: Hypothèse ou hypothèque.* Ed. Paul Vialleneix. Paris: Klincksieck, 1975. 182–195.

DeJean, Joan. *Fictions of Sappho, 1546–1937.* Chicago: University of Chicago Press, 1989.

———. "Staël's *Corinne*: The Novel's Other Dilemma." *Stanford French Review* 11 (Spring 1987): 77–87.

Dodge, Guy Howard. *Benjamin Constant's Philosophy of Liberalism: A Study in Politics and Religion.* Chapel Hill: University of North Carolina Press, 1980.

Dormoy-Savage, Nadine. "Identité et mimétisme dans quelques romans de George Sand." *George Sand.* Colloque de Cerisy. Ed. Simone Vierne. Paris: SEDES, 1983. 159–170.

Duras, Claire de. *Edouard.* Ed. Claudine Herrmann. Paris: Mercure de France, 1983.

———. *Olivier ou le secret.* Ed. Denise Virieux. Paris: Albert Corti, 1971.

———. *Ourika.* Ed. Claudine Herrmann. Paris: des femmes, 1979.

Eagleton, Terry. *The Rape of Clarissa: Writing, Sexuality, and Class Struggle in Samuel Richardson.* Minneapolis: University of Minnesota Press, 1982.

———. "Text, Ideology, Realism." In *Literature and Society.* Selected Papers from the English Institute, 1978. Ed. Edward W. Said. Baltimore: Johns Hopkins University Press, 1980. 149–173.

Epstein, Julia. "Either/Or—Neither/Both: Sexual Ambiguity and the Ide-ology of Gender." *Genders* 7 (Spring 1990): 99–142.

Ermarth, Elizabeth. "Fictional Consensus and Female Casualties." In *The Rep-resentation of Women in Fiction.* Selected Papers from the English Insti-tute, 1981. Ed. Carolyn G. Heilbrun and Margaret R. Higonnet. Baltimore: Johns Hopkins University Press, 1983. 1–18.

Evans, Martha Noel. "*Adolphe*'s Appeal to the Reader." *Romanic Review* 73 (May 1982): 302–313.

Fairlie, Alison. "Framework as a Suggestive Art in Constant's *Adolphe*." *Austra-lian Journal of French Studies* 16 (1979): 6–16.

Faludi, Susan. *Backlash: The Undeclared War against American Women.* New York: Crown, 1991.

Féletz, Abbé de. Review of *Corinne*. *Journal de l'Empire* (12 May 1807): 1–4.

Férard, E. A. "*Olivier* par Mme la Duchesse de Duras." *Le Figaro* (25 Jan., 1 Feb. 1930).

Feuillide, Capo de. Review of *Lélia*. *L'Europe littéraire* (22 Aug. 1833): 69–72.

Foucault, Michel. *The History of Sexuality.* Trans. Robert Hurley. New York: Random House, 1980.

Fraisse, Geneviève. *Muse de la raison: La Démocratie exclusive et la différence des sexes.* Aix-en-Provence: Alinéa, 1989.

Freud, Sigmund. "Creative Writers and Day-Dreaming." In *The Standard Edi-tion of the Complete Psychological Works of Sigmund Freud.* Trans. James Strachey. 24 vols. London: Hogarth Press, 1957. 9: 141–153.

Gans, Eric. "Le Secret d'Octave: Secret de Stendhal, secret du roman." *Revue des Sciences Humaines* 40, no. 157 (Jan.–Mar., 1975): 85–89.

Genette, Gérard. "Flaubert's Silences." *Figures of Literary Discourse*. New York: Columbia University Press, 1982. 183–202.

Gilbert, Sandra M., and Susan Gubar. "The Man on the Dump versus the United Dames of America; or, What Does Frank Lentricchia Want?" *Critical Inquiry* 14 (Winter 1988): 386–406.

———. *No Man's Land: The Place of the Woman Writer in the Twentieth Century.* Vol. 1: *The War of the Words.* New Haven: Yale University Press, 1988.

Gilot, Michel, and Jean Sgard. "La Vie intérieure et les mots." In *Le Préromantisme: Hypothèse ou hypothèque.* Ed. Paul Vialleneix. Paris: Klincksieck, 1975. 509–528.

Goldzick, Jean, and Gérard Gengembre. "L'Opinion dans *Corinne*." *Europe* 64 (Jan.–Feb. 1987): 48–57.

Gonin, Eve. *Le Point de vue d'Ellénore: Une Réécriture d' "Adolphe."* Paris: Albert Corti, 1981.

Gubar, Susan. "The Birth of the Artist as Heroine: (Re)Production, the *Künstlerroman* Tradition, and the Fiction of Katherine Mansfield." In *The Representation of Women in Fiction*. Selected Papers from the English Institute, 1981. Ed. Carolyn G. Heilbrun and Margaret R. Higonnet. Baltimore: Johns Hopkins University Press, 1983. 19–59.

Gutwirth, Madelyn. "*Corinne* et l'esthétique du camée." In *Le Préromantisme: Hypothèque ou hypothèse.* Ed. Paul Vialleneix. Paris: Klincksieck, 1975. 237–245.

———. "Forging a Vocation: Germaine de Staël on Fiction, Power, and Passion." *Bulletin of Research in the Humanities* 86 (1983–1985): 242–254.

———. *Madame de Staël, Novelist.* Urbana: University of Illinois Press, 1978.

———. "Madame de Staël, Rousseau, and the Woman Question." *PMLA* 86, no. 1 (1971): 100–109.

———. "Woman as Mediatrix: From Jean-Jacques Rousseau to Germaine de Staël." In *Woman as Mediatrix: Essays on 19th-Century European Women Writers.* Ed. Avriel H. Goldberger. New York: Greenwood Press, 1987. 13–29.

Hamm, Jean-Jacques. "Stendhal et Chateaubriand: Analyse d'une influence." In *Stendhal et le romantisme.* Ed. V. del Litto et al. Aran, Switz.: Editions du Grand Chêne, 1984. 103–112.

Herrmann, Claudine. "Corinne, femme de génie." *Cahiers staëliens*, n.s. 35 (1984): 60–76.

Hobson, Marian. "Theme and Structure in *Adolphe*." *Modern Language Review* 66 (1971): 306–314.

Hogsett, Charlotte. *The Literary Existence of Germaine de Staël.* Carbondale: Southern Illinois University Press, 1987.

Holmes, Glyn. *The Adolphe Type in French Fiction of the First Half of the Nineteenth Century.* Sherbrooke, Quebec: Editions Naaman, 1977.

Hoog, Armand. "Who Invented the 'Mal du Siècle'?" *Yale French Studies* 13 (1954): 42–51.

Huysmans, J.-K. *A Rebours.* Paris: 10/18, 1975.

Janeway, Elizabeth. "On the Power of the Weak." *Signs* 1 (Autumn 1981): 103–109.

Jeffords, Susan. "Performative Masculinities, or, 'After a Few Times You

Won't Be Afraid of Rape at All.'" *Discourse* 13 (Spring-Summer 1991): 102–118.

Jensen, Katharine. "Sex and Sensibility in *Armance*." Unpublished essay.

Johnson, Diane. "The I as Female: Elizabeth Hardwick." *Terrorists and Novelists*. New York: Knopf, 1982.

Johnson, Barbara. *The Critical Difference*. Baltimore: Johns Hopkins University Press, 1980.

Kadish, Doris. *Politicizing Gender: Narrative Strategies in the Aftermath of the French Revolution*. New Brunswick: Rutgers University Press, 1991.

Kelly, George Armstrong. "Constant and His Interpreters: A Second Visit." *Annales Benjamin Constant* 6 (1986): 81–89.

Kelly, Dorothy. *Fictional Genders: Role and Representation in Nineteenth-Century French Narrative*. Lincoln: University of Nebraska Press, 1989.

King, Norman. "Structures et stratégies d'*Adolphe*." In *Benjamin Constant, Madame de Staël, et le groupe de Coppet*. Ed. Etienne Hofmann. Oxford: Voltaire Foundation, 1982. 267–285.

Kirkpatrick, Susan. *Las Románticas: Women Writers and Subjectivity in Spain, 1835–1850*. Berkeley: University of California Press, 1989.

Kristeva, Julia. "The Bounded Text." In *Desire in Language: A Semiotic Approach to Literature and Art*. Trans. Thomas Gora, Alice Jardine, and Leon S. Roudiez. Ed. Leon S. Roudiez. New York: Columbia University Press, 1980. 36–63.

Labia, Jean-Jacques. "Le Recours au roman, ou l'impossibilité de la comédie au dix-neuvième siècle: L'Expérience inaugurale de Stendhal." In *Proceedings of the Xth Congress of the International Comparative Literature Association*. Ed. Anna Balakian. New York: Garland, 1985. 11–15.

Landes, Joan. *Women and the Public Sphere in the Age of the French Revolution*. Ithaca: Cornell University Press, 1988.

LeGates, Marlene. "The Cult of Womanhood in Eighteenth-Century Thought." *Eighteenth-Century Studies* 10 (1976): 21–39.

Lemoine-Guéry, Nadine. "La Femme froide chez Honoré de Balzac et George Sand." *Présence de George Sand* 14 (June 1982): 46–52.

Lentricchia, Frank. "Patriarchy against Itself—The Young Manhood of Wallace Stevens." *Critical Inquiry* 13 (Summer 1987): 742–786.

Lipking, Lawrence. "Aristotle's Sister: A Poetics of Abandonment." In *Canons*. Ed. Robert von Hallberg. Chicago: University of Chicago Press, 1983. 85–105.

Lough, John. *Writer and Public in France: From the Middle Ages to the Present Day*. Oxford: Clarendon Press, 1978.

Lyotard, Jean-François. "Sur la force des faibles," *L'Arc* 64 (1976): 4–12.

MacCannell, Juliet Flower. "Stendhal's Woman." *Semiotica* 48 (1984): 143–168.

"Male Subjectivity." *differences* 1: 3 (Fall 1989).

Maugue, Annelise. *L'Identité masculine en crise au tournant du siècle*. Paris: Rivages, 1987.

Maurois, André. *Lélia, ou la vie de George Sand*. Paris: Hachette, 1952.

Melzer, Sara, and Leslie Rabine, eds. *Rebel Daughters: Women and the French Revolution*. Oxford: Oxford University Press, 1992.

Mercken-Spaas, Godelieve. "Death and the Romantic Heroine: Chateaubriand and de Staël." In *Pre-Text/Text/Context: Essays in Nineteenth-Century*

French Literature. Ed. Robert L. Mitchell. Columbus: Ohio State University Press, 1980. 79–86.

Merlant, Joachim. Le Roman personnel de Rousseau à Fromentin. Paris: Hachette, 1905.

Miller, Nancy K. "The Exquisite Cadavers." Diacritics 5 (Winter 1975): 37–43.

———. The Heroine's Text: Readings in the French and English Novel, 1722–1782. New York: Columbia University Press, 1980.

———. "Les Liaisons dangereuses: Pas à pas." Modern Language Studies 12 (1982): 45–46.

———. "Men's Reading, Women's Writing: Gender and the Rise of the Novel," Yale French Studies 75 (1988): 40–55.

———. Subject to Change: Reading Feminist Writing. New York: Columbia University Press, 1988.

Modleski, Tania. Feminism without Women: Culture and Criticism in a "Postfeminist" Age. New York: Routledge, 1991.

Moers, Ellen. Foreword. Lelia. Trans. Maria Espinosa. Bloomington: Indiana University Press, 1978. vii–ix.

———. Literary Women: The Great Writers. Garden City, N.Y.: Anchor, 1977.

Mooij, Anne Louis Anton. Caractères principaux et tendances des romans psychologiques chez quelques femmes auteurs de Mme Riccoboni à Mme de Souza, 1757–1826. Groningen: Drukkerij de Waal, 1949.

Moskos, George. "Editing Ellénore: The Disappearing Feminine in Constant's Adolphe." Unpublished essay.

Mueller-Vollmer, Kurt. "Politique et esthétique: L'Idéalisme concret de Benjamin Constant, Guillaume de Humboldt et Madame de Staël." In Benjamin Constant, Madame de Staël, et le groupe de Coppet. Ed. Etienne Hofmann. Oxford: Voltaire Foundation, 1982. 453–473.

Musset, Alfred de. La Confession d'un enfant du siècle. Ed. Maurice Allem. Paris: Garnier, 1968.

Naginski, Isabelle Hoog. George Sand: Writing for Her Life. New Brunswick: Rutgers University Press, 1991.

Pailhès, G. La Duchesse de Duras et Chateaubriand, d'après des documents inédits. Paris: Perrin, 1910.

Petrey, Sandy. "George and Georgina Sand: Realist Gender in Indiana." In Sexuality and Textuality. Ed. Judith Still and Michael Worten. Manchester: Manchester University Press, forthcoming.

Pholien, Georges. "Adolphe et son public." Revue d'histoire littéraire de la France 85 (Jan.–Feb. 1985): 18–25.

Planté, Christine. La petite soeur de Balzac. Paris: Editions du Seuil, 1989.

Praz, Mario. "The Lady with the Lyre." In On Neoclassicism. Trans. Angus Davidson. Evanston: Northwestern University Press, 1969. 255–267.

Rabine, Leslie. "George Sand and the Myth of Femininity." Women and Literature 4, no. 2 (Fall 1976): 2–17.

Reboul, Pierre. Introduction. Lélia. Paris: Garnier, 1960. iii–lxviii.

Rogers, Nancy. "The Wasting Away of Romantic Heroines." Nineteenth-Century French Studies 11, nos. 3 and 4 (Spring–Summer 1983): 246–255.

Rollo, David. "The Phryné and the Muse: Onanism and Creativity in Chateaubriand's Mémoires d'Outre-Tombe and René." Nineteenth-Century French Studies 18 (Fall–Winter 1989–1990): 25–40.

Rosa, George M. "Byronism and 'Babilanisme' in *Armance*." *Modern Language Review* 77 (1982): 797–814.
———. "Writing the World: *Armance* and Byron's *Don Juan*." *Studi francesi* 31 (May–Aug. 1987): 217–229.
Ross, Marlon B. *The Contours of Masculine Desire: Romanticism and the Rise of Women's Poetry*. New York: Oxford University Press, 1989.
———. "Romantic Quest and Conquest: Troping Masculine Power in the Crisis of Poetic Identity." In *Romanticism and Feminism*. Ed. Anne K. Mellor. Bloomington: Indiana University Press, 1988. 26–51.
Rossard, Janine. *Pudeur et romantisme*. Paris: Nizet, 1982.
Rousseau, Jean-Jacques. *Les Confessions*. Paris: Flammarion, 1968.
Sade, Donatien Alphonse François de. *Justine ou les malheurs de la vertu*. Paris: Union Générale d'Editions, 1969.
Sainte-Beuve, Charles Augustin. "Du roman intime ou Mademoiselle de Liron." *Oeuvres*. 2 vols. Paris: Gallimard, 1960. 2: 1007–1024.
———. *Les Grands Écrivains français, XIXe siècle, Les Romanciers*. 2 vols. Ed. Maurice Allem. Paris: Garnier, 1927.
———. *Volupté*. Ed. André Guyaux. Paris: Gallimard, 1986.
Sand, George. "A propos de *Lélia* et de *Valentine*." Preface to *Romans et nouvelles* (1834). Rpt. in Sand, *Questions d'art et de littérature*. Paris: Calmann Lévy, 1878. 43–52.
———. *Lélia*. Ed. Pierre Reboul. Paris: Garnier, 1960.
———. *Lélia*. Trans. Maria Espinosa. Bloomington: Indiana University Press, 1978.
———. Préface. Senancour, *Obermann*. Paris: Charpentier, 1874. 1–14.
Sansone, Melinda. "*Lettres d'une Péruvienne*: The New Sentimental Plot and Its Feminist Implications." Unpublished essay.
———. "Possessing the Sentimental Tradition." Unpublished essay.
Schor, Naomi. *Breaking the Chain: Women, Theory and French Realist Fiction*. New York: Columbia University Press, 1985.
———. "Female Fetishism: The Case of George Sand." *Poetics Today* 6, nos. 1–2 (1985): 301–310.
———. *George Sand and Idealism*. New York: Columbia University Press, forthcoming.
———. "Idealism in the Novel: Recanonizing Sand," *Yale French Studies* 75 (1988): 56–73.
———. "*Lélia* and the Failures of Allegory." *L'Esprit Créateur* 29 (Fall 1989). 76–83.
———. "The Portrait of a Gentleman: Representing Men in (French) Women's Writing." *Representations* 20 (Fall 1987): 113–133.
———. "The Scandal of Realism." In *A New History of French Literature*. Ed. Denis Hollier. Cambridge: Harvard University Press, 1989. 656–661.
Schwartz, Lucy McCallum. "George Sand et le roman intime: Tradition and Innovation in 'Women's Literature,'" In *George Sand: Collected Essays*. Ed. Janis Glasgow. Troy, NY: Whitston, 1985. 220–226.
Sclippa, Nobert. *Texte et idéologie: Images de la noblesse et de la bourgeoisie dans le roman français des années 1750 à 1830*. New York: Peter Lang, 1987.
Sedgwick, Eve Kosofsky. *Between Men: English Literature and Male Homosocial Desire*. New York: Columbia University Press, 1985.

Segal, Naomi. *Narcissus and Echo: Women in the French 'Récit'*. Manchester: Manchester University Press, 1988.

Senancour, Etienne Pivert de. *Obermann*. Paris: Charpentier, 1874.

Showalter, Elaine. "Critical Cross-Dressing: Male Feminists and the Woman of the Year." *Raritan* 2, no. 2 (Fall 1983): 130–149.

———. *The Female Malady: Women, Madness, and English Culture, 1830–1980*. New York: Penguin Books, 1987.

———. *Sexual Anarchy: Gender and Culture at the Fin de Siècle*. New York: Viking, 1990.

Silverman, Kaja. "Historical Trauma and Male Subjectivity." In *Psychoanalysis and Cinema*. Ed. E. Ann Kaplan. New York: Routledge, 1990. 110–127.

Sivert, Eileen Boyd. "*Lélia* and Feminism." *Yale French Studies* 62 (1981): 45–66.

Spackman, Barbara. *Decadent Genealogies: The Rhetoric of Sickness from Baudelaire to D'Annunzio*. Ithaca: Cornell University Press, 1989.

Staël, Germaine de. *Corinne, or Italy*. Trans. and ed. Avriel H. Goldberger. New Brunswick: Rutgers University Press, 1987.

———. *Corinne, ou l'Italie*. 2 vols. Ed. Claudine Herrmann. Paris: des femmes, 1979.

———. *De l'Allemagne*. Ed. La comtesse de Pange and Simone Balayé. 2 vols. Paris: Hachette, 1958.

Starobinski, Jean. "Suicide et mélancolie chez Mme de Staël." In *Mme de Staël et l'Europe*. Paris: Klincksieck, 1970. 242–252.

Stendhal. *Armance, ou quelques scènes d'un salon de Paris en 1827*. Ed. Henri Martineau. Paris: Garnier, 1962.

———. *Armance, or Scenes from a Parisian Salon in 1827*, Trans. Gilbert and Suzanne Sale. London: Merlin, 1960.

———. *La Comédie est impossible en 1836. Mélanges* II: *Journalisme*. Geneva: Cercle du Bibliophile, 1972.

———. *Courrier anglais*. Ed. Henri Martineau. 5 vols. Paris: Le Divan, 1935–1936.

———. *De l'amour*. Ed. Henri Martineau. Paris: Garnier, 1959.

———. *Romans et nouvelles*. Paris: Gallimard, 1952.

Stewart, Grace. *A New Mythos: The Novel of the Artist as Heroine, 1877–1977*. St. Albans, Vt.: Eden Press, 1979.

Suleiman, Susan. *Authoritarian Fictions: The Ideological Novel as a Literary Genre*. New York: Columbia University Press, 1983.

———, and Inge Crosman. *The Reader in the Text*. Princeton: Princeton University Press, 1980.

Tanner, Tony. *Adultery in the Novel: Contract and Transgression*. Baltimore: Johns Hopkins University Press, 1979.

Temchin, Shelley I. "Straining the Structures of Romanticism: George Sand's *Lélia* Reconsidered." Ph.D. Diss., Tufts University, 1981.

Tenenbaum, Susan. "Liberal Heroines: Mme de Staël on the 'Woman Question' and the Modern State." *Annales Benjamin Constant* 5 (1985): 37–52.

Todd, Janet. *Sensibility: An Introduction*. London: Methuen, 1986.

Todorov, Tzvetan. "Benjamin Constant: Politique et amour." *Poétique* 14, no. 56 (1983): 485–510.

Truchet, Jacques. Introduction. *Théâtre du XVIIIᵉ siècle*. Vol. 1. Paris: Gallimard, 1972.

Vallois, Marie-Claire. *Fictions féminines: Mme de Staël et les voix de la Sibylle.* Saratoga: Anma Libri, 1978.

———. "Old Idols, New Subject: Germaine de Staël and Romanticism." In *Germaine de Staël: Crossing the Borders.* Ed. Madelyn Gutwirth, Avriel Goldberger, and Karyna Szmurlo. New Brunswick: Rutgers University Press, 1991. 82–97.

———. "Les Voi(es) de la Sibylle." *Stanford French Review* 6 (1982): 35–48.

Van Rossum-Guyon, Françoise. "A Propos d'*Indiana*: La Préface de 1832, problèmes du métadiscours." *George Sand.* Colloque de Cerisy. Ed. Simone Vierne. Paris: SEDES, 1983. 71–84.

Vialet, Michèle. "*Adolphe*: Echec en amour ou temporisation politique." *Annales Benjamin Constant* 5 (1985): 53–73.

Waller, Margaret. "Being René, Buying Atala: Alienated Subjects and Decorative Objects in Postrevolutionary France." In *Rebel Daughters: Women and the French Revolution.* Ed. Sara Melzer and Leslie Rabine. New York: Oxford University Press, 1992. 157–177.

———. "Cherchez la femme: Male Malady and Narrative Politics in the French Romantic Novel." *PMLA* 104 (Mar. 1989): 141–151.

———. "The Melancholy Man and the Lady with the Lyre: The Sexual Politics of Genius in Early Romantic Fiction and Painting." In *Selected Proceedings of the Sixteenth Annual Nineteenth-Century French Studies Colloquium.* Amsterdam: Rodopi, forthcoming.

Weil, Armand. Introduction. Chateaubriand. *René.* Paris: Droz, 1935. ix–lxv.

Winnett, Susan. "Coming Unstrung: Women, Men, Narrative, and Principles of Pleasure." *PMLA* 105 (May 1990): 505–518.

Yaeger, Patricia, and Beth Kowaleski-Wallace. *Refiguring the Father: New Feminist Readings of Patriarchy.* Carbondale: Southern Illinois University Press, 1989.

Zemek, Theodora. "Benjamin Constant, Adam Smith and the 'moule universel': The Impartial Spectator and His Social Framework." *Annales Benjamin Constant* 7 (1987): 49–63.

Index

Adolphe, 4, 45, 93–113; as autobiography, 105, 110–111; compared to Armance, 115, 122, 199n20; compared to Corinne, 70, 97, 98; compared to Lélia, 146, 155, 156, 160–161; compared to René, 94, 95, 98, 112; consequences for hero in, 14, 15, 95, 100–101; consequences for heroine in, 100–101, 104–105, 106, 160–161; death of heroine in, 106–107, 182, 196n4; double bind in, 95, 96, 97, 100–101; double talk in, 98, 109, 112–113, 120, 197n32; father in, 99; hero of, as patriarchal failure, 10, 11, 44, 99; hero's discursive privilege in, 98, 102–104, 108–109, 112–113; heroine's role in, 94, 98, 104–105, 107, 108, 190n21; homosocial bond in, 98, 99; and ideology of gender, 104, 108, 176, 189n6; and liberalism, 6, 93–98, 195n3; and libertinism, 6, 10, 94–95, 99–100, 109, 160; and paratext, 109–113; and plot, 25, 100–101, 104, 106–107, 107–108; as prototype, 205n5; reader response to, 105, 110. See also androcentrism

adultery, novel of, 179; role in novels of 1830s, 180

Aeneas, 128, 129, 149

alienation: and art, 87; and empowerment, 87, 88, 108, 146, 161; from father, 15, 18; of hero from patriarchal status quo, 11, 16, 18; and genius, 195n47; and incapacitation, 87. See also mal du siècle; mal du siècle hero; mal du siècle novel; writers

allegory, 144; and gender, 174; in Lélia, 168

Alletz, Edouard, 205n5

androcentrism: in Adolphe, 98, 112, 123–124, 198n34; in Armance, 115, 130, 190n26, 199n24; refusal of, in Corinne, 89; in René, 29, 35–36. See also mal du siècle novel

androgynes, 177

anonymity: and Beyle, 119; and Duras, 118; of woman writer, 121

anxiety: of male critics, 206n13; about virility, 205n8; of women writers, and plot, 24. See also Beyle; Constant; Dudevant; male authors; Sainte-Beuve; Staël

Armance, 4, 113, 114–135, 190n26; and class, 10, 115, 122, 125–126, 193n19; compared to Adolphe, 115, 122, 199n20; compared to Lélia, 156, 166; compared to René, 115; double talk in preface to, 120–121; exaggerated virilization of hero in, 122, 124; feminization of hero in, 122, 126, 127, 176; and fiction of female authorship, 113, 119–121, 131, 137; filial duty of hero in, 122, 124, 125–126, 200n31, 200n33; hero playing both male and female roles in, 129, 149; and impotence, 6, 9–10, 20, 129, 130–133, 205n8; and irony, 6, 115; mother in, 14, 122–124, 199n28; narrator in, 115, 123, 189n15; and plot, 127; power of hero in, 122–123,

woman of; heroine; spheres, separate; virilization of heroine

women, rights of: in contemporary U.S., 1; after French Revolution, 2; in 1830s, 181. *See also* gender, construction of

women writers: and alienation, 87; and anticonformism, 25; and anxiety about authorship, 24; attitudes toward, in 1830s, 176; in 1830s, 170; and feminist protest, 24, 25; and heroine's moral superiority, 86, 97, 192n17; and innovation, 188n35; and mal du siècle, 139; in male context, 4, 27; and

notion of self, 188n35; and plot, 193n25; prejudices against, 24; and representation of men, 12, 27, 188n37, 192n17; stereotypes of, 136, 201n1; as threat, 179. *See also* Beyle; Dudevant; Duras; male authors; Sainte-Beuve; Staël

Woolf, Virginia, 157

writers, as outsiders, 22–23; in nineteenth-century England, 22

writing: as feminization, 22, 183; as political dissidence, 21

Yaeger, Patricia, 194n41